Contemporary Classics of Children's Literature
Series Editor: Morag Styles

Alternative Worlds in Fantasy Fiction

Contemporary Classics of Children's Literature

Series Editor: Morag Styles

This exciting new series provides critical discussion of a range of contemporary classics of children's literature. The contributors are distinguished educationalists and academics from Britain, North America, Australia and elsewhere, as well as some of the foremost booksellers, literary journalists and librarians in the field. The work of leading authors and other outstanding fictional texts for young people (popular as well as literary) are considered on a genre or thematic basis. The format for each book includes an in-depth introduction to the key characteristics of the genre, where major works and great precursors are examined, and significant issues and ideas raised by the genre are explored. The series will provide essential reading for those working on undergraduate and higher degrees on children's literature. It avoids jargon and is accessible to interested readers, from parents, teachers and other professionals, to students and specialists in the field. Contemporary Classics of Children's Literature is a pioneering series, the first of its kind in Britain to give serious attention to the excellent writing being produced for children in recent years.

Also available in the series:
Kate Agnew and Geoff Fox: *Children at War*
Julia Eccleshare: *A Guide to the Harry Potter novels*
Nick Tucker and Nikki Gamble: *Family Fictions*
Kim Reynolds, Kevin McCarron and Geraldine Brennan: *Frightening Fiction*

Contemporary Classics of Children's Literature

ALTERNATIVE WORLDS IN FANTASY FICTION

Peter Hunt and Millicent Lenz

CONTINUUM
London and New York

Continuum
The Tower Building
11 York Road
London SE1 7NX

370 Lexington Avenue
New York
NY 10017–6503

www.continuumbooks.com

First published 2001

British Library Cataloguing-in-Publication Data
A catalogue record for this book is available from the British Library.

ISBN 0–8264–4936–0 (hardback)
      0–8264–4937–9 (paperback)

Typeset by YHT Ltd, London
Printed and bound in Great Britain by Creative Print and Design, Ebbw Vale

Contents

CHAPTER 1

Introduction: Fantasy and Alternative Worlds

Peter Hunt

'Now, what I want is, Facts. Teach these boys and girls nothing but
Facts. Facts alone are wanted in life. Plant nothing else, and root out
everything else. You can only form the minds of reasoning animals upon
Facts: nothing else will ever be of any service to them.'
Charles Dickens, Hard Times (1854)

Fantasy is the natural, the appropriate language for the recounting of the
spiritual journey and the struggle of good and evil in the soul.
Ursula K. Le Guin (1992: 64)

Fantasy is literature for teenagers
Brian Aldiss (quoted in Winoker, 1987: 39)

There's certainly prejudice in some quarters against fantasy, but this
tends to be from people who think it's all swords and dragons – which is
as silly as saying that 'Booker books' are all about foul-mouthed Scots
and lonely ladies taking tea on wet Thursdays. It seems to be suggested
that fantasy is some kind of fairy icing when, from a historical point of
view, it is the whole cake.
Terry Pratchett (Pratchett and Briggs, 1997: 467)

The paradoxes of fantasy

The first question about fantasy usually is: how seriously should we
take it?

In 1984, Ann Swinfen began her book *In Defence of Fantasy* by
noting that fantasy occupies 'a curiously ambivalent position ... in the
contemporary literary scene'(1); in 1988, Raymond Tallis began his *In
Defence of Realism* with the wry observation: 'that realism is outmoded
and the realistic novel a form that has had its day is a critical
commonplace'(1). Lucie Armitt, in 1996, took the opposite view:

> if you place 'fantastic' in a literary context ... suddenly we have a
> problem. Suddenly it is something dubious, embarrassing ...

> Suddenly we need to justify our interest in it ... [Fantasy] ... is that intangible source of unconscious fears and desires which fuels our dreams, our phobias and therefore our narrative fictions ... but its presumed association with the formulaic inevitably attracts two negative[s] ... : escapism and pulp fiction.(1)

Worse, it is associated with that still-marginalized literary form, children's literature.

Fantasy literature is either taken seriously (and enthusiastically), or seriously rejected. It is the root of all literature, an area of advanced literary experimentation, and essential to our mental health; *or* it is regressive, and associated with self-indulgent catharsis on the part of the writers; *or* it is linked to a ritualistic, epic, dehumanized world of predetermination and out of tune with post-romantic sensitivity: *or* it symbolizes the random world of the postmodern.

Or, quite possibly, all of these, for fantasy resists, and indeed mocks, the elaborate classification systems of academia that have grown up around it, just as it defies the view that its huge popularity is a sad reflection on the state of contemporary culture.

However, it is useful to take the three most common (if not the most damning) of opinions – that fantasy is formulaic, childish, and escapist, to see if they can be sustained – remembering that the one thing that can rarely be said of fantasy is that it has nothing to do with reality.

The problem of genre

Of types of fiction, fantasy is where the initial impulse of the writing and the constraints of genre clash most strongly. Personal, private, fantasy allows us to speculate, to explore possibilities, to indulge our private selves – to consider imaginatively things that cannot be (as opposed to speculation on things that *might* be, which produces science fiction): it would seem to offer worlds of infinite possibility, of expansiveness, of liberation.

And yet, the forms that fantasy takes – for all the endless ingenuity of the human imagination – are surprisingly limited. Fantasy seems to have, like the folk tales from which it sprang, a restricted number of recurrent motifs and elements: there are young, questing heroes, wise controlling sages, irredeemably evil monsters, and (although, mercifully fewer these days) damsels in distress (Propp, 1975). It might seem that the most visible form, 'sword and sorcery' genre fantasy, is doomed to die of repetition or parody – as in Terry Pratchett's 'Discworld' series, or Diana Wynne Jones's *The Tough Guide to Fantasyland* which mercilessly catalogues every cliché: 'Beer always foams and is invariably delivered in tankards' (1996: 30).

Such is the grip of formula, that it is almost as if one part of the human psyche is frightened of the other: imagination is too dangerous to wander unchained. (Of course, it may simply be that the very publicness of written fantasy simplifies it: it needs to be comprehensible to more than one person, and most private fantasies would need a good many footnotes were they to be made public in their raw state!) And yet, making sense of both the dark, unknown universe out there, and the perhaps worse demons within – making both humanly manageable – has been what storytelling and metaphor have always been about. Ritualization, then, is neither surprising, nor exclusive to fantasy. Original fantasy, however, as this book will demonstrate, is not hard to find, although it may have to work harder because of its awareness of its context.

There is, however, one area of formulaic writing that is increasingly difficult to justify: the treatment of gender. The hero tale, still the staple of contemporary fantasy, has been essentially a male preserve: in fantasies from *The Wind in the Willows*, *Winnie-the-Pooh*, *Peter Pan*, *The Hobbit*, the first three 'Earthsea' Books, and countless others, women are marginalized (Tenar) or mothers (Wendy, Kanga), or dangerous (Toad's bargewoman). As Ursula K. Le Guin said, ironically: 'Authority is male. It's a fact. My fantasy dutifully reported the fact. But is that all a fantasy does – report facts?' (1993: 11).

But despite all this, fantasy literature, whose wellsprings are most visibly subversive, continually strives to overcome (or exploit) both genrefication and the fact that commercialism finds it easier to sell the restricted and restricting rather than the dangerously unclassifiable.

The three major authors studied in the rest of this book are writers who have taken on what has been, in terms of genre and gender, an often limited form, and have moved it into new areas.

Fantasy and children
The second major criticism of fantasy is that it is childish. It is not surprising that fantasy and children's literature have been associated with each other, because both are essentially democratic forms – democratized by being outside the solipsistic system of high culture. The idea of a 'canon' – a group of superior texts whose superiority is validated by some set of privileged judges – is alien to both: and to both 'popular culture' is a rallying cry, rather than a contradiction in terms.

But there is no reason to suppose that children and fantasy have a natural connection, even if the struggle of imagination and generic constraints parallels the conflict between common concepts of the child and the adult – the expansive versus the repressed, freedom versus discipline, freshness versus familiarity. Thus J. R. R. Tolkien's famous dictum on the fairy tale can be applied to fantasy: 'the association of children and fairy stories is an accident of our domestic history. ... Children as a class neither like fairy-stories more nor understand them better than adults do' (1964: 34). In fact, the association of fantasy with children – and childishness – is quite bizarre, in that fantasy (at least as most often constructed) concentrates on worlds other than this one: alternative worlds – desirable, if unattainable options. Why should this be thought to be of interest to child readers? It is far more likely, as we shall see, with fantasists from MacDonald to Barrie and onwards, that it is adult writers who are interested in, or have a need for such alternatives. And so we might ask, is, to a developing child, this world not enough? And if it is not, is it because adults have closed off its inherent wonders? (Hence, perhaps, the criticism of C. S. Lewis that his 'Narnia' books reject the world as (God-)given world – albeit in favour of another, more mystic version.)

Thus, a great many fantasy worlds do not cater for a developing mind at all: the real world may be seen as being full of arbitrary, adult-controlled restrictions, but for this is substituted another world, often of even more arcane restrictions. Similarly, there has been, since the days of the first real example of a 'logically cohesive' alternative world (Sullivan, 1996: 307), William Morris's *The Wood Beyond the World* (1894), a tendency to exploit pseudo-medieval settings. This suggests a regressive element, a romantic yearning (by adults) for earlier 'innocence', for an alternative world where motivations, actions, needs and gratifications are simpler and more direct than in the desperately complex and subtle real world.

The paradox is that the appreciation of fantasy does involve (for children as well as adults) the use of and validation of romantically constructed 'child-like' talents – the joy of invention and discovery, the wonder at variety and ingenuity – the fresh view of the different, the other. The rejection of this as atavistic or childish by the 'sophisticated' adult reader has some interesting implications: as C. S. Lewis put it:

> To be concerned about being grown up, to admire the grown up because it is grown up, to blush at the suspicion of being childish; these are the marks of childhood and adolescence. When I became a man I put away childish things, including the fear of childishness and the desire to be very grown up. (1966: 25)

Adult criticism tends to resist this: invented worlds cannot be 'merely' places of wonder or delight: they must mean something else (morally, rather than inevitably) if they are to be interesting or valuable. Manlove's complimentary comment on Terry Pratchett's *The Colour of Magic*, that 'in a sense the real narrative ... is Pratchett continually outdoing himself' (1999: 136) can be taken as a negative criticism; analysts of Le Guin's writing concentrate on the *meaning* rather than the *fact* of her wonders.

This winds back to the relatively low cultural status of fantasy for adults – although, logically enough, fantasy for children has a respectable place in the (adult-nominated) children's canon. This low status is compounded by the fact that differences between fantasy and realism and between children's and adults' fantasy are confusingly similar, and hinge on *what is left out*.

If fantasy is a simplifying activity – with simple acts and resolutions – it can be seen as both an innocent activity and as a corrupting activity, depending on who is reading it. Thus, for example, in fantasies, good and evil are polarized in a way that they can perhaps never be – or should never be – and which all-too-dangerously are – in a mature real world. As Robert Louis Stevenson said, of what he regarded as a fantasy, *Treasure Island*, in a debate with Henry James over the 'adventure' novel:

> The characters need to be presented with but one class of qualities ... Danger is the matter with which this class of novel deals; fear, the passion with which it idly trifles; and the characters are portrayed only so far as they realise the sense of danger and provoke the sympathy of fear ... To add more traits, to be too clever, to start the hare of moral or intellectual interest while we are running the fox of material interest, is not to enrich but to stultify your tale. (Allott, 1965: 83)

Things that are very difficult, for example, notably, sexuality, are cleared away – in what may be an urge towards purity and innocence – or towards irresponsibility and (wilful) ignorance – all of which terms cluster perjoratively around 'childhood'. 'High' fantasy, for example, especially clears out sex – orcs may be savage, but they are not rapists – sex is shunted off into that specialized ghetto of pornography where real humans become ultimately degraded by being treated as anything but humans. (Or, alternatively, the users of such material are degraded by ignoring humanity; or natural and harmful urges are harmlessly sublimated ... and so on.)

In this formulation, then, fantasy is necessarily evasive and irresponsible – and simple. Bruno Bettelheim's book on the fairy tale, *The Uses of Enchantment* (1976), notoriously reduced the elements of what Philip Larkin called 'the collective myth-kitty' to a series of reactive elements; the reaction to this suggested that he had devalued the tales – but perhaps they actually are as simple as Bettelheim suggested, and the idea that they are profound and forceful is merely a defence (by the regressive).

Thus fantasy substitutes violence for discussion, friendship for love, romance for passion, magic for achievement – and even food for sex – especially in books ostensibly for children or for regressing adults, such as Grahame's *The Wind in the Willows*, or Eleanor Farjeon's *Martin Pippin in the Apple Orchard*. If some things are left out of children's fantasy because they are not relevant to children, or because authors wish to preserve the innocence/ignorance of childhood, and these are much the same things as are left out of adult genre fantasy, then it is not surprising that there has been confusion.

And, of course, with anything connected with childhood, the more alienated the thinking about it, the more romantic it becomes. Therefore one conventional explanation for the supposed preponderance of fantasy in children's books is that children are in some way closer to the unknown, the unseen, and the mystical. Children are equated with primitives, who have (it is assumed) a simple faith in animism and an inherent understanding of certain narrative patterns; or are equivalent to the 'folk' (a naive construction) who originated the folk tale, for whom the world outside the door of the hut was full of who knew what wonders and terrors.

More patronizing still is the view that for children the distinction between reality and unreality is blurred, and therefore they scarcely have to suspend belief. (This view is at the root of a great deal of careless and trivial writing.) As it is not clear at what developmental stage any of this is true, or ceases to be true, it might all be treated with a healthy scepticism. The romantic idea of 'child-like', meaning innocent (however 'innocence' is constructed) and mystic, has been imposed upon actuality: to the postmodern adult reader, absorption into a text while reading is unfashionable; children (and unfashionable readers) do it – and (therefore) it is childish to do it. Any suggestion that developing readers may be just as capable of dual readings as other readers undermines childhood as constructed.

Even the best writers cannot escape: as Le Guin observed:

> For fantasy is true, of course. It isn't factual, but it is true. Children know that. Adults know it too, and that is precisely why

many of them are afraid of fantasy. They know that its truth challenges, even threatens, all that is false, all that is phoney, unnecessary, and trivial in the life they have let themselves be forced into living. They are afraid of dragons because they are afraid of freedom. (1992: 40)

In short, the most damning criticism of fantasy is that it seems to be *merely* 'fun': and we live in a culture that finds it difficult to take fun seriously: as A. P. Herbert said: 'People must not do things for fun. We are not here for fun. There is no reference to fun in any Act of Parliament'. But, ironically, fantasy cannot be merely anything. The assumption that fantasy is childish because you may not need to know much about this world in order to read about an invented one overlooks the obvious fact that knowledge of this world is necessary to *invent* one. Fantasy is, because of its relationship to reality, very *knowing*: alternative worlds must *necessarily* be related to, and comment on, the real world.

Escapism and the reality of fantasy

Ursula K. Le Guin, in an article, 'Why Are Americans Afraid of Dragons?' in 1974, reported the experience of a friend:

Ten years ago I went to the children's room of the library of such-and-such a city, and asked for *The Hobbit*; and the librarian told me, 'Oh, we keep that only in the adult collection; we don't feel that escapism is good for children.' (1992: 34)

The common accusation that fantasy is not a good thing because it is escapist rests on the fallacy that it *is* necessarily escapist (quite apart from the implication that escapism is necessarily not a good thing). The idea of all fantasy as frivolous escapism is no more generally applicable than the suggestion that all fiction is escapist – and perhaps less so. Fantasy cannot be 'free-floating' or entirely original, unless we are prepared to learn a new language and new way of thinking to understand it. It must be understandable in terms of its relationship to, or deviance from, our known world.

The notion of impossibility in fantasy, then, must be ... more public than the schizophrenic's hallucination, yet less public than myth and religion. It must ... be part of an implied compact between author and reader – an agreement that whatever impossibilities we encounter will be made significant to us, but will retain enough of their idiosyncratic nature that we still recognise them to be impossible. (Wolfe, 1982: 3)

If there is virtually no connection between the real and the fantastic, except distortion, then we arrive at the absurd and nonsense.

Consequently we do not escape ourselves or our situation: fantasy has an inevitable role as a commentary on, or counterpart to, reality and realism. Far from being 'escapist' as Jill Paton Walsh observed,

> A work of fantasy compels a reader into a metaphorical state of mind. A work of realism, on the other hand, permits very literal-minded readings ... Even worse, it is possible to read a realistic book as though it were not fiction at all. (1981: 38)

Or, in Ursula K. Le Guin's terms:

> It is by such statements as 'Once upon a time there was a dragon', or 'In a hole in the ground there lived a hobbit' – it is by such beautiful non-facts that we fantastic human beings may arrive, in our peculiar fashion, at the truth. (1992: 40)

As a result, fantasy – things as they cannot be – is very often a very direct critique of things as they are, even if not directly intended to be so. As Tolkien observed of *The Lord of the Rings*,

> As for any inner meaning or 'message', it has in the intention of the author none. It is neither allegorical nor topical ... I cordially dislike allegory in all its manifestations, and always have done so since I grew old and wary enough to detect its presence. I much prefer history, true or feigned, with its varied applicability to the thought and experience of readers. I think that many confuse 'applicability' with 'allegory'; but the one resides in the freedom of the reader, and the other in the purposed domination of the author. (1978: 8–9)

Of course, what Tolkien says of applicability is true of any text – but his mention of allegory is significant. The domain of modern fantasy is related to a long history of myth, legend, folk-tale and wonder tale, not to mention religion and the occult – forms of narrative which many have seen as expressions of, or as being closely related to, deep and universal human drives. As Colin Manlove has noted (and as Alan Garner acknowledged of his first two fantasies), simply to populate a landscape with these elements does not ensure any vibrant link.

> Any number of Waste Lands, broken lances, grails, eucharistic or baptismal symbols may appear in a story without that story having any potent meaning. More than this, where a story does have significance attached to it ... the word is indeed 'attached', for

the meaning has been neither felt by the author nor vitally realised in the story. (1975: 11)

However, I would take issue with Manlove's idea that we can distinguish between those works of 'fancy' – comic or escapist fantasy, as opposed to the works of the imagination – which carry 'deeper' meaning. It is just such a fanciful – and elitist – canonical view that leads us into needlessly difficult waters.

Thus when Raymond Tallis says that 'a total disregard for the probable will present a serious obstacle to the free operation of the reader's intelligence and imagination' (1988: 193), I would agree. The point is that fantasy does not totally disregard such things. If it did, it would produce utterly incomprehensible and chaotic texts: fantasy *must* react. There must be a 'realistic' focalizer: for example, in Oz, however wild the premises of physical laws, the story centres on Dorothy and her desire to get back to her familiar home; on the Discworld, however spectacular the invention, the psychology of the characters is recognizable; in Le Guin's books, the Dragons – and the women – are understandable and are able to be empathized with, precisely because they are in contrast to the conventionally realistic texts; in Philip Pullman's *His Dark Materials*, the worlds Lyra discovers are always in tension with the world she knows, and the world we know.

In fact, such is the engagement with 'real' life and characters in much fantasy that, as Manlove noted, it

tends to be moral in character, depicting the different natures of good and evil, and centrally concerned with viewing conduct in ethical terms. (1982: 30–1)

(Even on the simplest symbolic levels, as we have seen in the case of gender, the prejudices of this world easily transfer to other worlds. Both Tolkien and Lewis use the East and the Dark (skinned) as symbols of evil – not to mention Garner's Svarts, Dahl's Oompa-Loompas, and Lofting's Jollijinkies.)

Fantasy, then, is relevant, and so when Tallis finally concedes that 'the quarrel ... is with those who invent (or more usually, crib) mysteries because they are insensitive to the mystery of daily life' (1988: 193) no serious reader of fantasy would disagree.

Marking the boundaries

It seems to be more or less traditional for books on fantasy to begin with a collection of definitions, marking out academic or conceptual territory – and, on the whole, it seems to be a fairly defensive exercise. After all, it can be argued that all fiction (and a good deal of non-fiction) is in a sense fantasy – especially 'realistic' fiction, which, fantastically, makes sense of the random narratives of life – not because events described could not happen in some wise, but because fiction narrates and makes sense of things in a way that is unavailable in reality. As Mark Twain said, 'Why *shouldn't* truth be stranger than fiction? Fiction, after all, has to make sense' (Winoker, 1987: 47). At a lesser extreme, one could reasonably include in the category of fantasy any fanciful tale, from myths to religious parables, from the folk tale to the absurd, from nursery rhymes to nonsense.

One difficulty is that 'fantasy' is the ultimately relative term: one person's fantasy is another person's norm – who would care to draw their own line between fantasy and reality? The other is that most definitions merely send us in pursuit of other words, such as 'impossible' and 'reality', which are at best moveable feasts. In any case, the unacademic reader might wonder, why define?

However, following tradition, here is a sample. For W. R. Irwin it is 'the literature of the impossible' (1976: 4); for Eric S. Rabkin: 'its polar opposite is reality' (1976: 14), for Colin Manlove, it is 'of another order of reality from that in which we exist and form our notions of possibility' (1975: 3) and 'a fiction involving the supernatural or impossible' (1999: 3). Brian Attebury attempts to make the term a little more self-referential: for him, fantasy violates 'what the author clearly believes to be natural law' (1980: 2); Le Guin turns it into a survival strategy: fantasy is

> a different approach to reality, an alternative technique for apprehending and coping with existence. It is not anti-rational, but para-rational; not realistic, but surrealistic, superrealistic; a heightening of reality. (1992: 79)

... and so on. (For an excellent selection, see Sullivan, 1992: 97–100.)

One of the most detailed definitions is Colin Manlove's (1975: 1–12): 'A fiction evoking wonder and containing a substantial and irreducible element of the supernatural and which the mortal characters in the story or the readers become on at least partially familiar terms'(1). This is concerned with drawing boundaries: thus it excludes *Orlando* (both by Virginia Woolf and Kathleen Hale) or *The Once and Future King*, on the grounds that the fantasy element is not the central concern of the books; and, more swingeingly, 'where the supernatural is seen as a symbolic extension of the purely human mind' – which excludes, for example, the 'Alice' books. Manlove quotes

Tolkien – 'since the fairy-story deals in "marvels", it cannot tolerate any frame or machinery suggesting that the whole story in which they occur is a figment or illusion' (1964: 6) – thus dismissing (again) the 'Alice' books or the whirlwind ride of John Masefield's *The Box of Delights* – and countless others.

I have a great deal of sympathy with this purist view in terms of academic manageability, but rather less with the oceans of ingenious ink that has been used to classify fantasy: an activity which goes against the general spirit of expansive extravagance, but is in concord with the game-playing, obsessive detailing of a certain kind of fantasy.

However, simply to list possibilities does at least demonstrate the richness of the subject. Colin Manlove (1999), for example, divides English fantasy into: secondary worlds, metaphysical, emotive, comic, subversive, and children's; Ruth Nadelman Lynn divides children's fantasy into allegory and fable, animal, ghost, humour, imaginary beings, magic adventure, secondary worlds, time travel, toys, and witchcraft and wizardry; Ann Swinfen, into animals, time, dual world, visionary, secondary worlds and so on.

The most fundamental difference might seem to be between fantasy set in 'this' world, where there is a tension between the 'normal' and the fantastic elements, and 'other' worlds in which the fantastic is the norm. In 'this' world, magic may just happen to exist (as in John Masefield's *The Midnight Folk*, or E. Nesbit's *Five Children and It*); there may be intrusions of magic into this world from a different plane (as in Alan Garner's *The Weirdstone of Brisingamen*) or a different world (Alan Garner's *Elidor*); or the transportation of characters into another, parallel world (*The Lion, the Witch and the Wardrobe*, Joy Chant's *Red Moon, Black Mountain*). (In this last connection, a good deal of ingenuity has been expended on the devices that move characters between the worlds (rings, wardrobes, mirrors, or in the case of Pratchett's *Johnny and the Bomb*, black plastic sacks).)

Very often, places are very precisely described or mapped, emphasizing the gap between the real and unreal worlds: thus Mary Norton's *The Borrowers*, Richard Adams's *Watership Down*, Garner's *The Weirdstone of Brisingamen*, or my *The Maps of Time* provide precise maps onto which fiction is superimposed – and where there are no maps, as in Kipling's *Puck of Pook's Hill*, there is a sense that the setting is 'real'.

It can be argued that one of the differences between American and British fantasy – and the predominance of 'other world' fantasies in the USA, derives from British writers' sense of place and historical presence. As Susan Cooper has said:

Britain has had people living in it for God knows how many hundreds or thousands of years, especially in Wales. You walk those mountains and the awareness of the past is all around you. And I intend to write from that kind of awareness. The magic, if you like, is all around. There is no moment at which one slips down the rabbit hole. (Harrison and Maguire, 1987: 202)

In more general terms, there are differences in the way 'other' worlds are realized: is the fantasy of other worlds symbolism with a place, or is it a place with symbolism attached? Do the ideas in the books come first, and is the fictive world then formed to accommodate them; or is the fantasy accommodated in our 'real' world; or is the fictive world created first and ideas generated subsequently? Robert Louis Stevenson was an enthusiast of the last of these:

It is my contention – my superstition, if you like – that who is faithful to his map, and consults it, and draws from it his inspiration ... gains positive support ... [E]ven with imaginary places, he will do well in the beginning to provide a map; as he studies it, relations will appear that he has not thought upon ... it will be found to be a mine of suggestion. (Salway, 1976: 419)

It is this kind of distinction that makes the worlds of *The Water Babies* or the 'Alice' books not worlds in the way in which the Discworld, or Middle Earth, or Earthsea, or Gormenghast can be said to be separate worlds. You could not *map* them – even when, as in *Through the Looking-Glass*, we are dealing with a chess game. This is also true of the 'Pooh' books and *The Wind in the Willows*. It is true that E. H. Shepard drew maps of both, but the 100-acre wood or the River Bank are not places which exist of themselves and in which therefore things can happen. The place – the weir, Poohsticks bridge, the Mad Hatter's tea table – spring up, as it were, when they are needed by the action. You cannot map the place where 'a boy and his bear will always be playing'; you cannot go back to the garden of live flowers, or give a map reference to Badger's back door. Like Grahame's 'economy of character', it doesn't matter: Shepherd's maps are, in a sense, arbitrary, and, perhaps, a little undermining.

The same nebulous geography is found in the 'world' of George MacDonald's *The Princess and the Goblin*, and *The Princess and Curdie* – and of many other books that inhabit what might be broadly called 'fairy-land'. It is a space where things happen, not a place of itself. In Macdonald's world, there is a castle, a wood, a mountain, caves – but these are only the spaces for action and allegory: there is no sense of them having a separate existence. And allegory is a one-dimensional form. Spenser's dragons have no existence beyond their immediate rationale.

Rather than legislate these worlds out of our field of discussion, we might simply note that their effect is likely to be different: some of the dissatisfaction that critics – if not real readers – have felt with Lewis's 'Narnia' – is for all that it tries to map itself, it is really a place of ideas.

On the other hand, we might feel that the kingdom of Roke existed before Ged and Tenar, and in this sense, exists after them. Le Guin claimed that she explored and found Earthsea, rather than creating it – although 'one gets a little jovial and irresponsible, given the freedom to create a world out of nothing at all (Power corrupts)' (1992: 46). The Hobbits walk an historical land, meticulously conceived. The Discworld can be – and has been – mapped. ('Where' these places 'exist' might divert classifiers amongst us for a moment: Middle Earth may have occupied the same space as we do now, once upon a time; Earthsea, in contrast to Discworld, has no edges – in line with science-fiction thinking Discworld occupies another, *possible* (however improbable) corner of the multiverse; Lloyd Alexander's Prydain although loosely based on Wales is never located anywhere.)

Because border disputes do not seem to us to be particularly useful, the 'alternative worlds' discussed in this book are not confined to those which exist in different, discrete worlds, such as Discworld, Earthsea, Prydain, Middle Earth. Rather, we take 'alternative' to mean alternative conceptual worlds, those which either – as in Pratchett's *Johnny and the Bomb* – exist down the other trouser leg of time, or exist as (a similar concept) Pullman's parallel universes in *His Dark Materials*. As Pullman has said:

> I am surely not the only writer who has the distinct sense that every sentence I write is surrounded by the ghosts of the sentences I could have written at that point but didn't. (1998: 47)

And two final points on classification.

We have not used the term 'secondary worlds', which is often used to mean discrete, other worlds, because it often seems to be based on a misreading of Tolkien's *Tree and Leaf*. In discussing 'literary belief' or 'the willing suspension of disbelief', which he finds an unsatisfactory term, Tolkien says:

> What really happens is that the story-maker proves a successful 'sub-creator'. He makes a Secondary World which your mind can

enter. Inside it, what he relates is 'true': it accords with the laws of that world. You therefore believe it, while you are, as it were, inside. The moment disbelief arises, the spell is broken; the magic, or rather art, has failed. You are then out in the Primary World again, looking at the little abortive Secondary World from outside. (1964: 36)

For Tolkien, all imaginary worlds – all fictions – are 'Secondary'.

Similarly, we have not concerned ourselves too rigorously with the distinctions between fantasy and science fiction (or science fantasy), because the two are intertwined, and all three of the writers studied in this book have been described as science-fiction writers. Definitions, are, as usual, notable for their exclusions:

Fantasy deals with the impossible and the inexplicable, while science fiction deals with a future that scientific or technological advances could or might make possible. (Lynn, 1983: ix)

The fantasist tries to re-create, the science-fiction writer to make the wholly new … The genre is fundamentally exploratory in character. (Manlove, 1982: 30–1)

Fantasy literature, then, the public face of play and desire, with its (productively) opposing drives of ingenuity and simplicity, freedom and control, covers a spectacular range. Some indication of its richness, and the kinds of cultural tensions it provokes, and the problems and pleasures that its readers might encounter, can be demonstrated by a brief outline history, and a closer look at some key, representative, texts.

The progress of fantasy

Origins and principles

Most elements of contemporary fantasy writing can be traced to very ancient examples: wizards and werewolves and witches come from ancient fears and power struggles, but we should be cautious not to assume that naming a thing gives it any significance. As Tolkien notes in *Tree and Leaf*, the game of derivations is a very dangerous, if not pointless one. If we allow that folk-tale elements crop up across the world in similar form, that is more likely to lead us to assumptions about the human psyche, or humans' reactions to nature, than to significant literary links. The larger the generalization about fantasy ('folk tales are about empowering the disempowered'), or the smaller the detail (see for example Stith Thompson's mammoth folk-lore motif index) the less, it seems to us, is being usefully said.

Secondly, as Sullivan points out (1992: 97–100), just as children's literature requires some concept of childhood before it can exist, fantasy requires some concept of realism before *it* can exist. Consequently, to trace a history of fantasy 'back' to *Beowulf* or *Arcadia* or Spenser's *The Faerie Queene*, or Shakespeare's *A Midsummer Night's Dream* is to ignore the status of the 'fantasy' that they portray. As Sullivan says,

> the contemporary fantasy writer's borrowing of material from medieval and ancient literatures for his modern texts auto-matically makes those older narratives no more fantasies than it makes them modern. (99)

Unlike the audience for early literature,

> the modern reader makes categorical distinctions between the possible (real) and the impossible (not-real) ... Thus fantasy literature set in a Secondary World where the fantastic (departures from consensus reality) occurs in believable ways, is a product of the nineteenth and twentieth centuries and should be approached as such. (100)

The modern reader might dismiss, for example, some of the responses to *Gulliver's Travels* when it was first published as naive: some of Swift's contemporaries believed that the lands he described actually existed, and why should they not? But both the conception and understanding of that book must have been influenced by the readers' world-view.

Fantasy into literature

Fantasy's role as a way (personally and collectively) of combating or coping with deprivation and repression, as well as desire, is clear in the folk tale, and, not surprisingly, such narratives were either absorbed into or silenced by society – notably through the puritan-evangelical religious hegemony of the seventeenth and eighteenth centuries, and by the pervading utilitarian attitude of mind in the nineteenth century.

'Primitive' fantasy was absorbed effortlessly into literature and drama from the oral tradition from the fourteenth through to the seventeenth centuries. For example, Caxton's *Reynard the Fox* (1481) was among the earliest printed books, and many of the great Tudor works, Sidney's *Arcadia* (1590), Spenser's *The Faerie Queene* (1589–96), and many of Shakespeare's plays, for example, *A Midsummer Night's Dream*, *As You Like It*, *The Tempest*, and even *King Lear*, are undoubtedly fantasies.

The fantastic was unexceptional. Objections to its various manifestations (folk tale, romances) in chapbooks were raised by puritan writers in the seventeenth century, despite, as in Bunyan's *The Pilgrim's Progress* (1678), the widespread fashion for fanciful religious allegory.

In the eighteenth century, the age of reason, the fantastic worlds of the romance gave way to the pragmatic naturalism of the novel. Consider *Gulliver's Travels* (1726) and *Robinson Crusoe* (1719). *Gulliver* uses fantasy in the cause of intricate and far-reaching satire – which has its roots in the sixteenth- and seventeenth-century fantastic satires of Cyrano de Bergerac, Rabelais, and Cervantes; in contrast, *Crusoe* is a pragmatic, naturalistic fantasy, with its roots in mercantile Protestantism. Both play on the credulity of their readers, but it was Defoe's model that dominated the century. The novel, although often incidentally using the grotesque or the romantic, became a naturalistic form, from Richardson, through Austen, and on into George Eliot and Hardy. Books with elements of fantasy became either 'popular' fiction (the gothic), or passing fashions (the oriental). Across the literary board, the improbable or the highly coloured, from Dickens to Conan Doyle (although with curious exceptions, such as *Wuthering Heights*) slid down the literary scale of repute.

In children's literature, the eighteenth and nineteenth centuries, the age of pragmatism, saw a battle between the fantastic on one side, and evangelism and flat-footed practicality on the other. Although the fairy-tale genre, created in effect in late seventeenth-century France had infiltrated British culture in the eighteenth century, it was symptomatic that Sarah Trimmer could attack a new edition of *Perrault's fairy tales* in 1803 on the grounds of 'exciting unreasonable and groundless fears' in children, and not supplying 'any moral instruction level to the infantine capacity'. Dickens, not surprisingly, weighed in, in 'Frauds on the Fairies' in 1853, with a splendidly ironic utilitarian defence, against George Cruikshank's sanitized and teetotal versions of fairy tales.

> In a utilitarian age, of all other times, it is a matter of grave importance that fairy tales should be respected ... Every one who has considered the subject knows full well that a nation without fancy, without some romance, never did, never can, never will, hold a great place under the sun.

Where fantasy was harnessed to evangelical ideas, there was no nonsense. Sarah Trimmer's *Fabulous Histories* (later *The History* [or *Story*] *of the Robins*) (1786) had a preface which made it quite clear that readers were not to believe what they read, not to consider the stories

> as containing the real conversations of Birds (for that it is impossible we should ever understand) but as a series of FABLES, intended to convey moral instruction applicable to themselves.

Over seventy years later, in A. L. O. E.'s (Charlotte Maria Tucker) introduction to her *The Rambles of a Rat* (1857), some firm distinctions were made:

> Let not my readers suppose that in writing *The Rambles of a Rat* I have simply been blowing bubbles of fancy for their amusement, to divert them during an idle hour. Like the hollow glass balls which children delight in, my bubbles of fancy have something solid within them – facts are enclosed in my fiction.

Fantasies of various kinds (such as the Grimm brothers' *German Popular Stories* (translated 1823)), were channelled towards children, partly by default, with the not unnatural result that in due course they re-surfaced in spectacular ways.

They formed the root of a subversive reaction to a utilitarian attitude of mind, with writers such as John Ruskin with *The King of the Golden River* (1851), and William Makepeace Thackeray with *The Rose and the Ring* (1855). The 'golden age of children's literature' which began in the 1860s, was dominated (in Britain, at least) by fantasies by Carroll, MacDonald, Kingsley, Molesworth, Farrow, Nesbit, Kipling, Potter and Grahame. Fantasy, absorbed by these writers as children, was often being used as sublimation, or a political tool, or a way of negotiating either the writers' relationships with children, or their relationships to their own childhoods.

Here, another distinction emerges. As a generalization, the alternative worlds of science fiction, developing at this period (see James, 1994: 12–28), seem to be outward-looking, speculative, consequential. E. A. Abbott's *Flatland: a Romance of Many Dimensions* (1884) a philosophical–mathematical *jeu d'esprit*, or H. G. Wells's *The Time Machine* (1895), a social parable, are both concerned to open our eyes to the world. In contrast, fantasy of this period, whether for adults or children, looked inward and backward, as a therapy or a retreat, generating such highly ambiguous phenomena as the 'beautiful child' cult.

The period also contained examples of compromise: the fantasy of both Mary Louisa Molesworth, especially in *The Tapestry Room* (1878) and *The Cuckoo Clock* (1877) and E[dith] Nesbit in books such as *Five*

Children and It (1902) developed the fantasy of magic intruding on this world.

Although the USA was even more dominated in the nineteenth century by the pragmatic than Britain (notably the educational work of Peter Parley (Samuel G[riswold] Goodrich)) there was something of a fantasy tradition – for example, Louisa M. Alcott's first book was *Flower Fables* (1855). In general, though, European fantasies did not transplant well; a notable example is James Kirke Paulding's (1778–1860) *A Christmas Gift from Fairyland* (1838), which combines the fairy tale, the moral tale and the tall tale, but is fundamentally a critique of non-American values. For example, one of the stories, 'The Fairy Experiment', follows the progress of a group of fairies from England who come to America to seek 'refuge from the persecutions of science and philosophy, two deadly foes to these playful fantasies, and airy inventions of the imagination'. However, the fairy king and queen are despotic and, as the narrator comments 'despotism cannot exist in our new world'. Good American values prevail, the king and queen go back to England – while the rest of the fairies form a republic, and Puck goes to live with the Indians.

Stories that feature other lands, rather than other worlds, included *The Last of the Huggermuggers, a Giant Story* (1855, dated 1856) by Christopher Pearse Cranch, one of the 'New England Romantics', combining elements from *Gulliver's Travels* and 'Jack and the Beanstalk' with a tough American boy-hero, Jacky Cable – 'Little Jacket'.

Twentieth-century fantasy

One of the most striking things about fantasy of the twentieth century is how often it both reflects and transcends its time.

Thus, for example, *The Magic Pudding* (1918), Norman Lindsay's 'little piece of piffle', has survived as classic farce, with Sam Sawnoff the Penguin, and Bill Barnacle and the koala Bunyip Bluegum, rhyming their way across the Australian outback in pursuit of Puddin' Thieves. Yet, at the same time, it can be read as a lament for the lost Australia: the final picture of a rural idyll (albeit in a tree) shows the threatening civilization of the city edging over the horizon.

If at the beginning of the century – even with the influence of Tarzan (from *Tarzan of the Apes*, 1914) and *The Wizard of Oz* – fantasy was not as popular in the USA as in Britain: it seems to have been fostered by the two World Wars, and later the Vietnam war. In the 1920s and 1930s, writers scarred in various ways by the First World War, notably A. A. Milne, J. R. R. Tolkien and Hugh Lofting, created escapist worlds, and in the unstable political climate, fantasy flourished with the work of Masefield, P. L. Travers and many others. (It can be argued that the idyllic psuedo-realist lands of childhood created by writers such as Ransome and Estes, and later Elizabeth Enright, were – or soon became – fantasies.)

Travers, with *Mary Poppins* (1934), and Masefield with *The Midnight Folk* (1927) and *The Box of Delights* (1935) both make use of a more or less random selection of magical and fantastic elements intruding on the present day, largely through eccentric intermediaries – Mary Poppins and Cole Hawlings. The weakness of *Mary Poppins* may well be, as Perry Nodelman suggests, not the rag-bag nature of the fantasy, but Travers' virtual deification of her central character, with the result that 'Mary Poppins is not so much a fantasy as it is propaganda for fantasy, fantasy at one remove and made to be an example of its own significance' (1989: 8–9). At the same time, the USA was producing urban fantasies, notably featuring Superman and Batman.

Perhaps the ultimate fantasy for its time can be seen in Katharine Tozer's *Mumfie Marches On* (1942), in which the amiable little elephant and his friends capture Hitler:

> The silence was shattered by a series of guttural cries, rising to shrieks as the Leader of all the Germans danced madly in the road, clawing at the sharp ends of his nose which was caught firmly in the vice-like grip of the rat-trap …
>
> 'Shut up,' said Jelly. 'We're not the Reichstag.' He took the yellow duster from his hat, and lifting the rat-trap, crammed the rag into the Führer's open mouth.
>
> 'Shan't be able to use that again.' he said regretfully.

If Mumfie is now more or less forgotten, the period produced a fantasy whose importance was not really recognized for nearly thirty years, an 'alternative world' fantasy, with its roots in legend rather than fairy tale, *The Hobbit, or There and Back Again* (1937).

British fantasy for children burgeoned after the Second World War, but the tone, rather than being retreatist, as after the First World War, was much more uneasy and unsettling. Alan Garner (*The Weirdstone of Brisingamen* (1960) and *The Moon of Gomrath* (1963)), Penelope Lively (*The Whispering Knights* (1971) and *The Wild Hunt of Hagworthy* (1971)) and Susan Cooper (*The Dark is Rising* (1965–77)) borrowed from Celtic and French romance sources to provide threatening and disruptive elements. The issues at stake are now generally much greater: battles between good and evil rage in and over our world. In *Silver on the Tree* (1977) Cooper explains a whole cosmography, which can stand as an example for many similar structures:

> This where we live is a world of men, ordinary men, and although in it there is the Old Magic of the earth, and the Wild Magic of living things, it is men who control what the world shall be like ... But beyond the world is the universe, bound by the law of the High Magic, as every universe must be. And beneath the High Magic are two ... poles ... that we call the Dark and the Light. No other power orders them. They merely exist. The Dark seeks by its dark nature to influence men so that in the end, through them, it may control the earth. The Light has the task of stopping that from happening.

But neither good nor evil will ever triumph totally, 'for there is something of each in every man'.

As with Tolkien and Lewis, and many others, Cooper follows Ursula K. Le Guin's dictum that 'The mythopoeticists err, I think, in using the archetype as a rigid, filled mold. If we see it only as a vital potentiality, it becomes a guide into mystery' (1993: 22).

Perhaps the best example of the dynamic between the real and the fantastic is Garner's *The Owl Service* (1967), which draws on a recurrent legend recorded in the Fourth Branch of the Welsh collection of legends, *The Mabinogi*. However, the central difficulty for readers unable to enter the implied solipsistic world of the child readers recurrent in such fantasies, is how to make the actions of the contemporary children seem important, or even particularly interesting, in the light of the great weight of mythic significance held in the stories of their predecessors – let alone the inevitability of the outcome. (This problem is notable in C. S. Lewis's 'Narnia' series.) The same is true of Garner's 'other world' fantasy, *Elidor* (1965), but like William Mayne's *Over the Hills and Far Away* (1968) the other world is so shadowy and symbolic that it is the interface between the two worlds that is most interesting.

Fantasy from the 1960s was dominated by the Tolkien phenomenon, and the many imitations of *The Lord of the Rings*. Perhaps the best of this genre (for children), is Lloyd Alexander's Chronicles of Prydain (from *The Book of Three* (1964)) which 'freely interweave material from all four branches of the Mabinogi' (Sullivan, 1989: 56) – but which in its ultimately democratic and even pacifist message provides a gloss on the Vietnam war.

At the other end of the scale (and, literally, in terms of scale) another form of alternative world is represented by Mary Norton, in her 'Borrowers' sequence (from *The Borrowers* (1952) to *The Borrowers*

Avenged (1982)). While Swift's *Gulliver's Travels* demonstrated the potency of the ingenious 'wonder' generated by scale changes, his purposes were intensely political. His more distinguished successors, such as T. H. White's eccentric *Mistress Masham's Repose* (1947), Norton's books, the eccentric 'Indian in the Cupboard' sequence of Lynn Reid Banks, through to Terry Pratchett's remarkable *The Carpet People* (1992) and *The Bromeliad* (1989–90) the idea of the miniature has led to a more general exploration of themes of power, loss, and so on. The fascinating case of the 'frames' around Norton's stories, designed to stress their verisimilitude, while appearing to cast doubt upon their existence, has a symbolic function: 'the gradual withdrawal of human narration from their story may well symbolize freeing the Borrowers from god-like human intervention' (Kuznets, 1985: 78).

This element of rejection of the human world (also seen in Lewis's 'Narnia' sequence) although set back in time, is characteristic of tensions in British fantasy of this period. The loss of empire, the loss of the old 'grand narratives', and the contrast between past glories and future changes can be seen in major fantasies such as Lucy M. Boston's *The Children of Green Knowe* (1954) or Philippa Pearce's *Tom's Midnight Garden* (1958). Both books demonstrate the potential of philosophy in fantasy, but concentrate on the regressive, nostalgic element of fantasy – which, as we have seen, is curiously un-childlike.

A similar tone can be seen in books for adults; Mervyn Peake's 'Titus Groan' trilogy (1946–59) or T. H. White's *Once and Future King* (1958) can be seen as very regressive and conservative; indeed they were regarded as essentially eccentric in the new realism of the 'angry' decade of the 1950s. It was not until the 1960s that adult fantasy in its most visible 'sword and sorcery' form began its rise in popularity – and was gradually paralleled by a rise in the respectability of the absurd – often associated with linguistic or narrative breakdown (for example, Beckett, Barthelme, Pynchon), 'magical realism' (Borges, Marquez), or to allegory, with an associated psychological breakdown (Angela Carter). The fantastic in these forms can be seen as essentially postmodern, and has been intellectually fashionable; but as Tom Shippey has pointed out:

> 'The fantastic', as academically defined and studied, is just not the same phenomenon as the bestseller genre of 'fantasy' now to be found in every bookshop. (1995: xi)

Commercial pressures consolidated the genrefication of fantasy for children towards the end of the twentieth century. Nonetheless, there was some outstanding original work, such as Diana Wynne Jones's

Archer's Goon (1984), Jan Mark's *They Do Things Differently There* (1994), or Margaret Mahy's *The Changeover* (1984), all moving children's fantasy towards the postmodern and the metafictive. The boundaries between reality and psychological fantasy have become increasingly unstable and blurred, notably in Gillian Cross's *Wolf* (1990), although such books were foreshadowed by the existential parable of Russell Hoban's *The Mouse and his Child* (1967), whose alternative world is a nightmare landscape of junk-yards, haunted by a manic obsessive, Manny Rat. This is a more explicit nightmare than Alice's dream, and symptomatic of the world that fantasy increasingly inhabits.

Despite such remarkable work, objections to fantasy remain. In 2000, there was a good deal of public debate over whether J. K. Rowling's *Harry Potter and the Prisoner of Azkaban*, or Seamus Heaney's translation of *Beowulf* should be awarded the prestigious British Whitbread Literary Prize. Much of the debate hinged on common confusions between popular and high culture, and Rowling's book was doubly condemned for being for children. It is, however, highly significant that nobody seems to have pointed out, during the Whitbread controversy, that both the competing texts were fantasies.

Fantasy, then is part of the fabric of literary culture. Although it is still sometimes argued, with Raymond Tallis, that 'Fantasy imposes a passivity on the reader: he either swallows what he is told or he is excluded from the story altogether' (1988: 192), C. S. Lewis's view seems likely to prevail:

> Of course, a given reader may be (some readers seem to be) interested in nothing else in the world except detailed studies of complex human personalities. If so, he has a good reason for not reading those kinds of works which neither demand nor admit it. He has no reason for condemning them, and indeed no qualification for speaking of them at all. We must not allow the novel of manners to give laws to all literature. (1966: 65)

Thus the kind of comment made by E. M. Forster in *Aspects of the Novel* (neatly stabbing the mode in the back as he did so) – that fantasy 'asks us to pay something extra. It compels us to an adjustment that is different to an adjustment required by a work of art' (1974: 113), can now be countered by Tom Shippey's view that

> it is quite certain that the modern fantasy genre contains within it a substantial part of the literary effort and literary skill of present-day English-speaking culture, and provides for millions of readers a distinctive literary reward. (1995: xxi)

Exploring alternative worlds: the key fantasies

The various complex ways in which writers have approached fantasy writing can be illustrated by looking at some key texts, from Kingsley's awkward, self-destructing use of the form, to J. K. Rowling's hard-edged and eclectic *Bildungsroman*. What emerges strongly is the complexity of these books, and the sheer fecundity of imagination, whether at the service of intellectualism or humour, generally defies or challenges classifications.

Charles Kingsley's *The Water Babies: A Fairy Tale for a Land-Baby* (1863) is a highly eccentric 'landmark' text, often claimed to have marked the beginning of the first 'golden age' of British children's literature (from the 1860s to the First World War). It is a curious performance, which might be excluded from a discussion of fantasy (under a definition such as Manlove's, cited above), on the grounds that its real preoccupations are Kingsley's hobbyhorses – issues such as child-welfare, children's reading, sexuality, evolution, redemption and purgatory. As a result, what seems at first sight to be a rambling excursion into a fantasy-land of mystic fairies, talking sea-creatures, and uneducated vegetables, becomes an extended illustrated lecture. Kingsley almost seems to go out of his way to devalue his own fantasy – the book ends: 'But remember always, as I told you at first, that this is all a fairy-tale, and only fun and pretence: and, therefore, you are not to believe a word of it, even if it is true.'

The Water Babies lurches between categories, from a realistic indictment of child-labour conditions, to whimsical fantasy, fuelled by undisciplined doses of scientific speculation and religious convictions. One critic has proposed that in *The Water Babies* Kingsley 'offers his most attractive, deceptively simple presentation of the argument that all purely scientific explanations of reality would benefit by being placed in the larger context of Christian revelation' and that 'science must be especially careful not to trample on the realms of imagination and religion' (Hawley, 1989: 20). For example, quoting Wordsworth's 'Ode: Intimations of Immortality':

> Our birth is but a sleep and a forgetting ...
> But trailing clouds of glory, do we come
> From God, who is our home

the narrator of *The Water Babies* goes on:

> there, you can know no more than that. But if I was you, I would
> believe that. For then the great fairy Science, who is likely to be
> queen of all the fairies for many a year to come, can only do you

good, and never do you harm; and instead of fancying, with some people, that your body makes your soul, as if a steam-engine could make its own coke; or, with some people, that your soul has nothing to do with your body, but is only stuck into it like a pin into a pin-cushion, to fall out with the first shake; – you will believe the one true ... doctrine of this wonderful fairy-tale; which is, that your soul makes your body, just as a snail makes his shell.

Fantasy is harnessed to both polemic and allegory, and the book exemplifies the ambivalent status of fantasy for children at this period. Humphrey Carpenter may have been exaggerating when he suggested that Kingsley was 'the first writer in England, perhaps the first in the world with the exception of Hans Andersen, to discover that a children's book can be the perfect vehicle for an adult's most personal and private concerns' (1987: 37); whether this is true or not, Kingsley is still operating in the didactic mode of a previous generation. Thus although the world of Tom the chimney sweep/water baby is mapped on to the everyday world – all the elements, from Harthover Hall to the oceans, are there only to deal with ideas.

The same can be said – although the ideas are ingeniously hidden – of the alternative worlds of Lewis Carroll's 'Alice' books. This is fantasy locked on to the real world; each book is a satire-allegory on politics, a commentary on Victorian mores, an empathetic view of the (female) child's position in Victorian society, and a sublimation of Carroll's own desires. Carroll's choice of (Sir) John Tenniel – a prominent political cartoonist – to illustrate the books was no accident, so dense (if gnomic) is the political reference. In fact, despite all appearances, the one thing that the books are emphatically *not*, is nonsense.

A comparison with Carroll's imitators, such as G. E. Farrow and his 'Wallypug of Why' books, demonstrates this. Farrow could handle verbal jokes in the Carrollian manner:

'Late again!' called out the Hall Porter ...

'How can I be late *again*,' asked Girlie angrily, 'when I've never been here at all before?'

'If you've not been here before, then you must have been behind,' said the Hall Porter, and if one is behind, they are late, don't you know?'

But, to take an obvious example, he makes virtually nothing of the implications of the fact (or fiction) that the Wallypug was 'a *kind of king*, governed by the people instead of governing them. He was obliged to spend his money as *they* decided, and was not allowed to do *anything* without their permission. In terms of definitions of fantasy, this may make the *Wallypug* purer than *Alice*, but far less effective.

As an adult's fantasy (albeit directed at a child) the 'Alice' books have an underlying seriousness, not to say grimness. Humphrey Carpenter suggested that 'it is not in itself very surprising that the books show, on their deepest level, an exploration of violence, death and Nothingness' because 'Comedy tends to lead in that direction' (1987: 62). He might, perhaps, have added that fantasy does the same.

The alternative worlds that Alice enters are grotesque parodies of Alice's 'normal' world, existing, perhaps, only in her mind. There is, therefore a paradox here in the use of the dream structure; does making the story a dream actually make it safer? Commonly, as we have seen, the dream is regarded as the most unsatisfactory of devices for fantasy, undermining the value of the action, or showing authorial lack of confidence. In *Alice's Adventures in Wonderland*, the coda, which patronizingly reduces Alice's complex mindscape to echoes, is close to disavowing the disturbing complexities of the book (as Carroll later did totally in his ultra-simplified version *The Nursery Alice* (1890):

> 'Oh, I've had such a curious dream!' said Alice ... and when she had finished, her sister kissed her, and said, 'It *was* a curious dream, dear, certainly; but now run in to your tea: it's getting late.' So Alice got up and ran off, thinking while she ran, as well she might, what a wonderful dream it had been ... But her sister sat still just as she had left her ... till she began dreaming after a fashion, and ... the whole place around her became alive with the strange creatures of her little sister's dream.

And it is all deconstructed:

> the rattling teacups would change to tinkling sheep-bells, and the Queen's shrill cries to the voice of the shepherd-boy – and the sneeze of the baby, the shriek of the Gryphon, and all the other queer noises, would change (she knew) to the confused clamour of the busy farm-yard.

In the original text, Alice's sister dreams 'a dream within the dream, as it were', about Alice's future. *Through the Looking Glass*, rather more confidently, ends with Alice's soliloquy: 'Let's consider who it was that dreamed it', and the last line of the final poem – 'Life, what is it but a dream?' – takes us out into profound waters.

As several critics have noted, the dream 'frames' seem to be 'unwriting' both Carroll's subversiveness, and the suspicion that he had approached too many taboo things too nearly. But, far from the dream being an undermining feature, it is an integral part of the nightmare: there is a sinister relationship between dream and reality. In *Through the Looking Glass*, Alice comes across the Red King, asleep:

> 'He's dreaming now,' said Tweedledee: 'and what do you think he's dreaming about?'
>
>   Alice said 'Nobody can guess that.'
>
>   'Why, about *you!*' Tweedledee exclaimed, clapping his hands triumphantly. 'And if he left off dreaming about you, where do you suppose you'd be ... You'd be nowhere. Why, you're only a sort of thing in his dream.'
>
>   'If that there King was to wake,' added Tweedledum, 'you'd go out – bang! – just like a candle.'

Gloss on Bishop Berkeley's point about all things being ideas in the mind of God, or not, there is a dark sense of humour at work here: this is fantasy at its most misleadingly serious.

Definitions of fantasy would seem to exclude everything that the 'Alice' books are: but they triumphantly vindicate their existence, whether we regard them as profoundly rooted in the elemental uses of fantasy, or complex *romans à clef*. But if they can be criticized in terms of fantasy, it might not be that ideas come first, or that the worlds are not fully realized, or that the books do not invoke wonder: it is the character (or lack of character) of Alice herself. Her value seems to exist only in the narrator's fondness for her: she is (as in Tallis's criticism of fantasy in general) 'unastonished by things' (1988: 206).

At the opposite extreme from 'Alice' in terms of purpose is probably the most famous American fantasy, L. Frank Baum's *The Wizard of Oz* (1900) and its many sequels. If Baum had an intricate satirical or personal purpose in writing his fantasy, it has escaped most readers. He intended, he said, to produce a tale that retained 'the wonderment and joy' of the old tales, with 'the heartache and nightmares left out'. If he did not quite succeed, at least the heartaches and the nightmares are dealt with in a fairly perfunctory manner. The fantasy of Oz, whatever criticisms may be aimed at the functional rather than elegant prose, or the simple sequencing (rather than plotting), is a fantasy that seems to (and apparently intends to) exploit impossibilities for their own sake. Dorothy and her friends and successors are whirled through a series of adventures, each more inventive than the next. On the one hand, as Perry Nodelman has said, there is the sheer exuberant richness of Baum's imagination. As one reads through any one of the Oz books, one cannot possibly tell what weird wonder is going to happen next ... The astonishing world Baum describes has no overriding law or principle except variety ... Baum does not often create his fantasy worlds and characters out of his previous knowledge of literature and mythology. (1989: 10, 11)

But, as we have seen, even the most innocent-seeming texts must be more than they appear to be: psychoanalytic critics could no doubt make a great deal out of winged monkeys or melting witches, and there has been a good deal of speculation as to whether Oz is a complex allegory of the USA. It seems likely that at least some of the impact of *The Wizard of Oz* derives from its concentration on Dorothy's quest to return to Kansas and Aunt Em – however hard, and sketchily described, that landscape is – and on the underlying tensions of the two landscapes.

Nevertheless, it may be Baum's overpowering inventiveness that has given the book its relatively lowly literary status: as John Goldthwaite said, he was 'the Edison of narrative fantasy, finding ways of lighting it up and making it talk that no one had ever thought of before' (1996: 211).

The far more subtle fantasy world of Beatrix Potter's 'little books', is an anthropomorphic land *superimposed* upon the everyday world of Sawrey and the English Lake District. From *The Tale of Peter Rabbit* (1902) to *The Tale of Little Pig Robinson* (1930) her books, as Peter Hollindale put it, can be read as 'conversations through the medium of fantasy' between 'the biological reality of the animal and the social behaviour of the human' (1999: 18). Sometimes the world is self-contained, as in the satire of *The Pie and the Patty-Pan* (1905), in which the houses of the real village are inhabited by animals who generally behave as humans, or in *Ginger and Pickles* (1909), where Potter's apparent whimsicality shows its characteristic hard edge:

Ginger and Pickles were the people who kept the shop. Ginger was a yellow tom-cat, and Pickles was a terrier.

The rabbits were always a little afraid of Pickles.

The shop was also patronized by mice – only the mice were rather afraid of Ginger.

Ginger usually requested Pickles to serve them, because he said it made his mouth water.

'I cannot bear,' said he, 'to see them going out at the door carrying their little parcels.'

Sometimes it overlaps with reality as when, in *The Tale of Peter Rabbit*, Mr MacGregor finds Peter's blue jacket. The animal world to some extent copies, to some extent mirrors the human: possibly Potter's major achievement was to make her characters both at once. The ironic treatment of human foibles may not qualify for some category of 'high' fantasy, but Potter's portrayals of horrors (as in *The Roly-Poly Pudding* (1908)), or violence (*The Tale of Mr Tod* (1912)) is no less telling for being in miniature, rather that on a vast canvas.

As we have seen (and as we shall see in the work of Terry Pratchett), the roles of the adult creator and the child readers add a very intricate level of complication to children's fantasy. The inherent ambivalence of the relationship is nowhere better demonstrated by the Neverland of J. M. Barrie in 'Peter Pan' (1904).

At first glance – or, perhaps, in collective folk-memory (and as depicted in the Walt Disney version) – Neverland seems to be composed of favourite elements of (British) children's games, where one can fight pirates and red Indians, and play with mermaids and feast with impunity. It is, one might think, an obvious children's fantasy – always to play safely, never to grow up. But, as Jacqueline Rose observed, by the time Barrie came to write a definitive prose text in 1911, after his own stage versions and various retellings, 'Peter Pan' 'had come to signify an innocence, or simplicity, which every line of Barrie's 1911 text belies' (1984: 67). For example, how many lost boys were there? In the second (or third) of Barrie's prose versions, *Peter and Wendy* (1911), Barrie explains:

> The boys on the island vary, of course, in numbers, according as they get killed and so on; and when they seem to be growing up, which is against the rules, Peter thins them out.

The difficult question of innocence is, as we have seen, central to the idea of children's fantasy, but in this case, whose fantasy is it? Is it actually the fantasy of a child never to grow up? As Tolkien remarked, alluding to the sterility of the fantasy that Barrie sets up: 'Children are meant to grow up, and not become Peter Pans' (1964: 42). It may be the adult observer, or the adult fantasist who actually gets satisfaction: the narrator's commentary on the story that Wendy tells the lost boys could sum up Barrie's (and many other people's) attitudes to fantasy:

> Off we skip like the most heartless things in the world, which is what children are, but so attractive; and we have an entirely selfish time; and then when we have need of special attention we

nobly return for it, confident that we shall be embraced rather than smacked.

Barrie's theatrical technique continually spills over into his prose, parodying itself, and forming another distancing element. Here, fantasy cannot be compared to the novel: cannot be criticized for failing to involve the reader with naturalistic characters. Rather, we are dealing with symbolic tragedy, with complex sublimations which need this kind of abstract world of fantasy in which to function – otherwise matters might be too painful.

'Peter Pan' has become part of international folklore, but Margery Fisher saw its influence as essentially pernicious, for it set a fashion for books

> isolating the young from the adult world ... Peter Pan is still a classic, if only for the terrifyingly true, bleak definition of a type always with us. As a story to offer to children it should be approached with caution, for there is much to dislike in its curiously twisted, self-conscious, indulgent humour. (1986: 8)

Like *The Wind in the Willows*, 'Peter Pan' is an adult's fantasy for an adult, about childhood, warped into the appearance of being for children. The 1953 Walt Disney film is among the least disturbing versions, scarcely raising the issues of isolation and loss which permeate the original, while the cartoon form more or less eradicates the unpleasant violence, and makes the 'frame' story more obviously a fantasy in its own right.

Barrie was clearly ambivalent about the text: having set up Neverland as the desirable playground, he ends the book (although not every version of the play) with the image of Peter Pan being excluded from the fantasy of family life: 'He had ecstasies innumerable that other children can never know; but he was looking through the window at the one joy from which he must be for ever barred.'

If Potter was using fantasy to deal with the adult world for children, and Barrie to deal with the relationship between adulthood and childhood for himself, Kenneth Grahame in *The Wind in the Willows* (1908) seems to have been using it to deal with an adult's problem with adulthood. Contrary to the understandable assumption that it is a children's book, a strong argument can be made that not only was it never actually intended for children (even the child to and for whom part of it was ostensibly written) but is the concretization a wish-fulfilment fantasy about Grahame's own frustrations and desires.

The Wind in the Willows can scarcely be said to be about animals at all. Early reviewers were not all misled by the apparent anthropomorphism: novelist Arnold Bennett reviewed it as 'an urbane exercise in irony at the expense of the English character,' (Hunt, 1994: 16, 17). The major characters (all male) can be seen as facets of Grahame's own character: as Margaret Meek observed, we 'encounter the same person, the author, variously disguised as a Rat, a Mole, a Badger, and a Toad, all equally egocentric and self-regarding' (1991: 25). The disguise encompasses the roles of independent bachelor, poet and sailor, liberated clerk, powerful, traditionalist squire, and rebellious child, all living in a fantasy world of privilege, where there are no responsibilities, and where women are objects of fear or derision.

And these animals occupy a highly ambiguous fantasy space, as much an 'other' world as that of Peter Rabbit or Bilbo Baggins. On one level it is England in 1908: the woods, the river, Toad Hall, the inn, the motor cars, the train, could all be seen in the real world *then*. E. H. Shepard, after all, drew it from the life in 1930. But the world that Rat and Mole and Badger inhabit is at once human size and animal size: Toad is the only animal who crosses over into the 'real' world of humans. But that 'real' world is grossly distorted: there is a magistrate's court straight out of Gilbert and Sullivan, a medieval prison; where it looks most 'real' – as with the barge woman or the gypsy, it adapts to radical and irrational changes of scale. Is it, then, magical, or allegorical, or symbolic, or all of these?

The Wind in the Willows emerges as a genuine *escapist* fantasy which demonstrates the impossibility of escape: here is a writer sublimating his fear of change and decay, of a Victorian world rapidly becoming unstable – with the labour movement, the women's movement, the motor car – creating a golden world which is, curiously, repressive in itself. Thus while it might be assumed to appeal to children because of its fantasy of anarchy and play, much of it may appeal more directly to nostalgic adults. Women, those awkwardly complicated and demanding creatures, are excluded; the political status quo, so threatened by the faceless masses of the Wild Wood is easily restored 'by matchless valour, consummate strategy, and a proper handling of sticks'; and a homoerotic pagan God rules.

The conventions of fantasy provide certain readers with vicarious gratification. Thus the emphasis upon food (rather than sex) throughout seems to symbolize a retreat towards an irresponsible life (otherwise known as childhood). One of Grahame's friends recalled

an occasion on which Grahame had borrowed a fourteenth-century cottage in the main street of Streatley, and they walked twenty miles along the Ridgeway before returning to 'chops, great chunks of cheese, new bread, great swills of beer, pipes, bed and heavenly sleep'. (Green, 1959: 126)

Whatever it is, *The Wind in the Willows* does not seem to be either about or for childhood – growth, personal adventure, development, and escape are all rigorously suppressed. At Mole's first meeting with Rat, when he is revelling in his liberation from domestic drudgery, he has his own fantasies – curiously, involved with leaving what is essentially a fantasy world – quashed:

'Beyond the Wild Wood comes the Wide World,' said the Rat. 'And that's something that doesn't matter, either to you or to me. I've never been there, and I'm never going, nor you either, if you've got any sense at all. Don't ever refer to it again, please. Now then! Here's our backwater at last, where we're going to lunch.'

Later, Mole himself represses Rat, almost seduced by the Sea Rat, and, obviously in the grip of a 'strange seizure'. Grahame's encounter with fantasies of all kinds, and his intense, not to say tortured use of the fantastic form is a complex, painful thing, and can hardly be accused of being either shallow or unengaging.

Of all the major fantasies, A. A. Milne's *Winnie-the-Pooh* (1926) and *The House at Pooh Corner* (1928) must seem as far from the sword-and-sorcery image of fantasy as it is possible to get. However, the alternative world of the books, although it may look like a slice of Sussex, is not the real Five-Hundred Acre Wood, but the Hundred Aker Wood, which is a very different thing. And so, what is happening in terms of fantasizing is every bit as complex, in terms of writer–adult–child relationships, and every bit as conventional in terms of characteristics, as larger-scale works. This may not seem like one of the grand heroic narratives – but it is a question of scale, and, perhaps, gender.

One difficulty of approaching the books has been summed up by Milne's biographer, Ann Thwaite:

But after *The Pooh Perplex*, Frederick Crews's 1963 parody of a student casebook, one cannot attempt the most rudimentary criticism without seeming to be joking. After 'The Hierarchy of Heroism in *Winnie-the-Pooh*', and 'A la recherche du Pooh perdu' ... one's pen freezes in one's hand ... Perhaps the great Heffalump expedition really is a paradigm of colonialism? ... You begin to wonder if those invented critics might not have something after all. (1991: 301)

Grasping the critical heffalump by the nose (or trunk), then, it can be argued that the Pooh books contain many conventional elements of fantasy – the anti-hero – who is weak but wise (Pooh), and his buddy (Piglet), the omniscient mage (Christopher Robin), the team of (male) supporters, the quests, and the excluded others. But the major difference is that while fear in *The Wind in the Willows* is clearly derived from the other, the outsiders – the wild-wooders, the women, humans in general, the foreign – here the serpents are part of Eden. Rabbit, Owl and Eeyore are the destructive *adult male* egos, but stuffed toys for all that; even Kanga (both female and foreign) is presented as a rather frightening figure of power. Rabbit spends his time spreading cynicism and fear ('You know how it is in the forest . . . One has to be careful'); Owl lives on pretence ('Owl took Christopher Robin's notice from Rabbit and looked at it nervously'); and Eeyore is Eeyore ('Hallo, Eeyore,' they called out cheerfully. 'Ah!' said Eeyore. 'Lost your way?'). In contrasting these characters with the child-toys (Pooh, Piglet, Tigger, Roo) Milne is reproducing the relationship between the heroes and villains of all fantasy, within a sealed world.

Milne's ambivalence, both about writing for children, and an adult's relationship to a retreatist world shows in the frames he places around the book. Christopher Robin's growing up means, in effect, a transition away from the world of fantasy: it is a loss, but a somewhat ambivalent loss, as though childhood were not essentially admirable.

> With his eyes on the world Christopher Robin put out a hand and felt for Pooh's paw.
> 'Pooh,' said Christopher Robin earnestly, 'if I – if I'm not quite –' he stopped and tried again – 'Pooh, *whatever* happens, you *will* understand, won't you?'
> 'Understand what?'

Fantasy cannot hide ambivalence like this – and indeed is often the place where it is to be found most painfully.

Of the inter-war fantasists, Tolkien is undoubtedly the most important for his influence on the genre, with *The Hobbit, or There and Back Again* (1937). But for all its influence, it is easy to see the same nostalgic, 'escapist' characteristics in Tolkien, Grahame and Milne: the world is moving on, and the bucolic world of the Hobbits is under threat – and, at the end of *The Return of the King*, the Shire is severely damaged by industrialization. But whereas in Milne there is a sense of moving on for Christopher Robin, the whole ethos of the Middle Earth cycle is of the good past that is being lost. Aragorn and Galadriel are but the lesser son and daughter of great peoples – and they are going to fade and die. The humans that come after the third age are short-lived and imperfect.

Rather than being a personal statement (as is much of the work of Macdonald and Carroll and Grahame – and Pratchett and Le Guin), the world of Middle Earth seems to be at root a ritual: everything is done for the sake of song and legend – characters are living out gnomic predictions, or consciously writing themselves into future history-books. As Bilbo says, at the end of *The Hobbit*:

> 'Then the prophecies of the old songs have turned out to be true, after a fashion!' said Bilbo.
>
> 'Of course!' said Gandalf. 'And why should not they prove true? Surely you don't disbelieve the prophecies, because you had a hand in bringing them about yourself? You don't really suppose, do you, that all your adventures and escapes were managed by mere luck, just for your sole benefit?'

It is all this, perhaps, that makes the books so disliked by commentators raised on the novel of character, or, indeed, any post-romantic humanist: violence, tempered with a little mystic philosophy, solves everything. No real passions arise anywhere – and least of all from the chronicler (who is acting out the traditions of ancient chroniclers); no real people are involved.

There is little question that Middle Earth, a complex creation, carefully worked out over many years, and based on language as much as geography is the fullest exemplar of the coherent alternative world yet – with the possible exception of the Discworld (although for some less-well-known examples, see Manlove, 1999: 37–63). And some of its appeal is this very intricacy: as Tolkien said: 'A lot of it, is just straight teen-age stuff. I didn't mean it to be, but it's perfect for them. I think they're attracted by things that give verisimilitude' (quoted in Manlove, 1975: 156).

The maleness of the world is not confined to its heroics: as in *The Wind in the Willows* we are largely free of the annoyances of the female or the personal; the pleasures of the Hobbits are childlike in appetite but adult in execution – pipes, beer, and so on – and as the books progress, the Hobbits have less and less to do with childhood.

In this context, such genuine emotions as there are, are very small-scale. Thus it could be argued that Sam Gamgee is the character who provides the link not only with childhood, but with some kind of identifiable reality. His role is essentially that of a child (or an adult's preferred image of a child), trusting, supportive, pragmatic, and eventually heroic: the difficulty is that he is simultaneously, like Mole, a regressive image for the adult; he knows his place (subordinate, rural, domestic). *The Hobbit* and *The Lord of the Rings* celebrate the success of the little person, the powerless who upset the counsels of the great – as a metaphor for Englishness of a kind, it is very potent. And yet its lack of passion – the kind of passion that lurks in 'Alice' or 'Peter Pan', or the Pooh books – remains a weakness for many readers.

Much 'high' fantasy operates in a pagan, unredeemed world; but, one might think, given that fantasy generally has a purpose, then what better purpose might there be than the celebration of religious faith, rather than the voyeuristic position of watching imaginary religions at work? And yet C. S. Lewis's 'Narnia' series remains problematic for critics on several counts. Tolkein, that builder of coherent worlds, did not approve of Lewis's (at least initially) scatter-gun approach: talking beasts from fable mix with hags and dwarves from legend, religious allegorical figures, and even that modern, partially commercial creation, Father Christmas.

The 'Narnia' books have been a publishing success story, selling steadily over fifty years, although banned here and there (for blasphemy). Some of the books, such as *The Silver Chair* (1953) and *The Horse and his Boy* (1954) are set entirely in Narnia; others pass between Narnia and the 'real' world. For Narnia is, genuinely, an alternative. The most obviously symbolic books are *The Lion, the Witch and the Wardrobe* (1950) and *The Last Battle* (1956) and also there are obvious moments, such as the lion–lamb transformation in *The Voyage of the 'Dawn Treader'* (1952). There is a re-working of Christ's passion, and, in *The Last Battle*, the end of the alternative world in favour of another:

> 'When Aslan said you could never go back to Narnia, he meant the Narnia you were thinking of. But that was not the real Narnia. That had a beginning and an end. It was only a shadow or a copy of the real Narnia which has always been here and always will be here; just as our own world, England and all, is only a shadow or copy of something in Aslan's real world ... ' The new [Narnia] was a deeper country: every rock and flower and blade of grass looked as if it meant more.

A sticking point is the resemblance of Lewis's Christian world to the pagan world it replaces, or overlays. The characters have no free will: the Christ-figure of Aslan is totally in control – and seems to play even more arbitrary games than the old Gods. But if this is acceptable in a thousand imaginary worlds, why should it be seen as debilitating here? It may be because the books seem to be about freedom and choice, but are actually about control. David Holbrook, in a famous critique of the books, suggested that structurally, 'nothing happens in the Narnia books except the build-up and confrontation with paranoically conceived menaces, from an aggressive posture of hate, leading towards conflict' (1976: 117). The patterns of legend, which countenance such simple remedies, do not sit well with Christianity (and this is quite apart from Holbrook's doubt whether 'the hate, fear and sadism in them is relieved by humanizing benignity' (124)).

John Goldthwaite has developed this attack, pointing out that Lewis's alternative world is a positive rejection of this one (in itself blasphemy), and the rejection is on a rather mean-minded basis: the alternative world 'allowed Lewis to leave out everything about the world that he disliked or to summon up what he disliked in such a way that he could knock it about however he wished' (1996: 224). Thus Goldthwaite feels that the books are actually profoundly anti-Christian, notably as Aslan travels his world casually excluding from the elect (who go to the ultimate alternative world, heaven) people of whom Lewis disapproves – for example, the 'dumpy, prim little girls with fat legs' in *Prince Caspian*, or the lipstick-wearing Susan of *The Last Battle*.

Ideology is inescapable in any text: Lewis's work demonstrates the complexities that follow when a specific philosophy meets quite different kinds of generic and cultural materials.

Fantasy, then, remains powerful, as demonstrated by the recent efforts in the USA to ban the work of J. K. Rowling – on the grounds that her books validate witchcraft. The world of Harry Potter might technically be described as a 'parallel' world, a wizardly world existing beside, and sometimes overlapping the everyday 'muggle' world. In *Harry Potter and the Philosopher's Stone* (1997), *Harry Potter and the Chamber of Secrets* (1998), *Harry Potter and the Prisoner of Azkaban* (1999) and *Harry Potter and the Goblet of Fire* (2000) intertextuality is inevitable, and managed intelligently – perhaps because, unlike many adult fantasies, it is essentially positive – even if it appears to be built upon regressive elements such as the school story and a sexist popular-culture hierarchy. The books' knowingness goes beyond intertextuality; their preoccupation, for example with levels of knowledge and surveillance, reflects very accurately the world of their readers. The books are essentially not escapist: far worse things happen, personally, to Harry than to Frodo or Bilbo. However symbolic Frodo's stabbing, it is nothing compared to Harry's parents' murder. In several significant ways, Rowling has changed fantasy, while holding on to such addictive details as are useful.

Introducing Pratchett, Le Guin, and Pullman

Fantasy, then, has a remarkable history, and a remarkable range. It is never innocent, very often highly complex, and contrary to a long tradition of religious disapproval, very often based on ethical premises. As Molson notes, 'ethical fantasy' is

> explicitly concerned with the existence of good and evil and the morality of human behaviour ... [it] takes for granted that good and evil exist and that there are substantive, discernible differences between them. [It assumes that] choosing between right and wrong and accepting the consequences of that choice are marks of maturity. (1982: 86)

It is also continuously re-inventing itself and challenging itself, and the three authors discussed in detail in this book have three things in common: they have absorbed the past of fantasy, they move it on in new directions, and they are formidably intelligent.

Terry Pratchett might have the toughest job in achieving (in the unlikely event of his wanting to do such a thing), literary respectability, as a comic fantasist. But he is also an inveterate satirist and hence, ironically enough, a realist:

> Originally I just wanted to write a sort of antidote to some of the worst kind of post-Tolkien fantasy, what I call the 'Belike, he will wax wroth' school of writing. I wanted the world to be fantastic but the people to be as realistic as possible. (Pratchett and Briggs, 1997: 472)

Pratchett is also a fascinating test-case for the debate about the distinction between literature for children and literature for adults.

Ursula K. Le Guin, a writer of serious purpose, has written for both:

> The real trouble isn't the money, it's the adult chauvinist piggery.
> 'You're a juvenile writer, aren't you?'
> Yeth Mummy.
> 'I love your books – the real ones, I mean, I haven't read the ones for children, of course!'
> Of courthe not, Daddy.
> 'It must be relaxing to write simple things for a change.'
> Sure, it's simple, writing for kids. Just as simple as bringing them up. (1992: 49)

Her concerns are both philosophical and social, and she has done a great deal to challenge the gender balance of certain types of fantasy.

And Philip Pullman?

I think the grand narratives aren't so much played out or exhausted in contemporary writing, as abandoned for ideological reasons ... Maybe the whole thing is weakened by a fatal lack of ambition. This is what I find most irritating in my contemporaries among writers: lack of ambition. They're not trying big things. They're doing little things and doing them well. (Parsons and Nicholson, 1999: 117)

Raymond Tallis observed, in his attack on fantasy, that 'it takes infinitely greater talent to imagine and express the consciousness of the person sitting opposite you in a train than to summon up ten thousand demons from some imaginary hell' (1988: 207, cf. Le Guin, 1992: 117). Perhaps – but it takes infinitely more talent still to imagine and express the consciousness of the demons. Fantasy treats of demons of one kind or another, and nowhere better than in the alternative worlds of Pratchett, and Le Guin and Pullman.

References

Allott, M. (1965) *Novelists on the Novel*, London: Routledge and Kegan Paul.

Armitt, L. (1996) *Theorising the Fantastic*, London: Arnold.

Attebury, B. (1980) *The Fantasy Tradition in American Literature: from Irving to Le Guin*, Bloomington: Indiana University Press.

Bettelheim, B. (1976) *The Uses of Enchantment*, London: Thames and Hudson.

Carpenter, H. (1987) *Secret Gardens*, London: Unwin Hyman.

Fisher, M. (1986) *Classics for Children and Young People*, South Woodchester: Thimble Press.

Forster, E. M. (1974) *Aspects of the Novel*, Harmondsworth: Penguin.

Goldthwaite, J. (1996) *The Natural History of Make-Believe*, New York: Oxford University Press.

Green, P. (1959) *Kenneth Grahame*, London: John Murray.

Harrison, B. and Maguire, G. (eds) (1987) *Innocence and Experience: Essays and Conversations on Children's Literature*, New York: Lothrop, Lee and Shepard.

Hawley, J. C. (1989) 'The *Water Babies* as catechetical paradigm', *Children's Literature Association Quarterly*, 14(1): 19–21.

Holbrook, D. (1976) 'The problem of C. S. Lewis', in G. Fox *et al.*, (eds), *Writers, Critics and Children*, New York: Agathon/London: Heinemann.

Hollindale, P. (1999) 'Aesop in the shadows. The annual Linder Memorial Lecture [on Beatrix Potter]', *Signal* 89: 115–32.

Hunt, P. (1994) *The Wind in the Willows. A Fragmented Arcadia*, New York: Twayne.

Irwin, W. R. (1976) *The Game of the Impossible*, Urbana: University of Illinois Press.

James, E. (1994) *Science Fiction in the Twentieth Century*, Oxford: Oxford University Press.

Kuznets, L. (1985) 'Permutations of frame in Mary Norton's "Borrowers" series', *Studies in the Literary Imagination*, 18(2): 65–78.

Le Guin, U. K. (1992) *The Language of the Night. Essays on Fantasy and Science Fiction*, second edition, New York: HarperCollins.

Le Guin, U. K. (1993) *Earthsea Revisioned*, Cambridge: Children's Literature New England in association with Green Bay Publications.

Lewis, C. S. (1966) 'On three ways of writing for children', in W. Hooper (ed.) *Of Other Worlds*, London: Geoffrey Bles.

Lynn, R. N. (1983) *Fantasy for Children. An Annotated Checklist and Reference Guide* (2nd edition), New York: R. R. Bowker.

Manlove, C. N. (1975) *Modern Fantasy: Five Studies*, Cambridge: Cambridge University Press.

Manlove, C. N. (1982) 'On the nature of fantasy', in R. C. Schlobin (ed.), *The Aesthetics of Fantasy Literature and Art*, Notre Dame: University of Notre Dame Press/Brighton: Harvester Press: 16–35.

Manlove, C. N. (1999) *The Fantasy Literature of England*, London: Macmillan.

Meek, M. (1991) 'The limits of delight', *Books for Keeps*, 68: 24–5. [Reprinted in C. Powling (ed.) (1994), *The Best of Books for Keeps*, London: The Bodley Head: 27–31.]

Molson, F. J. (1982) 'Ethical fantasy for children', in R. C. Schlobin (ed.), *The Aesthetics of Fantasy Literature and Art*, Notre Dame: University of Notre Dame Press/Brighton: Harvester Press: 82–104.

Nodelman, P. (1989) 'Introduction: On words and pictures, neglected noteworthies, and touchstones in training', in P. Nodelman (ed.) *Touchstones: Reflections on the Best in Children's Literature*, Vol. 3, West Lafayette: Children's Literature Association: 1–13.

Parsons, W. and Nicholson, C. (1999) 'Talking to Philip Pullman: An interview', *The Lion and the Unicorn*, 23(1): 116–34.

Pratchett, T. and Briggs, S. (1997) *The Discworld Companion*, London: Vista.

Propp, V. (1975) *Morphology of the Folk Tale* (trans. L. Scott), Austin: University of Texas Press.

Pullman, P. (1998) 'Let's write it in red: the Patrick Hardy Lecture', *Signal*, 85: 44–62.

Rabkin, E. S. (1976) *The Fantastic in Literature*, Princeton: Princeton

University Press.

Rose, J. (1984) *The Case of Peter Pan*, London: Macmillan.

Salway, L. (ed.) (1976) *A Peculiar Gift: Nineteenth Century Writings on Books for Children*, Harmondsworth: Kestrel (Penguin).

Schlobin, R. C. (ed.) (1982) *The Aesthetics of Fantasy Literature and Art*, Notre Dame: University of Notre Dame Press/Brighton: Harvester Press.

Shippey, T. (1995) 'Introduction', *The Oxford Book of Fantasy Stories*, Oxford: Oxford University Press.

Sullivan III, C. W. (1989) *Welsh Celtic Myth in Modern Fantasy*, Westport: Greenwood Press.

Sullivan III, C. W. (1992) 'Fantasy', in D. Butts (ed.), *Stories and Society. Children's Literature in its Social Context*, London: Macmillan: 97–111.

Sullivan III, C. W. (1996) 'High fantasy' in P. Hunt (ed.) *International Companion Encyclopedia of Children's Literature*, London: Routledge: 303–13.

Swinfen, A. (1984) *In Defence of Fantasy. A Study of the Genre in English and American Literature since 1945*, London: Routledge and Kegan Paul.

Tallis, R. (1988) *In Defence of Realism*, London: Edward Arnold.

Thompson, S. (1932–6) *Motif-Index of Folk-Literature: a Classification of Narrative Elements in Folk-Tales, Ballads, Myths, Fables, Medieval Romances, Exempla, Fabliaux, Jest-Books, and Local Legends* (6 volumes), Helsinki: Suomlainen Tiedeakatemia.

Thwaite, A. (1991) *A. A. Milne. His Life*, London: Faber and Faber.

Tolkien, J. R. R. (1964) 'On fairy stories', in *Tree and Leaf*, London: Allen and Unwin.

Tolkien, J. R. R. (1978) *The Lord of the Rings*, London: Allen and Unwin.

Walsh, J. P. (1981) 'The art of realism', in B. Hearne and M. Kaye (eds), *Celebrating Children's Books*, New York: Lothrop, Lee and Shepard: 35–44.

Winoker, J. (1987) *Writers on Writing*, London: Headline.

Wolfe, G. K. (1982) 'The encounter with fantasy', in R. C. Schlobin (ed.) *The Aesthetics of Fantasy Literature and Art*, Notre Dame: University of Notre Dame Press/Brighton: Harvester Press: 1–15.

Wynne Jones, D. (1996) *The Tough Guide to Fantasyland*, London: Vista.

Further reading

Allison, A. (2000) *Russell Hoban/Forty Years. Essays on his Writings for Children*, New York: Garland.

Apter, T. E. (1982) *Fantasy Literature. An Approach to Reality*, London: Macmillan.

Barron, N. (1990) *Fantasy Literature. A Reader's Guide*, New York: Garland.

Brooke-Rose, C. (1981) *A Rhetoric of the Unreal. Studies in Narrative and Structure, Especially of the Fantastic*, Cambridge: Cambridge University Press.

Cohen, M. (1995) *Lewis Carroll. A Biography*, London: Macmillan.

Cornwell, N. (1990) *The Literary Fantastic. From Gothic to Postmodernism*, Hemel Hempstead: Harvester Wheatsheaf.

Cunningham, V. (1985) 'Soiled fairy. *The Water Babies* in its time', *Essays in Criticism* 35: 121–48.

Dusinberre, J. (1987) *Alice to the Lighthouse. Children's Books and Radical Experiments in Art*, London: Macmillan.

Egoff, S. A. (1988) *Worlds Within*, Chicago: American Library Association.

Gardner, M. (ed.) (2000) *The Annotated Alice. The Definitive Edition*, New York: Norton.

Harvey, D. (1985) *The Song of Middle-Earth. J. R. R. Tolkien's Themes, Symbols, and Myths*, London: Allen and Unwin.

Hetherington, J. (1973) *Norman Lindsay: The Embattled Olympian*, Melbourne: Oxford University Press.

Hulme, K. (1984) *Fantasy and Mimesis: Responses to Reality in Western Literature*, New York: Methuen.

Jackson, R. (1981) *Fantasy: The Literature of Subversion*, London: Methuen.

Manlove, C. N. (1983) *The Impulse of Fantasy Literature*, London: Macmillan.

Nikolajeva, M. (1988) *The Magic Code*, Goteborg: Almqvist and Wiksell International.

Scott, C. (1997) 'High and wild magic, the moral universe, and the electronic superhighway: reflections of change in Susan Cooper's fantasy literature', in S. L. Beckett (ed.), *Reflections of Change. Children's Literature Since 1945*, Westport: Greenwood Press: 91–7.

Smith, K. P. (1993) *The Fabulous Realm. A Literary-Historical Approach to British Fantasy 1780–1990*, Metuchen: Scarecrow Press.

Sullivan III, C. W. (1995) 'Cultural worldview: marginalizing the fantastic in the seventeenth century', *Paradoxa*, 1(3): 287–300.

Todorov, T. (1973) *The Fantastic: A Structural Approach to a Literary*

Genre (Trans. R. Howard) Press of Case Western Reserve University.

West, M. I. (1989) *Before Oz. Juvenile Fantasy Stories from Nineteenth-Century America*, Hamden: Archon.

Wilkie, C. (1989) *Through the Narrow Gate: The Mythological Consciousness of Russell Hoban*, Rutherford: Fairleigh Dickinson University Press.

CHAPTER 2

Ursula K. Le Guin

Millicent Lenz

What Earthsea is about

The 'big' questions
In *A Wizard of Earthsea* (1968) Le Guin confronts the big existential
question: how to respond to the Biblical knowledge, 'Dust thou art,
and to dust thou shalt return' (Genesis 3:19). Le Guin's direct
approach to the topic of personal death and what lies beyond it
distinguishes her and certain other fantasists – J. R. R. Tolkien among
them – from most writers in this secular age, when concepts of death
and the hereafter, so much a part of our ancestors' daily psychological
landscape, have become a *terra incognita* (see Esmonde, 1987). Death
has been treated superficially in both 'realistic' fiction and factual
books, which present it as a problem to be solved (the bibliotherapeutic
approach) or as an occasion for 'soap-operatic sermons' (invariably
avoiding the question of a possible after-life altogether) (see
Abramson, 1974). Death is reduced to 'the great fertilizer' that makes
the flowers grow. Thus it is left to the fantasists, specialists in unknown
lands, to deal with the mystery of death and the puzzle of immortality
as components of a personal vision of life. J. R. R. Tolkien, for example,
in *The Lord of the Rings*, shows how 'mortality is indeed a gift and not a
curse' (Esmonde, 1987: 35–7) through the contrast between elves,
who are immortal, and humans, who must die. Like Tolkien, Le Guin
in the original trilogy (which includes *A Wizard of Earthsea* (1968), *The*

Tombs of Atuan (1971) and *The Farthest Shore* (1972)) highlights the paradox of the 'doom' or 'gift' of death and faces it without despair. Esmonde notes Le Guin's use of the concept of reincarnation to explore 'the relationship of life, death, and the hereafter' (39). The wizards or mages of Earthsea must maintain the Balance, the Equilibrium of all things, including the Balance between life and death, for without Balance, whether on the individual or social level, the entire realm is doomed.

A second big question raised in the Earthsea cycle concerns how a young person may learn wisdom and attain 'generativity,' passing the legacy of experience on to others. My approach will trace the psychological growth and development of the protagonists, how they gain self-knowledge and wisdom, how mentoring and life experiences contribute to their learning, and how they may teach others. I will also consider gender-based differences: clearly the acquisition of self-knowledge and 'wisdom' involves quite different processes for Ged, the wizard of Earthsea, and Tenar, the priestess of *The Tombs of Atuan*.

For a broader perspective, it is helpful to contrast the patterns in male and female initiation stories. Brian Attebery's remark in *The Fantasy Tradition in American Literature* (1980), that *The Farthest Shore* is a quest whereas *The Tombs of Atuan* is a story of rescue, shows that he views the story of *The Tombs of Atuan* (perhaps unconsciously) from the male perspective of Ged. Attebery's later book, *Strategies of Fantasy* (1992), perhaps influenced by feminist literary criticism, reveals much more insight into Tenar's experience. He categorizes *A Wizard of Earthsea* as belonging to a tale-type known as the 'sorcerer's apprentice', wherein the male hero begins in obscurity, attracts attention to his gifts, leaves the domestic setting, is apprenticed to a male 'master' who endows him with a new name, attends an all-male school, commits an act of disobedience resulting in disaster, wanders the world to find a remedy for the evil he has unleashed, is tempted by a witch, bests a dragon, and finally overcomes evil. What the typical male hero must learn is *limits*: He begins as arrogant, impulsive, and ambitious; he ends in self-mastery, finally realizing his only true adversary is himself. This pattern has been traced many times, notably by such ethnologists as Van Gennep and Joseph Campbell, both fundamentally concerned with males and their changes of status.

Attebery contrasts this with the pattern for female passage to maturity, drawing upon Bruce Lincoln's *Emerging from the Chrysalis: Studies in Rituals of Women's Initiation* (1981). Lincoln identifies three stages for women's rites of passage: 'enclosure, metamorphoses (or magnification), and emergence'. Often the girl is secluded in her own home, at or before her first menses. There she takes on a new identity, perhaps that of a culture goddess, being robed in a special costume for the ceremonial assumption of her new persona; then emerges into society, carrying the gifts of fertility and order associated with the mythic figure she represents (Attebery, 1992: 91). Female rituals in traditional societies centre more on marking the onset of menstruation than on the element of 'spiritual revelation' found in the puberty rites of boys (see Eliade, 1958).

Tenar's coming-of-age in *The Tombs of Atuan* diverges in several respects from Lincoln's pattern. She is forced to become Arha, a life-denying 'culture goddess', and her true identity is restored partly through the mediation of Ged, partly by her own efforts. Attebery assesses Arha's task as 'unleashing' herself rather than mastering herself (self-mastery being the 'male' task, throwing off the traces the 'female' one). He finds Kossil to be as 'fearsome as any fairytale stepmother' and notes that Tenar reaches adulthood only over Kossil's dead body (1992: 88, 98–9).

Le Guin's worldbuilding: the genesis of Earthsea, its magic of language and names

Le Guin 'discovered' rather than 'invented' Earthsea, for she is an 'explorer,' not an 'engineer' (Le Guin, 1989c: 44). Elements of Earthsea were drawn from two stories, a 'grim' one, 'The Word of Unbinding' (1964b) and a 'lighthearted' one, 'The Rule of Names' (1964a). The latter is set on an island, with a dragon, Mr Underhill (true name 'Yevaud') from a westerly isle, Pendor. Later Le Guin wrote a story (never published) about a prince in search of the Ultimate, who encounters a colony of raft people, settles with them as the 'ultimate' until he discovers there are more remote sea-people inhabiting the sea, and joins them. Le Guin jests: 'I think the implication was that (not being a merman) he'll wear out eventually, and sink, and find the ultimate Ultimate.' (The raft-colony was eventually incorporated into *The Farthest Shore*.)

When the publisher of Parnassus Press invited her in 1967 to write a book 'for older kids' (beyond the picture book level), the result was a mix of archetypal ingredients: islands, magic, and above all wizards. Her minimal former acquaintance with wizards had consisted only of 'usually elderly or ageless Gandalfs,' and she asked herself, what they were 'before they had white beards? How did they learn what is obviously an erudite and dangerous art? Are there colleges for young wizards? And so on' (1989c: 44–6).

The basic story of *A Wizard of Earthsea* came to her as a 'voyage' in a spiral pattern, with mental pictures of the islands where the young wizard would travel, three named for her three then young children (their 'baby' names), and other names chosen on the basis of their 'sounding' right. Given the primacy of sound to her writing, correct pronunciation is *de rigueur*. She notes that 'Ged' should be pronounced with a hard 'g', not with a soft as in 'Jed', which, she remarks 'sounds like a mountain moonshiner to me' (1989c: 46).

Earthsea's 'groundrules' are first that words and names are the basis of magic, and second that everything has a secret name – both beliefs harking back to those of tribal societies, reflecting Le Guin's anthropological bent. The fully fleshed-out setting is complemented by a rich history, told in songs, such as the epic 'Deed of Ged,' set in a time so remote that the reader has a sense of peering into the 'dark backward and abysm of time'.

Peoples and cultures of Earthsea

An island culture, Earthsea's isolated communities are 'stable, homogeneous, and self-absorbed' (Attebery, 1980: 169). Most islanders speak 'Hardic,' derived from dragon speech, the exceptions being the residents of the wicked realms of the Kargad Empire and Osskil, whose eccentricity of language emphasizes their isolation from the culture of the archipelago as a whole. As part of the Kargad Empire, Atuan is peopled by pale, fair-haired folk, Tenar included; Ged and most of the Earthsea inhabitants are coppery brown in colour, with black hair, like Native Americans (Attebery, 1980: 172). As for governance, a king and local burghers wield secular power, but the *real* power – knowledge – belongs to the wizards. The throne is vacant at the time of *A Wizard of Earthsea*, and the action of the first three books moves towards Arren's enthroning at Havnor.

Settings of Earthsea narratives

A strong 'spirit of place,' achieved through vivid details and visualization (detailed maps accompany the narratives), lends immediacy to this high fantasy set in an alternative world. Brian Attebery finds a possible 'real-world' model for Earthsea in the Indonesian archipelago, though Earthsea's climate seems more European and its animals and plants are of mixed origin, some imaginary (such as the 'otak', and at least one, 'kingsfoil', borrowed from Tolkien), others familiar. Atuan seems to resemble the eastern desert area of Oregon (Le Guin's adopted home), not sandy but overgrown with 'scrub' and featuring mountains to the West. The total landscape is, however, markedly original, with its temples, monoliths, and priestesses (see Manguel and Guadalupi, 1980 for a gazetteer).

Geography in Earthsea is rich in symbolic significance, the sea being less under control of humans and thus associated with superhuman and nonhuman powers, the land being home to both people of virtue and miscreants. On a psychological level, the islands of Earthsea represent disparate, individual modes of human consciousness; the shared rituals of the inhabitants help to create community despite differences. The setting on islands in an archipelago suggests 'a subterranean or archetypal connection of public events ... in this seemingly medieval, romance-soaked Bronze Age world' (Barrow and Barrow, 1991: 25). Douglas Barbour finds in Earthsea 'a single civilization,' wide enough to contain people of extreme differences in education, social and economic standing, and ethnicity, and thus resembling Medieval Europe during the twelfth century, 'where high learning and philosophy could be found in the same village with complete ignorance, where material, scientific progress had barely begun, where the great part of the population were peasants' (Barbour, 1974: 121).

Gifts and shadows: two 'chains' of metaphors in the Earthsea cycle
Le Guin's poetic, richly textured narratives are full of metaphor, and repeated occurrences of two 'chains' of metaphors underpin the structure of the entire cycle: the metaphors of the 'Gift' or 'Exchange', and the metaphor of 'Shadow'. The 'chain of gifts' was noted by George Slusser: he traces the progress of the actual Ring of Erreth–Akbe and observes the social effects of gifts: 'True harmony ... comes only from the gift freely given' (1976: 39). Elizabeth Cummins explores gifts in a more abstract sense, such as Ged's 'gift' of spells to protect Pechvarry's boats in A Wizard of Earthsea (Cummins, 1990: 94) which the latter reciprocates with lessons in boatbuilding and sailing. She observes that 'the exchange of gifts is a manifestation of the trust that makes human community possible' (35, 46). The many types of exchanges in Earthsea have been noted by W. A. Senior: bartering, selling, thieving (a negative exchange), trades, but primarily gifts and returns: 'from physical objects, to names, to magical spells, to abstractions such as friendship and sacrifice' (1996: 102). Drawing upon Marcel Mauss, who observed that 'in archaic societies all gifts carry a spiritual import or content and entail the giver offering a piece of himself', Senior concludes that gifts in the Earthsea cycle serve two major functions: to encapsulate 'the macrocosmic system of Balance' that governs and stabilizes the world; and to chart Ged's 'development, moral growth, and integration' (104) into what Robert Scholes has called 'a dynamic balanced system, not subject to capricious miracles of any deity', but

rather to its natural laws – which include the laws of magic – and to all aspects of 'the great Balance or Equilibrium, which is the order of this cosmos' (Scholes, 1986: 36–7).

The significance of the many occurrences of Shadows – which form another and contrasting 'chain' – has been still more fully analysed from a variety of critical angles (most often the Jungian), but there has been no prior attempt to show the interplay between these two metaphors. The Shadow in one of its meanings may represent the 'withholding' of relationship, the denial of 'giving', and hence it stands at the opposite end of the psychological spectrum from 'gift-giving' and the mutuality such giving implies.

A Wizard of Earthsea

The emergent wizard, 'Duny' to 'Ged'
Before *Tehanu*, Le Guin famously said that the (then) trilogy is 'about art, the creative experience, the creative process' – the 'magician' and the artist being of one species, both types of the Trickster (1989c: 48). Thus, *A Wizard of Earthsea* is on one level an 'artist' novel, wherein an alienated outsider undergoes an inner struggle to achieve the self-discipline he needs to control his 'magic' powers. This process, a kind of *Bildungsroman* in a fantasy setting, can be seen as the organizing thread of the narrative.

Ged begins like many mythical heroes: humble origins, half-orphaned, harshly treated, a childhood called by psychoanalytical critics 'a portrait of hidden need' (Barrow and Barrow, 1991: 25). He is, however, rich in psychic gifts, which his witch-aunt calls 'the makings of power' (*A Wizard of Earthsea*: 14), and from her he learns the rudiments of the magic arts. The danger posed by her superficial knowledge is clear: she is ignorant of 'the Balance and the Pattern which the true wizard knows and serves, and which keep him from using his spells unless real need demands' (16). She does nonetheless teach the child – known then as Duny – 'honest craft' and the epic songs of their oral culture (17), including 'The Deed of Erreth–Akbe', shaping his imagination to heroic ends.

The stages in his movement towards maturity are marked by his changes in name: first Duny; then the nickname 'Sparrowhawk' (from the birds of prey that frequent the fields where he plays); then his True Name, bestowed by Ogion, 'Ged'. A village hero at an early age, Sparrowhawk saves his community from the fierce Kargad invaders through 'fogweaving', a trickster skill that may recall Homer's wily Odysseus.

Shadow as key metaphor: Le Guin's 'The Child and the Shadow'
The Taoist and Jungian implications of Le Guin's use of shadow and
light are illuminated in her essay, 'The child and the shadow,' but
whereas Jung concentrated on facing one's shadow as a mid-life crisis,
Le Guin sees it as a task of adolescence. She decries writers of realistic
fiction who attempt to teach children the truth about good and evil
through 'superficialities of the collective consciousness, [the] simplistic
moralism [of] the baddies and the goodies'. 'Problem books', she feels,
miss the point, 'as if evil were a problem, something that can be solved,
that has an answer, like a problem in fifth grade arithmetic'. Such a
'realistic' approach to evil fails to confront what evil actually is: 'all the
pain and suffering and waste and loss and injustice we will meet all our
lives long, and must face and cope with over and over and over, and
admit, and live with, in order to live human lives at all' (1975: 147).
The child needs

> knowledge; he needs self-knowledge. He needs to see himself and
> the shadow he casts. That is something he can face, his own
> shadow; and he can learn to control it and to be guided by it. So
> that when he grows up into his strength and responsibility as an
> adult in society, he will be less inclined, perhaps, either to give up
> in despair or to deny what he sees, when he must face the evil
> that is done in the world, and the injustices and grief and
> suffering that we all must bear, and the final shadow at the end of
> all. (147–8)

Ogion's mentorship of Ged: overtones of Taoism
Ged takes with him to Re Albi (The Eagle's Nest, Ogion's home), his
meagre belongings, all gifts: the bronze sword from his father, the
hand-me-down coat from the tanner's widow, and a becharmed alder-
stick from his witch-aunt (A Wizard: 26). Ogion the Silent subtly
models the art of patience for the impetuous youth: 'Manhood,' he tells
Ged, 'is patience. Mastery is nine times patience' (28). Never one to
write down to her audience, Le Guin presents in Earthsea (though in
simpler narrative form), the important themes of her writings for
adults, including, as Douglas Barbour notes, a completely realized
alternative world where Taoism is rendered in a way wholly consistent
with Earthsea's 'laws' (Barbour, 1974: 119–21).

> Earthsea's magic 'Equilibrium' is the Earthsea equivalent of the
> Way, the Tao, for upon this Equilibrium everything depends, as
> everything depends upon the Tao ... To use Equilibrium for

selfish reasons is to break its deep laws: this is the lesson Ged must suffer so greatly to learn. (Barbour, 1974: 120)

Ogion's wise passivity reflects the Buddhist idea of inaction, a concept readers of Western background may find less compelling than Ged's desire to seize the moment and act decisively. Ogion's asceticism and closeness to the animal world (he shares his dwelling with goats) connect him also to the pastoral 'green world' of romance. Ogion occupies a liminal position, 'poised between the world of the human and the world of the nonhuman' (Selinger, 1988: 32–3) and thus he is able to mediate between the two.

Pivotal points of the spiralling plot: the apprentice wizard's temptations and choices

Ged's first 'fall' combines disobedience (tampering with the forbidden Lore Books) with the careless use of language (perilous in a world built upon True Speech), and the dire outcome is a hideous shadow – 'a shapeless clot of shadow darker than the darkness' (A *Wizard*: 34), his own personal Frankenstein's monster. Eleanor Cameron notes two lessons Ged learns of Ogion:

> The first: that naming sets limits to power, and that he who knows a man's true name (i.e. his true being) holds that man's life in his keeping. The second: that danger must surround power as shadow does light, and that sorcery is not a game played for pleasure or for praise. (1971: 133)

Ogion's reprimand to Ged for neglecting mindfulness in wielding the power of sorcery states a central theme:

> 'Have you never thought how danger must surround power as shadow does light? This sorcery is not a game we play for pleasure or praise. Think of this: that every word, every act of our Art is said and is done either for good, or for evil. Before you speak or do you must know the price that is to pay!' (A *Wizard*: 35)

Faced with a crucial choice of life – Ogion's pastoral way of humility, hermitage, and silence; or the way of the bright enchantments of the Wizards on Roke – Ged predictably chooses the latter, the choice appropriate to his stage in life.

Ged's crossing the threshold of the School on Roke carries the metaphorical significance of 'liminality', a state of 'in-betweenness'. The door exemplifies Le Guin's symbolic use of thresholds: its two faces, the one artfully fashioned of ivory, cut from a tooth of the Great

Dragon, the other of polished, translucent horn, allude, as Tavormina (1988) has pointed out, to Virgil's *Aeneid* (6: 893–8), where true and false dreams are linked with the twin Gates of Sleep, the gate of translucent horn (open to light) signifying the truthful, and the gate of ivory (opaque) the false dreams (Tavormina: *passim*). Ged's sense of the shadow at his heels forebodes trouble, but the shadow is destined also to play a less obvious role – as a guide into the regions of the deeper self (Le Guin, 1975: 143).

The burst of birdsong when Ged meets the Archmage Nemmerle (with his Raven) marks a new growth in the ability to understand the language of the natural world . A beautiful unitary moment, when Ged seems to himself to be 'a word spoken by the sunlight' (*A Wizard*: 48), is broken by the sharp dissonance of the Raven's croaking, 'Terrenon ussbuk! ... Terrenon ussbuk orrek!' (49). Craig and Diana Barrows' interpretation is pertinent: in Jungian theory, birds, as 'symbols of transcendence ... release a person from 'any confining pattern of existence, as he moves toward a superior or more mature stage in his development' ... The raven relates to the witch who has tempted Ged in the past and will tempt him in the future' (Barrow and Barrow, 1991: 27). Ogion's note of introduction foretells Ged's exceptional destiny: in runes it declares '*I send you one who will be greatest of the wizards of Gont, if the wind blow true*' (*A Wizard*: 48).

Jungian psychology also explains Ged's overreaction to his fellow student, the polite but disdainful Jasper: because Ged has not yet admitted his own 'shadow' into consciousness, he projects it upon another, thereby blocking his own growth. Fortunately, Ged is not isolated in his apprenticeship; he gains a true friend in Vetch, who bestows the gift of trust and offers his True Name – Estarriol – in exchange for Ged's own (84); Vetch offers to the half-orphaned Ged a certain stability and rootedness. Ged finds comfort also in his 'otak', a small rodent who becomes his animal guide, a motif familiar from folklore. Vetch views the otak's favouring of Ged as a sign that he is one to whom 'Old Powers' of stone and spring – meaning dragons – will speak in human tongue. Jasper, in contrast, taunts Ged for keeping a rat as his 'familiar' (67). Ged's bestowing of the otak's true name, 'Hoeg' (62) seals their mutually sustaining relationship.

Master Changer imposes on Ged the 'prohibition' that is a familiar feature of traditional tales:

> 'You must not change one thing, one pebble, one grain of sand, until you know what good and evil will follow on that act. The world is in balance, in Equilibrium. A wizard's power of Changing

and of Summoning can shake the balance of the world. It is dangerous, that power. It is most perilous. It must follow knowledge and serve need. To light a candle is to cast a shadow.' (57)

This gnomic echo of a medieval proverb employs an ambiguous metaphor, for as the Jungian critic Edgar C. Bailey, Jr. has commented, although the repressed and unacknowledged shadow can lead to loss of control and hence the potential of evil, the shadow is also a source of tremendous creative energy. 'To be born, to be human, to act ... is to do evil – or at least to be capable of it' (Bailey, 1980: 257). On the one hand, Master Changer warns of the peril of ignoring *limits* on the mage's power; on the other, Ged's violation of the prohibition in a sense constitutes the 'fortunate fall' vital to his growth. Thinking he can 'balance the world as seemed best to him, and drive back darkness with his own light' (*A Wizard*: 57), Ged is blinded by hubris to the peril within. Le Guin's 'The child and the shadow' tells us that the unrecognized shadow becomes stronger, until it can become 'a menace, an intolerable load, a threat within the soul'. Paradoxically, though the shadow is 'inferior, primitive, awkward, animallike, childlike,' it is also 'powerful, vital, spontaneous' and moreover, absolutely necessary, for 'without it, the person is nothing. What is a body that casts no shadow? Nothing, a formlessness, two-dimensional, a comic-strip character' (143). To withdraw his projected shadow, a process necessary to his own psychological wholeness, Ged must bring it to consciousness (Bailey, 1980: 255, drawing on Jung). This he is not yet able to do.

Ged must also learn mindfulness in the use of names. As T. A. Shippey has noted, the processes of magic in Earthsea depend on a concept prominent in early modern anthropology, the 'Rumpelstiltskin' theory

> that every person, place, or thing possesses a true name distinct from its name in ordinary human language; and that knowing the true name, the *signifiant*, gives the mage power over the thing itself, the *signifié*. (1977: 151)

Elizabeth Cogell connects Le Guin's emphasis on names to the influence of her father's anthropological research (1983: xvi). Her mother, who authored two juvenile books about the Native American, Ishi – *Ishi, Last of His Tribe* (fiction, made into a film of the same name) and *Ishi in Two Worlds* (nonfiction), doubtless also had a significant influence (See Kroeber, T., 1961, 1964 and Kroeber, A. L., 1976).

Ged's second fall into temptation occurs at a place highly charged with symbolism: the dark enchanted ground of Roke Knoll, where the tree roots reach 'down even to the old, blind, secret fires at the world's core' (*A Wizard*: 74). The repetition of the pattern of his first 'fall' illustrates what Bernard Selinger calls the 'normal' structure of Le Guin's novels: 'radial, circling about, repeating and elaborating the central theme', using a key image around which the rest of the novel revolves (1988: 23). As a consequence of his second act of rash disobedience, Ged's shadow is driven within, resulting in depression, loss of creativity, and dulling of intellect. A tale from the *Matter of Dragons*, involving a 'speaking stone' in a far northern land (86), foreshadows the test Ged will face in his encounter with the Stone of Terrenon.

Ged's subsequent adventures: learning on the job, gifts as tokens of relationship

Ged's subsequent adventures constitute 'experiential' learning. From his vain effort to save Pechvarry's son Ioeth from death and from the loving touch of the otak's tongue that restores him to life (98), Ged's concept of wisdom is altered: wisdom does not consist in setting oneself apart from other living beings, nor in attempting to challenge the laws of nature (that mortals die). Rather, a human being must strive in humility 'to learn what can be learned, in silence, from the eyes of animals, the flight of birds, and slow gestures of trees' (98).

The new wizard's saving of the community of Low Torning from the dragons of Pendor parallels the dragon encounter of the quest romance. However, Le Guin's dragons are not to be confused with the dragons of the Christian tradition, representatives of fallen nature. (*Tehanu* gives the common genealogy of dragons and humans.) For the first time, Ged becomes aware of what the Romantic poets called the sublime, an ancient power surpassing human comprehension. By his wits he wins out over Yevaud (107), resisting the temptation to learn from the Dragon the name of the shadow (108). Unwittingly, Yevaud supplies Ged a vital bit of information (a 'gift' of sorts): the shadow *does* have a name! Ged's dragon-slaying becomes legendary and is celebrated in the Song of Sparrowhawk.

At the Court of Terrenon in the North, the pattern of peril is repeated: Lady Serret, Queen of Terrenon, is his earlier temptress, the daughter of the Lord of Re Albi (139), and with her evil lord, Benderesk, tends the ancient Stone of Terrenon, made when the world was made, which imprisons within it an 'old and terrible spirit' (132). In a psychoanalytical interpretation, the Stone of Terrenon is 'a projection of the blackest part of Ged's own character, his desire for power and dominion' (Barrow and Barrow, 1991: 30). Stone in Jungian theory represents, says Marie-Louise von Franz, 'what is perhaps the simplest and deepest experience – the experience of something eternal that man can have in those moments when he feels immortal and unalterable' (quoted from Jung in Barrow and Barrow: 30). This is Ged's greatest temptation – to succumb to the desire to 'feel' immortal and unalterable, to deny death.

His return to Re Albi in the shape of a falcon brings him full circle. Ogion's telling of the parable of Bordger of Way, who took on a bear-shape too often, until 'the bear grew in him and the man died' (*A Wizard*: 143), warns Ged of the peril of remaining too long in animal form. Ged must do as Ogion says: '"Turn around ... You must hunt the hunter."' Only by returning to the original spring of his soul's strength (146), and following his terror to its source and confronting it (166), can he hope to win over it. Ogion's gifts of simple Gontish attire (149) (reclothing Ged in his natural identity) and a meticulously crafted staff of yew (148) mark another stage in the young wizard's growth, making them tokens of 'renewal and engagement with others' (Senior, 1996: 107).

Ged's active pursuit of the shadow leads to the 'robinsonade' episode, his shipwreck on a reef inhabited by two old people, the 'prince and princess of Desolation' (162). Senior's comment sums up the significance of the exchanged gifts: 'In this possessionless world on a forgotten island, the spirit behind the gift of the Ring matches its importance and power, for these aged, marooned children have almost nothing to give and were long ago deprived of the world of gifts itself,' and when Ged reciprocates with the gift of fresh water (giving the reef a new name, 'Springwater Isle' (*A Wizard*: 162)), this exchange 'binds Ged to these castaways for life, since their story now becomes an integral part of his' (Senior: 106). The reunion with Vetch, and their shared voyage towards the unknown, is preceded by another meaningful exchange: when Ged compassionately heals an old man's cataracts, he is rewarded with a new vessel, named 'Lookfar' by the giver, who remarks: '"I had forgotten how much light there is in the world, till you gave it back to me."' The spiritual principle of reciprocity is at work: Ged has endowed another with light, and thus prepares himself for overcoming the Shadow (*A Wizard*: 170–1).

The eerie journey into waters to the east towards the foreboding point where light and darkness meet is a 'threshold' experience of a new sort, comparable to wavering in that shadowy state between life and death, a metaphorical 'Lastland', before launching into the unknown Open Sea.

The sea that turns to sand: Ged's 'recognition' scene
C. G. Jung in *Essays on Analytical Psychology* spoke of an individual's need to integrate the psyche's 'negative side' to attain wholeness, and the related need to bring the 'shadowed' content of the psyche to consciousness, 'so as to produce a tension of opposites, without which no forward movement is possible' (quoted in Bailey, 1980: 255). Jung's statement applies to Ged, who as the sea turns to sand is both literally and figuratively 'stuck' in the 'sand' of his own unacknowledged darkness.

As Ged walks across the sea of sand, he meets the Shadow in its different manifestations: first a hateful-looking Jasper, then Pechvarry, then Skiorh, and finally, 'a fearful face he did not know, man or monster, with writhing lips and eyes that were like pits going back into black emptiness'. Only when they meet face-to-face and speak at once the same word, ' "Ged" ' (*A Wizard*: 201), are the seeming opposites unified and made whole (201–2).

Vetch witnesses to

> the truth, that Ged had neither lost nor won, but, naming the shadow of his death with his own name, had made himself whole: a man, who, knowing his whole true self, cannot be used or possessed by any power other than himself, and whose life therefore is lived for life's sake and never in the service of ruin or pain, or hatred, or the dark (203).

Taoist philosophy permeates the novel and dominates in the ending: 'Insofar as [Ged] acts for others, and only insofar as he does so, he acts, most truly, for himself' (Barbour, 1974: 121).

Coming full circle, the book closes with Estarriol's song, the epigraph to the book. 'Only in silence the word, | only in dark the light, | only in dying life: | bright the hawk's flight | on the empty sky. – The Creation of Ea.'

The Tombs of Atuan

Thanatos enshrined, choice denied
Fresh ocean breezes fill *A Wizard of Earthsea* and *The Farthest Shore*, but *The Tombs of Atuan* is 'thick with the heaviness of earth' (Nicholls, 1974: 72, 74). Atuan's background images are of 'isolation, darkness, perversity – seen in the neutering of slaves, the wasting of lives, the 'dedication of the Kargish religion to age, fear, and death' (Attebery, 1980: 176). There are other contrasts as well. Whereas Sparrowhawk could choose between a school for wizardry or a pastoral life, Tenar is virtually kidnapped into a life of slavery at the Tombs. Whereas Ged must face his mortality, Tenar/Arha must struggle to be free of a false

'immortality' as the endlessly reincarnated One Priestess. Awakened out of the dust of the Tombs, she chooses life (*eros* in the broadest sense) over *thanatos* (fixation on death). Whereas Gont and Roke are full of light and air, Atuan is, in W. A. Senior's words, a harsh, sterile world where 'the standard pattern is taking, not giving. Children are taken, lives are taken, light is taken, obedience is extracted, emotion is obliterated, identity is erased, and names themselves are eradicated, but nothing is given in return' (1996: 107). Arha's childhood is more deprived than Ged's, for she lacks even a witch-aunt or an otak, or any mentor like Ogion. The pathos of her sacrifice is underscored by contrast to Penthe, who is 'round and full of life and juice as one of her golden apples, beautiful to see'. Through Penthe, Arha can see a world she is denied, 'A whole new planet hanging huge and populous right outside the window, an entirely strange world, one in which the gods did not matter' (*The Tombs of Atuan*: 46).

The walled place: Arha's 'education'
Arha's strict 'education' (more precisely, 'indoctrination') includes the sacred songs and dances, the history of the Kargad lands, and (for Arha alone) the secret rites of the Nameless Ones, taught by Thar. Her narrow attitudes are played against Penthe's love of change and difference and daring (21), and her growing haughtiness shows in her boast that she is the 'One Priestess', not to be bothered by 'old women and half-men' (a thrust at Manan) (22–3). Kossil's ignorant assertion that the 'pirates' of the outer lands are ' "black and vile. I have never seen one …" ' (58) brings out the prejudice of Atuan's culture.

A silent crossing into womanhood: the emptiness of Arha's 'powers'
The narrative skips the interval between Arha's twelfth and fifteenth year, passing over the critical age of fourteen, when girls are considered adults (23). The silence concerning Arha's initiation into womanhood, contrasting with the public ceremony surrounding Ged's coming into manhood, implies cultural neglect of rites of passage for females. In Tenar/Arha's case, as Slusser observes, a 'person of great strength and imagination' is left with no life-affirming cultural support; he compares her being 'eaten', consumed by darkness, to 'Blake's "marriage hearse", the corruption of life at its source' (Slusser, 1976: 39–40).

Although the priestesses superficially appear to represent female dominance, in fact their cult is declining, as shown by the God-Kings' contempt for the old deities. Despite her presumed 'power', Arha finds her life intensely boring, and, according to Kargad belief, is doomed to be reborn as Herself (*The Tombs of Atuan*: 53) in an endless cycle. One of her duties is to preside over the deaths of those found guilty of sacrilege (32) – a repugnant task reflecting her culture's fixation on *thanatos*.

The labyrinth: a maze of meanings

The labyrinth, a major metaphor of the novel, is a 'vast, meaningless web of ways', designed 'to weary and confuse', and in the end, 'a great trap' (62). In psychological symbolism, it signifies the unconscious and remoteness from the wellspring of life (Pail Diel, *Le Symbolism dans la mythologie grecque*, quoted in Cirlot, 1971: 175). In exploring this maze, Arha probes her own inner realm, the subconscious. From a Jungian point of view, Arha can be seen as beginning her process of 'individuation'; this process remains unconscious until Ged calls her by her true name, Tenar (see Barrow and Barrow, 1991: 34). In mythical terms, the labyrinth is associated with seeking, movement and danger, and stands in contrast to the primal cave image, associated with security, peace, and refuge (Gebser, 1992: 62).

Jean Gebser calls the labyrinth the counter-image of the cave, and believes it represents the yearning for greater awareness, 'the possibility of advancing rather than returning into unconsciousness and time-lessness ... The labyrinth is a way, if still a confused way, into awareness' (63). Arha's descent into the labyrinth is an interior, female parallel to the male heroic journey in search of the 'dragon', for it is an attempt to face and transform what the poet Rainer Maria Rilke called 'the erroneous zone within' (in his poem 'An den Engel,' ['To the Angel,'] quoted in Gebser: 62). The beginning of awareness is signalled by a dim light (Ged's) in the cavern of the Undertomb. The image of the labyrinth evokes the classical myth of Theseus, to whom Ariadne gave a thread, a symbol of consciousness, to help him escape from the Minotaur; this is echoed in Arha's ball of yarn that helps her find her way (*The Tombs of Atuan*: 74).

From Arha to Tenar: confronting herself

Ged's appearance means radical change for Arha – pivotal decisions and new ambivalent emotions. Fear causes her to try to deny his magical powers, and her desire that he should live vies with her impulse to kill him. She is drawn to him partly because he brings difference into her world of sameness, partly because she wants to witness his sorcerer's 'tricks'. Her serious threat to kill him if he does not 'perform' for her has a game aspect: 'They tossed his life back and forth between them like a ball, playing' (97). When she requests '"something worth seeing"', his trick of illusion is metaphorically significant: he changes her black attire into a silken gown like that of a princess. As 'something worth seeing,' he tells her, ' "I show you yourself" ' (98).

Mirroring Tenar to herself, Ged is reciprocating her gift of a cloak with something much more valuable, a vision of her own worth, but the self-knowledge means she must risk the spying Kossil's treachery. When Ged calls her 'Tenar' (105) (giving her also his own true name), she finds the strength to assert her own identity.

Well acquainted with the Dark Powers, Ged unmasks the Nameless Ones, those who ' "hate the light: the brief, bright light of our mortality ... they are not gods .... All their power is to darken and destroy" ' (118). Reflecting Le Guin's Taoist philosophy, he tells Tenar the earth is both beautiful and ' "terrible ... dark and cruel" ' (118), but that ' "You are free ... You were taught to be a slave, but you have broken free" ' (118–19).

The Ring of Erreth-Akbe: thefts and gifts

Arha commits robbery twice, first taking Ged's staff and then tearing the silver chain (not knowing it is really a piece of the broken Ring) from his neck. Ged steals the half of the Ring of Erreth-Akbe which is the object of his quest. The scene of Tenar's discovery of the Ring's significance and the mutual exchange of the segments between her and Ged is the pivotal 'gift' motif of the book (120 ff.). When the ring is rejoined (127–9), Tenar faces a crucial choice: she opts in favour of life and her true identity. When Ged makes the Ring whole by patterning and places it on her arm, he symbolically gives wholeness to both Tenar and the world of Earthsea (129).

Escape and earthquake: the weight of liberty

Manan's character from the outset is ambiguous; he is both Tenar's 'protector' and her keeper. The horror of his end is mitigated by his guilt in trying to push Ged to his death (131). The earthquake which follows – an expression of the anger of the dark powers – toppling and swallowing the Tombstones (137), brings the action to a dramatic climax.

Tenar's acceptance of her new freedom is difficult: her great joy in the replenishing energy of the natural world struggles against her impulse to kill Ged because she knows he will pursue the heroic path and abandon her (155). What to make of these reactions has spurred critical debates: is her murderous impulse a sign of female weakness, an inability to carry on an independent life? Responding with understanding, Ged ignores the dagger, trustingly urges her on, and the moment passes. Tenar feels that 'a dark hand had let go its lifelong hold upon her heart' (156). She is feeling 'the weight of liberty' (157). As Erich Neumann put it:

> In reality we are dealing with the existential fact that the ego and individual that emerge from a phase of containment, whether in a gradual and imperceptible process of development or in sudden 'birth', experience the situation as rejection. Consequently we find a subjective experience of distress, suffering and helplessness in every crucial transition to a new sphere of existence. (*The Great Mother*, quoted in Jenkins, 1985: 27)

Communities of women and communities of men: contrasts
Since Le Guin portrays the Tombs' community of priestesses as evil and twisted, in contrast to the community of men on Roke, who are creative and mutually supportive, does this mean, as Cordelia Sherman has suggested, that 'the subliminal message of *The Tombs of Atuan* seems to be that women living without men must become twisted and purposeless, while men living without women can be productive and strong'? (26). On the other hand, Sherman notes that Tenar is not a passive 'heroine,' who waits for Ged to rescue her; on the contrary, she shows exceptional courage in fighting the Nameless Ones, actively helps to restore wholeness to the Ring, and plays a strong part in the growth of her own character (1987: 26–7).

Lois Kuznets has expressed disappointment in *The Tombs of Atuan* for failing to use its plot potential to construct a 'new' role for young women; rather, it 'actually depicts the suppression of a female cult' and its 'all-female community (except for eunuchs) is endowed with a menace not at all evident in the all-male school for wizards that Ged attends' (1985: 32).

Tenar's awakening to her sexuality
Le Guin has famously said that *The Tombs of Atuan* is 'about' sexuality ('Dreams Must Explain Themselves,' in 1989c: 50) and presumably (since she does not describe their relationship in physical terms) she is speaking of 'the sense in which Tenar's healing is dependent upon her response to Ged' (Jenkins, 1985: 26). Tenar must trust him, respond positively and warmly to him, if the two of them are to escape from the Tombs. She does not 'fall in love' with him in the usual romantic sense, but through him confronts all that is 'outside herself, bigger than herself, more important than herself' (26). Michelle Landsberg points out that Ged offers Tenar 'friendship, not sexual love' (1987: 82), and

although Tenar is naturally drawn to her rescuer, only one sentence expresses her dawning romantic feeling: 'Never could she have said what was in her heart as she watched him in the firelight, in the mountain dusk' (145–6). The emotional reserve reflects a truth about young girls, namely their 'tentativeness' *vis-à-vis* 'the psychological necessity of connecting with other humans by sharing experiences and language' (Reid, 1997: 39).

The history of the Ring; the growth of Ged; the shadowy future of Tenar

King Thoreg's story, central to the plot, relating the full history of the Ring of Erreth-Akbe, confirms the identity of the pathetic couple on the reef now named 'Springwater Isle' (*The Tombs of Atuan*: 158–60), and artfully connects the story of *Wizard* to that of *Tombs*.

Ged's considerable growth in compassion for Tenar and in the capacity to give of himself is evident when he tells her she was ' "made to hold light" '; and though she has been a ' "lamp unlit," ' her lamp ' "will burn out of the wind a while" ', meaning he will bring her to a place of refuge on the isle of Gont (162). Tenar has made immense strides towards self-knowledge, but Le Guin does not furnish any clues for her future (as she did for Ged at the close of *A Wizard of Earthsea*), and this omission speaks volumes. Elizabeth Cummins observes: 'Le Guin has created a woman and then was unable to imagine an appropriate place for her in the hierarchical, male world she had created' (1990: 156). *Tehanu* would change all that.

The Farthest Shore

From inner to public world

The Farthest Shore shifts the drama of restoring wholeness from the inner and interpersonal levels into the larger arena of public life. Shirley Toulson says the novel depicts how 'when the people turn away from the old rites, spells and traditions, and grab at a security and immortality of their own making, the equilibrium is shaken' (1973: 780). In a similar vein, Suzanne Elizabeth Reid emphasizes Le Guin's concept of the art of wizardry as 'looking for the outside edge', exercising the imagination to pay attention to both the concrete things of the world and one's inner realities, making connections and drawing upon 'emotions, memories, and experiences to go beyond superficialities' (1997: 40–1). She adds, 'Magic fades when the will to listen and learn the true names of the things of life pales.' Earthsea's inhabitants are spellbound by an illusion, seduced by 'a false dream outside of life, the dream of eternal security', and they no longer live with a sense of 'dangerous exploration', 'living wholly and passionately as do artists and magicians' (41).

The journey to the 'farthest shore', a metaphor for the land of the dead, traverses an Earthsea wherein people who were once proud and creative have been reduced to hallucinating drug addicts and peddlers of nondescript trash. 'Only the sea-people', says Toulson, escape the malaise, for only they 'accept inevitable danger and death.' Danger and death being undeniable components of life, Earthsea is fast becoming a spiritual wasteland. The spirits of the dead have no peace, and those who have not yet died exist in silent desperation: 'the sluice-gates of the world [separating life and death] must be closed again before all the real life is drained through them' (Toulson, 1973: 780). Compared to the two previous books, *The Farthest Shore* presents the reader with a larger and more imperilled universe, and its ecological implications may speak more directly to youth of the twenty-first century.

Le Guin on *The Farthest Shore*: other critics' perspectives

Le Guin has said that *The Farthest Shore* is 'about death', not death as an abstract reality, but rather the individual's awareness of personal mortality, which marks the moment of childhood's end. Because it is 'about the thing you do not live through and survive,' she considers it less 'well built' and 'complete' (1989c: 50). Some critics have echoed this view, perhaps finding the novel too metaphysical for their tastes. Michele Landsberg remarks that it is 'the most complex and the least satisfying' of Le Guin's Earthsea books, despite the 'most original and magnificent dragons in literature, ancient and thunderously immense creatures whose eyes glitter with a remote and ironic amusement at the doings of men' (1987: 179). Peter Nicholls finds a similarity between both the epic themes of Le Guin and Tolkien (specifically *Lord of the Rings*) and their shared fascination with dragons as embodying 'ancient knowledge and power', and he praises *The Farthest Shore* as 'a muted triumph, a quiet lyric,' admiring Le Guin's boldness in vividly portraying a descent into the underworld (1974: 71), a topic rare in literature for the young.

Prince Arren, the oracle of his destiny, and his marvellous sword of Serriadh

Prince Arren's quest is the traditional heroic one, wherein the external voyage mirrors an internal growth towards maturity, self-knowledge, and acceptance of personal mortality. Prince Arren (a name meaning 'sword') has been the subject of a prophecy made by Maharion ('He shall inherit my throne who has crossed the dark land living and come to the far shores of the day' (*The Farthest Shore*: 20)). Like King Arthur, Arren is the bearer of an enchanted sword, a marvellous weapon that can be wielded only 'in the service of life', never in blood-lust or revenge or greed (34–5).

Intimations of apocalyptic ruin and the call to adventure

Earthsea is in 'end time' mode (26): the Master Patterner can see no pattern, and instead perceives ' "fear. There is fear at the roots" ' (15). He is speaking of the roots of the world tree itself, the cosmic tree called Yggdrasil in Nordic mythology, whose roots reach down to the very core of Earth. Ged too senses impending disaster: ' "There is a dimming of the sun. I feel, my lords – I feel as if we who sit here talking, were all wounded mortally, and while we talk and talk our blood runs softly from our veins" ' (28–9), and wills to trace the 'trouble' to its source (28) with Arren at his side; the young man feels 'as if the Archmage had named him son of myth, inheritor of dreams' (24). Acceptance of the call to adventure is Arren's 'first step out of childhood' (11).

Gifts in *The Farthest Shore*

The basis of the social/political relationships between mages and kings is in a 'gift' of loyalty: The Masters of Roke, equal in rank to the great princes, serve the king 'by an act of fealty, by *heart's gift*', not by constraint (17). The 'loyalty' that makes order possible is 'the supreme gift', for it preserves the kingdom. Arren's fealty to Ged repeats the gift pattern on a personal scale. Personal gifts also play a part: Arren's purchase (34) of a silver brooch for his mother being one example. Throughout the Earthsea of *The Farthest Shore*, however, gifts and exchanges are becoming corrupt, and the loss of identity and joy (Senior, 1996: 109) results from the human obsession with 'power over life – endless wealth, unassailable safety, immortality', culminating in greed (41) – symptoms of the loss of Balance where values are concerned.

Holding despair at bay: the tale of Cob

Ged's discourse on the forbidden Lore of Paln, leads to the tale of the Grey Mage of Paln (whose use-name, 'Cob', means 'spider' (as in 'cobweb')), an evil, misguided wizard who angered Ged by his frivolous use of magic as 'a mere trick to entertain the idle' (85); the angry Ged had forced Cob – knowing his inordinate terror of death – to go with him into the Dry Land, winning his undying hatred. Cob has violated nature by opening a hole between the worlds, in a vengeful attempt to cheat death. Ged's part in making Cob into the Dark Mage suggests that Cob is Ged's shadow or *doppelgänger*.

Characters and events on the quest

In Hort Town, now a 'Vanity Fair' full of cheap illusions, a 'dream city' with no 'centre' (58), the once powerful wizard Hare says, ' "I remember being alive" ' (54–5); he is but one example of people seduced by Cob into thinking they could outwit Death. Lorbanery's once marvellous silk looms are silent, covered with spider webs, emblems of inertia and despair (88). The madwoman Akaren and her equally mad son, Sopli, (95–6) illustrate what Arren calls the absence of 'joy in life' (98). The mad Sopli ironically loses his life because of his irrational fear of drowning. Finally Arren himself falls into despair, doubting Ged and believing they too will die, and for nothing (122).

In contrast, the Raft People, some of Le Guin's most original inventions, live above this decay. Their participation in the Long Dance can be seen as a celebration of life, moving on 'fragile rafts' in a limitless ocean, dancing 'above the hollow place, above the terrible abyss' (Wood, 1979: 176), above the trap of 'nothingness' that haunts this blighted Earthsea.

Arren's 'healing': lessons from Ged

Ged lectures Arren on the principle of Balance and the need to resist 'doing good' for its own sake: instead, act only when necessary (*The Farthest Shore*: 75): the ' "first lesson on Roke, and the last, is *Do what is needful*. And no more!" ' (150). A second principle views knowledge of death as a 'gift' bestowing selfhood. Selfhood is difficult, but is beyond all price: ' "our torment, and our treasure, and our humanity" ' (138). As Elizabeth Cummins observes, the psychological healing process for Arren follows the pattern set with Ged and Tenar: 'In all three psychological healing begins when the problem and solution can be named, when the admission of weakness becomes strength' (1990: 54). Third, Ged teaches Arren the value of a trusting relationship (*The Farthest Shore*: 136), saying unequivocally, ' "I will trust you, son of Morred" '. The roles of mentor and apprentice are undergoing a transformation into mutuality (138). A fourth lesson is Ged's revelation of the 'Anti-King', the traitor self that lives in all of us, ' "in the dark, like the worm in the apple" ', seeking endless self-perpetuation, whose voice we must resist (153–4).

Orm Embar and 'the dragons' run': Cob's 'remains'

Guided by Orm (cf. Old English *wyrm*, dragon or serpent) Embar to Selidor, Arren experiences the sublime when he sees 'how small a thing a man is, how frail and how terrible,' in contrast to the dragon hovering above, filling half the sky (172). The dragon's use of '*Agni*' is left unglossed by Le Guin, though Perry Nodelman points out its resemblance to the Latin *agnus*, or lamb, and speculates on some possible implications of Christ-like innocence (1995: 196). The dragon's Old Speech adds a flavour of incantation, plus an orphic ambiguity ('"no and yes"', *The Farthest Shore*: 173) in its pronouncements. Orm Embar's heroic self-immolation leaves Cob's 'remains' crushed, revealing his empty eye-sockets (192). Elizabeth Cummins explains: 'Symbolically ... [Cob] has sacrificed his self ("I"), his ability to see the power of light, his ability to see the natural environment and the human community' (1990: 55).

The Stone of Shelieth

The Stone is a 'truth-telling' rock-crystal, used for divination (158). Two of the Masters of Roke see contradictory visions in the Stone: the Master Changer sees the sea as it was 'before the Making,' the Master Summoner sees 'the Unmaking' (161). Crow and Erlich suggest that Segoy's 'Making' of Earthsea through Old Speech, is 'mythologically, the birth of consciousness ... The existence of the world depends on man's consciousness' – an idea that pervades Western philosophy since Kant. Hence, the human capacity to destroy the world is 'twofold.' It can take the form of abusing nature (bad ecology), or neglecting 'the responsibility to create one's own human being', and in either case, the whole of creation is jeopardized (213). What the mages see in the Stone of Shelieth is alternative versions of the catastrophe that comes about when human beings refuse to do two things only they can do – give conscious attention to all the myriad forms of the created world, and utter the words that bring the world to consciousness.

Le Guin's concept of the Dry Lands; the closing of the hole between worlds

Peter Nicholls calls Le Guin's portrayal of the afterworld in Earthsea neither a state of nirvana nor a traditional 'heaven' or 'hell'; he deems it 'quite deeply un-Christian,' yet also not 'anti-Christian'; rather, it is something closer to the ancient Greek Hades. Le Guin clearly values life in the present world, and in the epigraph to A *Wizard of Earthsea*, the phrase 'only in dying life' means that 'the keenness of living is kept sharp by the imminence of death' (Nicholls, 1974: 78–9). The Dry

Lands evoke the Waste Land of T. S. Eliot, in turn based upon the tradition of depicting spiritual *acedia*, despair, as a lifeless desert.

At the dry, barren 'fulcrum of the world' (*The Farthest Shore*: 176), Ged closes the hole between the worlds, signifying through Agnen, the Rune of Ending, his restoration of wholeness to Earthsea. With the closing of this unnatural door, Ged incidentally releases Cob, whose eyes are inexplicably restored and freed of anger, hate, or grief (209). The *doppelgänger* wins release along with his 'original.'

The victory of consciousness; Ged's farewell to his wizardry; Arren's symbolic role fulfilled

Ged's Herculean effort has cost him his wizard's power (219), but his achievement has restored the wholeness of the realm of Earthsea: an artist nearing old age, Ged succeeds in 'assisting an entire country in dealing with a crisis of language' (Cummins, 1990: 60–1). Language had to be newly empowered, for the health and wholeness of Earthsea depends upon human consciousness, and human consciousness in turn requires words to name the things of the world and thereby bring them to awareness. Why Ged could do this, and no other, is explained in his comment to Arren: ' "I desire nothing beyond my art" ' (*The Farthest Shore*: 150). Pure of heart and single in purpose, he is ready for the simple life on Gont.

Arren's achievement is also great: he has grown from a naive idolization of Ged to being able to see him 'for the first time whole, as he was' (187). Knowledge of the 'true' Ged correlates with Arren's knowledge of himself. He is now ready to become King of Earthsea. His true victory, however, is not in being crowned at Havnor, but was achieved, as Margaret Esmonde says, on Selidor, 'where grasping a stone brought back from his conquest of the Mountains of Pain, he knows he has achieved a true victory over self, although there is no one to praise him' (1979: 29).

Homecoming

Kalessin, a monumental dragon still more ancient than Orm Embar, takes each of the protagonists to their respective destinations: ' "I have brought the young king to his kingdom, and the old man to his home." ' Master Doorkeeper notes of Ged, ' "He has done with doing. He goes home" ' (221–2).

TEHANU

Its relevance to contemporary times

Tenar, after the close of *The Tombs of Atuan*, 'put all magery behind her and chose the classic path to happiness: To live unknown' (Dirda, 1990: 9). Despite her choice Tenar/Goha ('Goha' meaning in the Gontish language 'a little white web-spinning spider' (*Tehanu*: 1) is swept up in events of an epic dimension through her relationship with the child Therru – meaning 'burned,' or 'flame,' a name bestowed by Tenar. The child becomes the pivotal figure in the transition from the old, exhausted Earthsea to the new world that is being born: the 'in-between' time of the setting makes it comparable to our own era.

Near the end of his life, Jung compared our age to the beginning of the Christian era two centuries ago:

> [A] mood of universal destruction and renewal ... has set its mark on our age. This mood makes itself felt everywhere, politically, socially, and philosophically. We are living in what the Greeks called the *kairos* – the right moment – for a 'metamorphosis of the gods,' of the fundamental principles and symbols. (quoted in Tarnas, 1993: 412)

Richard Tarnas sees the pertinence of Jung's comment to our time: 'The crisis of modern man is an essentially masculine crisis ... [in which] as Jung prophesied, an epochal shift is taking place in the contemporary psyche, a reconciliation between the two great polarities, a union of opposites: a *hieros gamos* (sacred marriage) between the long-dominant but now alienated masculine and the long-suppressed but now ascending feminine.' The contemporary struggle is to bring forth something fundamentally new in human history: 'We seem to be witnessing, suffering, the birth labour of a new reality, a new form of human existence, a "child" that would be the fruit of this great archetypal marriage, and that would bear within itself all its antecedents in a new form' (442–4). Tarnas's words can give perspective to Le Guin's 'reconciliation between the two great polarities of masculine and feminine in *Tehanu*, as well as the 'child' Tehanu herself as an 'antecedent' of a new form (if not a metamorphosis of the gods, perhaps a regendering and reimagining of their 'species').

Critical controversy over Tehanu's relationship to the trilogy

Tehanu, following *The Farthest Shore* after a gap of eighteen years, has received a varied critical reception. Some feel the trilogy was a complete work of art and are uncomfortable with the added book; for example John Clute, who finds it 'a forcible – and at times decidedly bad-tempered – deconstruction of its predecessors', and though he understands the rationale for Le Guin's unmasking of the 'inherently male' order of the previous books, he clearly would rather she had not 'deconstructed paradise' (Clute, 1990: 1409).

His opinion is shared by Ann Welton, who allows the considerable truth of the book, but finds it not wholly 'of a piece' with the trilogy: she believes 'the characters and *mise-en-scène*' 'are from Earthsea, [but] the message comes from someplace else', perhaps from Le Guin's short fiction and essays of the previous fourteen years (Welton, 1991: 18, 15). Others rejoice that Tenar's and Ged's stories are continued into middle age and, like Robin McKinley (herself an outstanding author of books for children, such as *Beauty*), praise *Tehanu*'s clearsighted 'recognition of the necessary and life-giving contributions of female magic – sometimes disguised as domesticity'. McKinley qualifies her praise with her assertion that 'Young readers of the Earthsea trilogy should be obliged to wait a decade or two before they read it. Adults may read the quartet as a finished work' (McKinley, 1990).

Others agree that *Tehanu* is more suited to adults than children, for it bears less resemblance to high fantasy (to their mind exclusively children's fare) than to the supposedly 'adult' novel. Dirda goes so far as to say it 'builds to a climax of almost pornographic horror, nearly too shocking for its supposedly young adult pages' (1990: 9).

There are those who argue to the contrary – that it supplies what is lacking in the preceding books, a female heroic. Some foreshadowing of *Tehanu*, albeit subconscious on Le Guin's part, occurs in *The Farthest Shore*, where the lonely Ged, desiring to go 'home' to see Tenar and Ogion, says, 'And maybe there I would learn at last what no act or art or power can teach me, what I have never learned' (*The Farthest Shore*: 176–7). A connection can also be made between *The Farthest Shore* and *Tehanu* in the progressively 'deepening gloom' of the cycle, which as T. A. Shippey says, reflects 'America in the aftermath of Vietnam: exhausted, distrustful, uncertain' (1977: 158–9).

Len Hatfield in 'From master to brother: shifting the balance of authority in Ursula K. Le Guin's *Farthest Shore* and *Tehanu*' (1993), believes that the implicit subversions of patriarchy in the original trilogy are simply made explicit in the last book. Perry Nodelman responded to Hatfield's article with a brilliant piece of Earthsea 'archaeology' in which he maintains that *Tehanu* can be read 'not as an explicit statement of formerly implicit themes, but rather, as a profound criticism and reversal of what went before'. Moreover, Le

Guin shows 'how much supposedly universal archetypes can change in a decade and a half', thus revealing 'the transitory nature of all the supposedly eternal assumptions human beings make about gender and sexuality', and portraying 'the continual process by which all of us constantly reinvent the past' (1995: 181, 198–9).

Holly Littlefield has demonstrated a continuity between the earlier Tenar, a fifteen-year-old girl who was able 'to outwit, entrap, and control' Ged, the most powerful wizard in Earthsea, and the Tenar of twenty years later, who addresses social issues, especially the imbalances of power between men and women (1995: 248, 252). Le Guin, she says, cannot reconstruct the Earthsea she created nearly three decades ago, but instead has written a mature response to it, reflecting women's experience in that world and offering some pungent criticism of it. Tenar's personal choice exalts loving relationships over Ogion's world of wizardly books and spells: as she says, ' "I wanted to live. I wanted a man. I wanted my children. I wanted my life" ' (*Tehanu*: 51). Despite her misogynist training in her prior life, she now feels 'the need to become more deeply connected to her own inner power as a woman' (Littlefield, 1995: 254).

Le Guin has expressed the philosophy of *Tehanu* elsewhere, for instance, in a 1986 commencement address to young women at Bryn Mawr: 'I hope you don't try to take your strength from men, or from a man. Secondhand experience breaks down ... I hope you'll take and make your own soul, that you'll feel your life for yourself pain by pain and joy by joy'. These were words that she believed Tenar might have said to the young women of Earthsea (1989a: 158).

How Tehanu differs from its predecessors in the Earthsea cycle
Tehanu differs from its three predecessors in several ways. First, Tenar, whose growth towards maturity was initiated by Ged's quest in *The Tombs of Atuan*, is now the centre of attention, no romantic heroine, but a middle-aged woman with her own kind of courage. Contemporary feminist theory and several of Le Guin's essays, plus her *Earthsea Revisioned*, provide illuminating background on why Le Guin essentially 'rewrote' the trilogy by adding the fourth volume. For example, the essay 'The Space Crone' explores the three stages of a woman's life: virgin, wife-mother, crone – the three aspects of the Triple Goddess, traditionally represented by Diana, Venus, and Hecate. The failure of the contemporary world to honour all three goddesses means that 'The entire life of a woman from ten or twelve through seventy or eighty has become secular, uniform, changeless'. Le Guin affirms the need to recapture the value of the last stage of a woman's life, when she must

become pregnant with herself, despite society's failure to value this lonely achievement; only old women, she says, have experienced and accepted to the utmost the 'essential quality' of the human condition (5–6). Not yet in the crone category (she uses this term to refer to the older Aunty Moss) Tenar is however in the process of giving birth to herself, and from a larger perspective, she is, together with the dragon Kaliessen and Therru/Tehanu, a kind of cultural mid-wife, assisting at the birth of a new world.

Lissa Paul describes the 'cultural shift' inherent in *Tehanu*: Tenar marks Le Guin's abandonment of the male romantic hero in favour of a 'feminist, pro-creative, recreative hero, not pure' (as the conventional romantic hero must be), but 'whole'. The dragon has undergone a parallel transformation, from a nemesis into a 'familiar', a 'guide for the new female hero'. Le Guin moves beyond the conventional hierarchical order of high fantasy into 'a new world where the search is for wildness, a "new order of freedom"' (Paul, 1996: 105. See *Tehanu*: 18, 26).

Both Tenar and Ged have suffered through many changes since *Tombs*, where Ged had initiated Arha/Tenar into selfhood and awakened her sexuality. In *Tehanu* it is Tenar who initiates Ged to sexuality and the satisfactions of ordinary domestic life. (Mages are required to be sexually abstinent, in accordance with the tradition of purity, embodied for example in Parsifal, though interestingly, this prohibition does not apply to witches.) In one of her sallies into humour, speaking of the absence of sex in the earlier Earthsea books, Le Guin observes in *Earthsea Revisioned* that the working title for *Tehanu* was in fact 'Better Late Than Never' (1993: 15).

Another major difference lies in Ged's loss of magic; he must now accommodate to this and, no longer the 'Alpha Male,' must seek what comforts he can in humility and simple tasks. (Michael Dirda has contrasted the ageing ex-mage with the aged Ulysses in Tennyson's poem, who 'sails off into the sunset, to certain death, proclaiming heroic verse: "To strive, to seek, to find, and not yield." But Ged feels nothing of this' (1990: 9).)

Lastly, Therru/Tehanu enters as a new, world-changing character destined to become the new female archmage, transforming the old Earthsea into a world that is yet-to-be-defined.

Le Guin on revisiting Earthsea: the need for 'Revisioning'
The main points that Le Guin makes in her account of her purpose in writing *Tehanu*, expressed in *Earthsea Revisioned*, can be summarized here. First, the 'gendered' character of the 'hero-tale' in the Western world, traditionally male and concerned with the 'validation of

manhood,' is structured as a quest with women as 'sidekicks' (5). Second, at the time she began to write, artists were supposed to ignore gender, but this ideal of the 'androgynous' artist's mind was – and is – problematical, for ' [t]he standards themselves were gendered' – the 'universally human' was gendered male. As she says: 'My Earthsea trilogy is part of this male tradition – that is why I had to write this fourth volume. Because I changed. I had to show the other side' (quoted in Tax, 1990: 75). No longer an 'artificial man,' she desired to 'revision' Earthsea through a woman's eyes, redefining 'action, decision, and power' through relationships, as women experience them. In Tenar's world, as today, 'History is no longer about great men. The important choices and decisions may be obscure ones, not recognized or applauded by society.' The virtues of Ged in *Tehanu* are 'no longer the traditional male heroic ones: power as domination over others, unassailable strength, and the generosity of the rich' (1993: 12– 14).

As Meredith Tax remarks, Le Guin wants us to ask, 'who did the dishes for all those feasts in Tolkien? And how can any of us – even men who share housework – be heroes when we have to spend so much time caring for house and children? And without heroes, how can evil be defeated?' For in *Tehanu* there is a sense of the growing strength of evil and a loss of the power to challenge it. Ged has lost his power, Tenar has given hers up to 'marry and have kids', and the central symbol of the book is 'a burned, abused child'. However, because this is fantasy, not realistic fiction, 'there are dragons', and in Le Guin's universe, dragons signal hope (Tax, 1990: 75).

The shared human–dragon history: the tale of the woman of Kemay
The tale of the old fisherwoman of Kemay tells the shared history of dragons and humans: Once both were of the same winged race and spoke the same Language of the Making, but they grew apart: 'the wild ones' became dragons, and the 'wise' ones, the gatherers of treasure and learning, became the human folk. Some of the humans 'saved the learning of the dragons – the True Language of the Making – and these are now the wizards'. Still others remained 'both human and dragon,' keeping their wings, and these great winged beings are both wild and wise, having human minds and dragon hearts (*Tehanu*: 11–12). Le Guin's dragons are far removed from the malevolent creatures of the medieval European imagination, closer to 'oriental lineage,' in Richard F. Patteson's phrase, and thus, stand for 'a nature in which savagery is a necessary part of the whole – something to be respected more than feared' (1985: 246). In fact, in this last book of Earthsea, the chief

dragon leads the humans in defeating the evil mage, Aspen.

In *Earthsea Revisioned* Le Guin further explains the evolution of dragons in the cycle. In the trilogy, they were 'above all, wildness. What is *not owned*.' Tenar makes a connection to 'wildness' – and thus to dragons – through her adoption of Therru. Therru is 'the key to this book. Until I saw Therru, until she chose me, there was no book.' With only one seeing eye, Therru 'sees with the eye of the spirit as well as the eye of the flesh' (19, 25), and she knows dragon language without needing to learn it. (Compare the children in Le Guin's picture book, *Fire and Stone*, where only they comprehend what the dragon says.) Her 'Third Eye,' a sign of extrahuman powers (Cirlot, 1971: 100) explains Ogion's words, ' "*they will fear her*," ' and why he urges Tenar, ' "Teach her, Tenar ... Teach her all!" ' (*Tehanu*: 21). In a folklore context, Ogion's prophecy 'adheres to the falling-word myth and foretells the coming of the avatar who will reverse the pattern of decline' (Senior, 1996: 110).

Reunited with Ged, teaching Therru

Both Therru and Ged learn about 'the womanly arts of survival: cooking, animal husbandry, and patience,' what Littlefield has called the 'less-sanitized side of life' that teaches compassion (quoted in Reid, 1997: 46) from Tenar. Tenar however is no 'angel in the house,' and occasionally seethes with bitterness and disillusionment over the lack of respect for the vulnerable, especially women and children. In response to critical comments on the negativity in the portrayal of men in the book, Le Guin has cited the exceptions: Ogion, the young king Arren, and Ged – who has lost his 'job' and is learning new virtues. As for Spark, he may be 'a selfish lout', but Le Guin counters, 'Are all sons good, then, all wise, all generous? Tenar blames herself for Spark's weakness (just like a woman!) but I blame the society that spoiled the boy by giving him unearned power' (1993: 14). Tenar shows sensitivity to Ged's dilemma in losing his wizard's staff: she says to Aunty Moss, ' "All I understand about living is having your work to do, and being able to do it. That's the pleasure, and the glory, and all" ' (97). In contrast to Tenar's alienation from her son (she does not know his 'true name'), the warmth and depth of the bond between Tenar and Ged grows, culminating when Tenar, looking at him in the light of a rose and gold dawn, says, ' "I have loved you since I first saw you" ', whereupon he responds with an intimate kiss, saying, ' "Life-giver" ' (214).

Fan and double vision: Tenar and Therru and their dragon 'powers'
The dragon motif and the theme of gifts are evident in the visit to Fan,
whose prize possession, acquired as a gift, is his eponymous, marvellous
fan. This two-sided piece of *trompe l'oeil* art, has on one side a gorgeous
image of 'delicately painted men and women ... The towers and
bridges and banners of Havnor,' and on the other an image of dragons,
which when held up to the light showed 'the men and women were
winged, and the dragons looked with human eyes' (*Tehanu*: 104–5). It
represents in Le Guin's words 'double vision, two things seen as one.'
(1993: 21). The dragons remain mysterious, even to their creator, but
clearly Therru/Tehanu has the double vision to 'see' both the human
and dragon worlds, and Tenar is 'a woman dragons would talk to'
(*Tehanu*: 62), who can do something male wizards cannot: look into
the dragon's eye and live (37–8). The reason is that she has not been
seduced by the need to wield power; therefore, she is free to connect
with 'a different world, a free world, where things can be changed,
remade' (Le Guin, 1993: 23).

Liminality in Tehanu
Kathleen Spencer's writings on Le Guin have explored the 'liminality'
of her typical 'anthropological hero' in her science fiction – a solitary
individual who reaches out to the 'alien,' and in the process of so
doing, becomes an agent of creative social change (1980: 34). Spencer
applies the social anthropology of Victor Witter Turner to Le Guin's
science fiction; Turner himself borrowed the term 'liminal' from
Arnold van Gennep's writings on rites of passage, and modified *liminal*
to elucidate his theory of ritual processes and symbolic behaviour in
human culture. (Spencer, 1980: 34; Turner, 1978: 249). Spencer's
comments on Le Guin's science fiction are relevant to the characters of
Earthsea, since Le Guin has identified the central theme of the cycle as
'Power' (Loer, 1990: 38) and issues of power must be faced by 'liminars'
on the periphery of the established order. All of the protagonists in the
Earthsea cycle are liminal, but none more so than Therru, who has
kinship with both the human and the dragon worlds, and thus can
meaningfully communicate between the two species who were once
one. (Le Guin's *Catwings* series illustrates 'liminality' on the picture
book level, where cats with wings – a kind of hybrid species – relate to
children who feel themselves marginalized and provide animal guides
'through a shadowy, urban landscape of archetypal evils' (Lindow,
1997a).)
    Therru, having been marginalized from both the human and dragon
worlds, and knowing the languages of both, is positioned to bring about

a new era, a time envisioned in Ogion's dying exclamation, ' "*All changed!*" ' (*Tehanu*: 23). Of both human and dragon lineage, she will be able to go 'beyond the old order in which men were taught to own and dominate and women were taught to collude with them: the order of oppression' (Le Guin, 1993: 23–4). The parallels to today's anxieties can be seen in Beech's comments on Tenar's world: ' "[It is] . . . a time of ruining, the end of an age . . . We must turn to the center again or be lost . . . We must find our heart, our strength" ' (*Tehanu*: 15). Though a sorcerer, Beech has no clue to the significance of the Master Patterner's cryptic prophecy of ' "*a woman on Gont*" ' (142). Therru/ Tehanu's mediation between the human and dragon worlds climaxes in Kaliessen's (Segoy's) battle with the false mage Aspen (true name 'Erisen'), after which Therru is given her new name, 'Tehanu' (in Kargish, 'The Heart of the Swan', and Hardic, 'the Arrow').

A new pastoral life, a new world to come
The abode of the newly-constituted family – Tenar, Ged and Therru – is Ogion's house, a neat metaphor of the transformation of his era into theirs. This setting and their newly chosen occupation as goatherds give a pastoral conclusion to what began as heroic fantasy. Tenar and Ged have come a long way from the Tombs of Atuan, and they now have the 'gift' of the dragon's child, left in their care for a time. Tehanu must eventually return to Kaliessen, but for the present, as the dragon remarks to her, ' "Thou hast work to do here" ' (225). Instead of heroic rewards, Ged and Tenar have achieved wholeness, ripeness, and harmony with the natural rhythms of a mountain home. The child, however, holds the promise of a breakthrough to a new world we can only imagine.

Earthsea for today
The Earthsea books portray their protagonists' growth and development from childhood through adolescence to maturity, and their respective quests to find answers to the existential questions of life, death, and the hereafter. Though expressed through the fantasy or 'dream' genre, this existential level of meaning mirrors, on a psychological level, the realistic *Bildungsroman* or novel of education. The characters face crucial moments of decision, 'pivotal' choices, in response to certain universals of the human condition. The relationships between the characters also play a vital role in their coming to wholeness. Though there are parallels between the alternative world of Earthsea and the world of the reader in contemporary times, there are also definitive, illuminating differences that lend themselves to comparison and contrast between the 'worlds'.

Earthsea

1. A realm of magical arts, based on the power of language, derived from the Old Speech of dragons, wherein to speak is to create.
2. An agrarian society, with limited commerce, where most people live simple lives in harmony with nature.
3. A class society, hierarchical and patriarchal in structure, headed by a king in Havnor, to whom wizards give the 'heart's gift' of fealty; in *Tehanu*, however, a questioning of rigidly defined male and female roles and leanings towards gender equality.
4. For the priestly, wizardly class, valuing of an abstinent, monastic path; simplicity and asceticism (compare Buddhism); denial of the passions; sublimation of sexual desires into service of heroic ideals (compare the knight of courtly romance).
5. A close relationship to the animal world; animals in a daemonic relationship with mages (compare Native American beliefs); nonetheless, animals viewed ambiguously: shapeshifters who stay too long in animal form risk losing their humanity.
6. A high value placed on metaphysical awareness: people's lives permeated with spiritual reality; the unlearned exhibit superstition and a naive belief in 'spells'.
7. Protagonists of 'liminal' status, standing between two 'worlds' and mediating between them.

'Realistic' contemporary world

1. An abundance of technological 'marvels' instead of 'magic'.
2. A predominantly urban society, highly materialistic, with most people removed from the natural world.
3. Democracy valued, though corporations and the military wield great political power; in the advanced nations, economy shifting from industrial to 'information age'.
4. Male dominance in many areas; movement towards a gender-equal society in more advanced and enlightened parts of the world.
5. Materialistic values 'rule', although some individuals opt for a simpler life close to nature; great yearning for richer spiritual life manifested in sales of 'soul' books, attraction to Eastern religions.
6. Increasing attention to the need for deeper ecological awareness; the 'green' revolution; renewed interest in herbal remedies; animal rights movement; most people however remote from rhythms of natural world.
7. An urgent need to develop people able to serve as 'mediators' of cultural understanding, such as Le Guin's 'liminal' figures, to bridge differences, whether social, political, or gender-based.

Earthsea and its readers

Given the fact that Le Guin's Earthsea novels offer many 'teachable moments,' I wish to explore a few answers to the question, 'What do the four books of the Earthsea cycle offer to today's readers?' (In addition, of course, to the sheer pleasure of the stories!) Judging from the electronically posted reader reviews, 'today's readers' of the cycle are an eclectic group, ranging from sixth graders (assigned by their teachers to read, usually, A *Wizard of Earthsea*) to adults mesmerized by the entire 'quartet,' such as one who speaks of the trilogy as 'a Jungian joy' and *Tehanu* as 'a text for the new millennium' in its introduction of 'the Anima as coeval healer and warrior' (Amazon. com, a reader from Los Angeles, posted 12 December 1997).

Wendy Jago's 'A *Wizard of Earthsea* and the charge of escapism' (1972) pointed out how the novel can contribute to a child's knowledge about growing up, apprenticeship, and facing mortality (also in the form of deathseeking impulses); much can be gleaned as well from Le Guin's artful use of language. Geoff Fox's 'Notes on "teaching" A *Wizard of Earthsea*' (1973) describes a variety of practical activities for teachers to use with young children: discussion, choral work, drama, artwork, game making and writing – both prose and verse – all tested in the classroom.

Others have noted how the books 'model' teaching. In 'A review of "Earthsea"' in *Growing Point*, Margery Fisher speaks of the 'element of loving pedagogy, of a human desire to instruct and strengthen,' shown in Ged's 'instinct to teach, to reach out in kindness, and share his experience and knowledge with others' (1977: 3119). Margaret Miles expresses her belief that the Earthsea books treat education in the most basic sense, portraying the way that 'how and what you are taught brings you to the point of learning to define who and what you are.' Ged, a student in the first book, teaches Tenar in the second, and both continue to learn as they in turn teach the young Lebannen and Therru, 'who will shape the powers of the world to come' (Miles, 1991: 301).

Respect for the power of language and the valuing of rhetoric

Reams could be written on the lyrical and orphic qualities of Le Guin's language in the Earthsea books. Here is a sampling of the critical responses it has evoked. Fred Inglis says Le Guin gives children a way of understanding that 'the most universal of human gifts, language, is also the most wonderful' (1981: 245–6). He quotes the passage in A *Wizard of Earthsea* in which the young Sparrowhawk looks into Ogion's lore book and, struck by the antiquity and mythic quality of the contents, experiences a peculiarly ghostly feeling: 'Small and strange was the writing, overwritten and interlined by many hands, and all those hands were dust now' (A *Wizard of Earthsea*: 34). This is the voice of one who understands the magic of language and its persistence over time, and 'makes language, as it always was and is for Magi, the special preoccupation of her hero-intellectual' (Inglis, 1981: 246).

Another characteristic of Le Guin's style is the creation of new words, vital to the building of new fictive worlds. Richard Ohmann says: 'A writer cannot escape the boundaries set by his tongue, except by creating new words, by uprooting normal syntax, or by building metaphors, each of which is a new ontological discovery' (Ohmann, 1972: 43). Just one example of a new word is the name of the cycle itself, 'Earthsea,' bringing together the components of land and ocean into linguistic unity, expressive of the underlying metaphysical oneness. The names of her dragons, such as Orm Embar and Kaliessen, resonate with a dragonish quality, showing her musical ear and prowess as a wordsmith. Her fondness for a word like 'rune' gives an Old English flavour to her 'wordhoard'; John R. Pfeiffer places the trilogy within the tradition of the oral epic, detailing Le Guin's use of Old English poetics: formulaic language, alliteration, kennings, gnomic expressions, and repetition (although this evidence has been questioned, see White, 1999: 24–5). Pfeiffer sees Ged's maturation 'in terms of his growing command of speech and language. Put another way, the message of [A *Wizard of Earthsea*] is that the achievement of the fully human experience requires the mastery of speech as the means for creating that experience'. Through Ged, young readers can see the importance of mastering rhetoric. Pfeiffer also insists that the Earthsea narratives need to be *heard* (1979: 124, 116).

Ecological dimensions

Volumes could be written on the pertinence of Le Guin's Earthsea to present-day ecological concerns. Here there is room for only a few suggestions that may spur further thought. Brian Attebery points to an analogy between Le Guin's portrayal of 'the psychic cost of seemingly effortless meddling with the world' (nearly fatal for the inept wizard) and the human and environmental cost of misused technologies (Attebery, 1980: 173). Since 'magic' can be viewed as technology whose *modus operandi* is not yet understood, the analogy seems especially pertinent. Although Le Guin has been called by some an 'ecofeminist,' there are good reasons to refrain from applying such a limiting label; neither the 'ecologist' nor 'feminist' label fits:

Because Le Guin creates entire cultures and environments, her work does lend itself to ecofeminist interpretations, but ecology is not as important to her work as is anthropology. If I had to identify Le Guin with a particular brand of feminism, it would be one that hasn't yet been invented. (White, 1999: 116)

Seeing beyond appearances

Tenar comforts the despairing Ged, telling him he needs time to heal from his experience of death (in *The Farthest Shore*), and he replies, ' "Like the child? ... I don't know ... Why you took her, knowing that she cannot be healed. Knowing what her life must be." ' His words anger Tenar, for he has failed to see beyond appearances (*Tehanu*: 74–5); instead, he has responded like the unlearned Tiff, who surreptitiously makes the sign to avert evil when Therru passes, showing that 'Like most people, Tiff believed that you are what happens to you' (161). *Tehanu* as a whole validates a much different perspective: it is the 'maimed child' with a vision that comprehends the inner essence who brings rescue and the promise of renewed life. In our day of overemphasis on superficialities of 'beauty', there is a deep wisdom here for the child whose only ideal of beauty may be a Barbie or Ken doll. Le Guin's portrait of the abused child carries a message of hope for the self-healing and self-affirmation of the wronged individual. In her article, 'Ursula Le Guin's Earthsea: rescuing the damaged child,' Sandra J. Lindow traces the 'maimed child' as a recurrent image throughout the Earthsea books, pointing out that both Ged and Tenar suffered abuse in childhood and that, in rescuing Therru, Tenar is psychologically reclaiming the child she once was (1997b: 10–13).

Envisioning a future of peace and harmony

In *Earthsea Revisioned*, Le Guin says that when writing *Tehanu*, she saw 'a new world, or maybe only gulfs of sunlit air' (26). Her characteristic self-deprecation does not diminish her accomplishment in leaving a reader of the entire cycle with what J. R. R. Tolkien called 'a lifting of the heart' (Tolkien, 1965: 69). Though she chose to incorporate in *Tehanu* elements of social criticism, commonly (and mistakenly) thought to be more germane to the realistic novel than to heroic fantasy, the close of the story belongs definitely to the tradition of *eucatastrophe*, the happy ending, noted by Tolkien as a necessary element of fantasy (68). This sense of newness of life is sorely needed today, at the start of a new century, when prophecies of disaster on a cosmic scale vie with pipedreams of unimaginable wealth and unprecedented 'progress.' Le Guin's vision is neither utopian nor dystopian, but rather what may be called 'melioristic,' meaning tending to betterment through human effort – or maybe through the opening of human hearts. Perhaps it is Le Guin's 'mediating' protagonists, the *liminars* who are isolated without being alienated and can further understanding between seemingly incompatible peoples, who are her most precious 'gift' to a vision of peace.

Through her Earthsea books, readers can stretch the limits of their own lives and experiment with alternative cultures in worlds rich and strange.

References

Abramson, J. (1974) 'Facing the other fact of life: death in recent children's fiction,' *School Library Journal* 21(4): 31–3.

Attebery, B. (1980) *The Fantasy Tradition in American Literature: From Irving to Le Guin*, Bloomington, IN: Indiana University Press.

Attebery, B. (1992) *Strategies of Fantasy*, Bloomington, IN: Indiana University Press.

Bailey, E. C. (1980) 'Shadows in Earthsea: Le Guin's use of a Jungian archetype,' *Extrapolation* 21(3): 254–61.

Barbour, D. (1974) 'On Ursula K. Le Guin's A *Wizard of Earthsea*,' *Riverside Quarterly* 6: 119–23.

Barrow, C. and Barrow, D. (1991) 'Le Guin's Earthsea: voyages in consciousness,' *Extrapolation* 32: 20–44.

Cameron, E. (1971) 'High fantasy: a wizard of Earthsea,' *The Horn Book Magazine* 47: 129–38.

Cirlot, J. E. (1971) A *Dictionary of Symbols*, Second edition (trans. Jack Sage), New York: Philosophical Library; London: Routledge and Kegan Paul, 1962.

Clute, J. (1990) 'Deconstructing paradise,' *The Times Literary Supplement*, 4578, 28 December: 1409.

Cogell, E. (1983) *Ursula K. Le Guin: Primary and Secondary Bibliography*, Boston: G. K. Hall.

Crow, J. N. and Erlich, R. D. (1979) 'Words of binding: patterns of integration in the Earthsea trilogy,' in *Ursula K. Le Guin*, ed. J. D. Olander and M. H. Greenberg, Writers of the 21st Century Series, New York: Taplinger: 200–24.

Cummins, E. (1990) *Understanding Ursula K. Le Guin*, Columbia: University of South Carolina Press.

Dirda, M. (1990) 'The twilight of an age of magic,' *Book World – The Washington Post*, 25 February: 1, 9.

Eliade, M. (1958) *Rites and Symbols of Initiation: The Mysteries of Birth and Death,* New York: Harper.

Esmonde, M. (1979) 'The master pattern: the psychological journey,' in *Ursula K. Le Guin,* ed. J. D. Olander and M. H. Greenberg, Writers of the 21st Century Series, New York: Taplinger: 11–35.

Esmonde, M. (1987) 'Beyond the circles of the world: death and the hereafter in children's literature,' in *Webs and Wardrobes: Humanist and Religious Worldview in Children's Literature,* ed. J. O'Beirne Milner and L. F. Morcock Milner, Lanham, MD: University Press of America: 33–42.

Fisher, M. (1977) 'A review of "Earthsea"', *Growing Point* 16(1): 3119.

Fox, G. (1973) 'Notes on "teaching" *A Wizard of Earthsea,*' *Children's Literature in Education* 11(2): 58–67.

Frye, N. (1957) *Anatomy of Criticism,* Princeton, NJ: Princeton University Press.

Gebser, J. (1992) 'Cave and labyrinth' (trans. Georg Feuerstein), *Parabola: The Magazine of Myth and Tradition,* 17(2): 61–3.

Hatfield, L. (1993) 'From master to brother: shifting the balance of authority in Ursula K. Le Guin's *Farthest Shore* and *Tehanu,*' *Children's Literature* 21: 43–65.

Inglis, F. (1981) *The Promise of Happiness: Value and Meaning in Children's Fiction,* Cambridge: Cambridge University Press.

Jago, W. (1972) '*A Wizard of Earthsea* and the Charge of Escapism,' *Children's Literature in Education* 3(8): 21–9.

Jenkins, S. (1985) 'Growing up in Earthsea,' *Children's Literature in Education,* 16(1): 21–31.

Jung, C. G., von Franz, M. L., Henderson, J. L. *et al.* (1964) *Man and His Symbols,* Garden City, NY: J. C. Ferguson Publishing Company.

Kroeber, A. L. (1976) *Handbook of the Indians of California,* New York: Dover.

Kroeber, T. (1961) *Ishi in Two Worlds: A Biography of the Last Wild Indian in North America,* Berkeley, CA: University of California; Cambridge: Cambridge University Press.

Kroeber, T. (1964) *Ishi, Last of His Tribe,* Berkeley, CA: Parnassus.

Kuznets, L. (1985) 'High fantasy in America: a study of Lloyd Alexander, Ursula Le Guin, and Susan Cooper,' *The Lion and the Unicorn* 9: 19–35.

Landsberg, M. (1987) *Reading for the Love of It: Best Books for Young Readers,* New York: Prentice Hall.

Le Guin, U. K. (1964a) 'The rule of names,' *Fantastic* 13: 79–88.

Le Guin, U. K. (1964b) 'The word of unbinding,' *Fantastic* 13: 67–73.

Le Guin, U. K. (1968) *A Wizard of Earthsea,* Berkeley, CA: Parnassus Press.

Le Guin, U. K. (1971) *The Tombs of Atuan*, New York: Atheneum.

Le Guin, U. K. (1972) *The Farthest Shore*, New York: Atheneum.

Le Guin, U. K. (1975) 'The child and the shadow', *Quarterly Journal of the Library of Congress* 32: 139–48.

Le Guin, U. K. (1989a) *Dancing at the Edge of the World: Thoughts on Words, Women, Places*, New York: Grove Press.

Le Guin, U. K. (1989b) *Fire and Stone*, New York: Atheneum.

Le Guin, U. K. (1989c) *The Language of the Night: Essays on Fantasy and Science Fiction*, revised edition, London: Women's Press; New York: Harper Collins.

Le Guin, U. K. (1990) *Tehanu: The Last Book of Earthsea*, New York: Atheneum.

Le Guin, U. K. (1993) *Earthsea Revisioned*. Cambridge: Green Bay Publications in association with Children's Literature New England.

Lincoln, B. (1981) *Emerging from the Chrysalis: Studies in Rituals of Women's Initiation*, Cambridge, MA: Harvard University Press.

Lindow, S. (1997a) 'Trauma and recovery in Ursula K. Le Guin's *Wonderful Alexander*: animal as guide through the inner space of the unconscious,' *Foundation* 70: 32–8.

Lindow, S. J. (1997b) 'Ursula Le Guin's Earthsea: rescuing the damaged child,' *New York Review of Science Fiction* 9(5): 1, 10–13.

Loer, S. (1990) '"Earthsea" story focuses on the power of women,' Review of *Tehanu*, *Boston Globe*, 21 May: 38.

Littlefield, H. (1995) 'Unlearning patriarchy: Ursula Le Guin's feminist consciousness in *The Tombs of Atuan* and *Tehanu*,' *Extrapolation* 36(3): 244–58.

Manguel, A. and Guadalupi, G. (1980) *The Dictionary of Imaginary Places*, New York: Macmillan.

Mauss, M. (1990) *The Gift: The Form and Reason for Exchange in Archaic Societies*, (trans. W. D. Halls), New York: Norton.

McKinley, R. (1990) 'The woman wizards's triumph,' *New York Times Book Review*, 20 May: 38.

Miles, M. (1991) '"Earthsea Revisited" revisited,' *VOYA: Voice of Youth Advocates* 14: 301.

Nicholls, P. (1974) 'Showing children the value of death: a review of *The Farthest Shore* by Ursula K. Le Guin', *Foundation* 5(5): 71–80.

Nodelman, P. (1995) 'Reinventing the past: gender in Ursula K. Le Guin's *Tehanu* and the Earthsea "trilogy"', *Children's Literature* 23: 179–201.

Ohmann, R. (1972) 'Prolegomena to the analysis of prose style,' in *Essays in Stylistic Analysis*, ed. Howard S. Babb, New York: Harcourt Brace Jovanovich.

Patteson, R. F. (1985) 'Le Guin's Earthsea trilogy: the psychology of fantasy,' in *The Scope of the Fantastic – Culture, Biography, Themes, Children's Literature*, ed. R. A. Collins and H. D. Pearce, Westport, CT: Greenwood Press: 239–47.

Paul, L. (1996) 'Feminist criticism: from sex role stereotyping to subjectivity,' in *International Companion Encyclopedia of Children's Literature*, ed. P. Hunt, London and New York: Routledge: 101–12.

Pfeiffer, J. R. (1979) 'But dragons have keen ears: on hearing Earthsea with recollections of *Beowulf*,' in *Ursula K. Le Guin: Voyager to Inner Lands and to Outer Space*, ed. J. De Bolt, Port Washington, NY: Kennikat Press: 115–27.

Reid, S. E. (1997) *Presenting Ursula K. Le Guin*, New York: Twayne Publishers; London: Prentice Hall International. Twayne United States Authors Series, No. 677. Young Adult Authors.

Scholes, R. (1986) 'The good witch of the west,' *Ursula K. Le Guin*, ed. H. Bloom, New York: Chelsea: 35–46.

Selinger, B. (1988) *Le Guin and Identity in Contemporary Fiction*, Ann Arbor, MI: UMI Research Press.

Senior, W. A. (1996) 'Cultural anthropology and rituals in Ursula K. Le Guin's Earthsea,' *Mosaic* 29(4): 101–12.

Sherman, C. (1987) 'The princess and the wizard: the fantasy worlds of Ursula K. Le Guin and George MacDonald, *CHLAQ* 12(1): 24–7.

Shippey, T. A. (1977) 'The magic art and the evolution of words: Ursula Le Guin's Earthsea trilogy,' *Mosaic* 10: 147–63.

Slusser, G. E. (1976) *The Farthest Shores of Ursula K. Le Guin*, The Milford Series: Popular Writers of Today, Vol. 3, San Bernardino, CA, R. Reginald, The Borgo Press.

Spencer, K. (1980) 'Exiles and envoys: the SF of Ursula K. Le Guin,' *Foundation* 20: 32–43.

Tarnas, R. (1993) *The Passion of the Western Mind: Understanding the Ideas That Have Shaped Our World View*, New York: Ballantine Books.

Tavormina, M. T. (1988) 'A gate of horn and ivory: dreaming true and false in Earthsea,' *Extrapolation* 29: 338–48.

Tax, M. (1990) 'Fantasy island,' *The Village Voice*, 34(44) 30 October: 75.

Tolkien, J. R. R. (1965) *Tree and Leaf*, Boston: Houghton Mifflin.

Toulson, S. (1973) 'Childhood haunts,' *New Statesman* 85(2201) 25 May: 780, 782.

Turner, V. W. (1978) *Image and Pilgrimage in Christian Culture*, New York: Columbia University Press. Lectures on the History of Religions, New Series, 11.

Welton, A. (1991) 'Earthsea revisited: *Tehanu* and feminism,' *VOYA, Voice of Youth Advocates* 14(1): 14, 16, 18.

White, D. R. (1999) *Dancing with Dragons: Ursula K. Le Guin and the Critics*, Columbia, SC: Camden House.

Wood, S. (1979) 'Discovering worlds: the fiction of Ursula K. Le Guin,' in *Voices for the Future: Essays on Major Science Fiction Writers*, Vol. 2, ed. T. D. Clareson, Bowling Green University Popular Press: 154–79.

Further reading

By Ursula K. Le Guin (a selection)

Very Far Away from Anywhere Else, New York, Atheneum, 1976, published in England as *A Very Long Way from Anywhere Else*, London, Gollancz, 1976.

Solomon Leviathan's Nine Hundred Thirty-First Trip around the World, illustrated by Alicia Austin, New Castle, VA, Puffin, 1976; Cheap Street, 1983. (Originally published in collection *Puffin's Pleasures*.)

Leese Webster, illustrated by James Brunsman, New York, Atheneum, 1979.

The Adventures of Cobbler's Rune, illustrated by Austin, Cheap Street, 1982.

Adventures in Kroy, Cheap Street, 1982.

A Visit from Dr Katz, illustrated by Ann Barrow, New York, Atheneum, 1988, published as *Dr Katz*, London, Collins, 1988.

Catwings, illustrated by S. D. Schindler, New York, Orchard Books, 1988.

Catwings Return, illustrated by S. D. Schindler, Orchard Books, 1989.

Fish Soup, illustrated by Patrick Wynne, New York, Atheneum, 1992.

A Ride on the Red Mare's Back, illustrated with paintings by Julie Downing, New York, Orchard Books, 1992.

Wonderful Alexander and the Catwings, illustrated by S. D. Schindler, New York, Orchard Books, 1994.

Jane on Her Own: A Catwings Tale, illustrated by S. D. Schindler, New York, Orchard Books, 1999.

Websites

Scholarly articles

http://scholar.lib.vt.edu/ejournals/ALAN/spring96/griffin.html by Jan M. Griffin, 'Ursula Le Guin's Magical World of Earthsea,' which appeared in *Alan Review* 23(3) (Spring 1996).

http://www.teleport.com/~aaugiee/leguin.shtml
'A Literary Analysis of Ursula K. LeGuin,' by Justin Day (Previously titled 'Ursula K. Le Guin: Symbolism, Theme, and Mythology In the Earthsea Trilogy'). Concise exposition of the symbolism, mythology, and themes in the Earthsea books (updated to include *Tehanu*).

'Fan' sites

1. *The Dragon of Solea's guide to Earthsea*
http://web.a-znet.com/ganieda/earthsea/earthsea.htm
Graphically beautiful, this will appeal to the image-oriented. A kind of concordance to Earthsea, including Names, Places, Chants, Plants, Animals, 'The Wisdom of Earthsea,' this is maintained by a fan, Shannon, of Ithaca, NY (see the site for details, click 'About the Dragon').

2. *Le Guin's World*
surf.to/le.guin
or http://hem.passagen.se/peson42/lgw/main.html
Useful links.

3. *The unofficial Ursula K. Le Guin homepage*, maintained by Laura Quilter, with an angle on Le Guin as a feminist, has links to published interviews:
http://www.wenet.net/~lquilter/femsf/authors/leguin/
and one section gives one-sentence reader's annotations of Le Guin's children's (picture) books:
http://www.wenet.net/~lquilter/femsf/authors/leguin/juvenile.htm

Miscellaneous
http://www.pacifict.com/ron/Mills.html
'A Left-Handed Commencement Address' delivered in 1983 at Mills College (inspirational, succinct, aimed at women).

'Ursula K. Le Guin, A Noted Portland Author Talks About Storytelling Aimed At Exacting Readers, The Pint-Sized Kind.' By Cheryl Bowlan
Delightful site, devoted to Le Guin's picture books, especially the *Catwings* series. Worth a visit despite the commercial headers.

Brief biography and critical overview: Ursula K. LeGuin

Ursula K. Le Guin, born in 1929 in Berkeley, California, daughter of Alfred L. Le Guin (an anthropologist) and Theodora Covel Brown (a writer; maiden name, Kracaw). Her early years were spent in the academic milieu of the University of California at Berkeley, where her imagination was fired by literature – the folklore of Celtic and Teutonic writers, the works of Hans Christian Andersen, Lord Dunsany, and J. R. R. Tolkien – and anthropological writings such as Sir James Frazer's *Golden Bough*.

She earned an undergraduate degree from Radcliffe (1951), and her master's degree from Columbia (1952) was in Romance Literatures of the Middle Ages and Renaissance, specializing in French. She has taught French at Mercer University in Georgia (1954–5) and the University of Idaho (1956) and has been a visiting lecturer and writer at Portland State University, University of California at San Diego, University of Reading in England, and many other places. A frequent guest of honour at science fiction conventions, she has also been a creative consultant for the Public Broadcasting Service, working on the television production of *The Lathe of Heaven* (1979). Her affiliations have included, among others, memberships in Writers Guild, PEN, Science Fiction Research Association, Science Fiction and Fantasy Writers of America, Amnesty International of the USA, National Abortion Rights Action League, National Organization for Women, Nature Conservancy, Planned Parenthood Federation of America, Women's International League for Peace and Freedom, and Phi Beta Kappa.

She married Charles Alfred Le Guin (a historian), 22 December 1953, and they have three children: Elisabeth, Caroline, and Theodore. Settling with her husband in Portland, Oregon, she continued to write while working and raising a family. Before turning to the novel, she wrote poetry, and her narrative style retains a remarkable clarity, evocative precision, and lyricism. Le Guin's writings in science fiction and fantasy invent new alternative worlds, representing new possibilities for self and society, often implicitly critiquing contemporary culture. Often, her tales are set in an alien world and trace the protagonist's efforts to mediate between vastly different peoples. The reconciliation of the alienated and sundered worlds typically comes by means of a conceptual breakthrough.

Her first published novel, the space opera *Rocannon's World* (1966; rev. 1977), prefigures several abiding themes that carry through to the Earthsea series: learning to 'bridge' between one's own culture and an alien one, and the power of mutual 'gifts' – which may be non-material or material in nature – to create and sustain relationships. In *Rocannon's World* an ethnographer is marooned on a primitive planet, suffers difficulty in navigating a strange culture, but finally, in return for opening himself to the new world, receives the gift of 'mindspeech' or telepathy. In *The Left Hand of Darkness* (1969), which won both Hugo and Nebula awards, Le Guin relates the story of an ethnologist who visits Gethen, a planet whose people are androgynous; neuter most of the time, they can become either male or female at intervals in their sexual cycles. Since the Gethenians appear at first to be like people in our world, and are only gradually revealed to be fundamentally different, the effect is a 'cognitive estrangement' that heightens the impact. This first novel in the Hainish series invites speculation on the nature of sex and sexism in contemporary society, as well as cultural chauvinism in a generic sense, in contrast to the Gethenian society where individual identities and social status are free from stereotypes of gender. In a departure from conventional novelistic form, the narrative is interwoven with ethnological reports, retellings of indigenous religious ceremonies, legends and myths, and diary entries. This novel is interlaced with one of Le Guin's recurring themes, namely that unity evolves from the interaction and balance between opposites: sameness and difference, male and female, the familiar and the alien.

By 1970 Le Guin had become one of the most esteemed writers of science fiction; and while her reputation transcends genre, her science fiction writings have won five Hugos and four Nebula awards and she has received more attention from the academic community than most other modern science fiction writers.

Her work incorporates an ideal of balance or 'Equilibrium': in the psyche, between the rational and the intuitive; in gender, between male and female; in the natural world, termed 'ecology'. Her Earthsea books reflect her typical strategy of shaping a story around recurrent motifs, in a pattern aptly called 'spiralling,' adding richness and density by means of new juxtapositions. Le Guin's stories have combined traditional elements of fantasy with elements of science fiction, creating alternative societies, sometimes incorporating psychic phenomena, such as telepathy ('mindspeech' in *Rocannon's World*), precognition and clairvoyance.

Her motifs are drawn from the paired archetypal symbols common to poetry, myth and romance: darkness and light, male and female, speech and silence, seen not as opposed polarities, but rather as twin parts of a balanced, meaningful whole. Her dualism is not that of Western philosophy, Hegelian or Marxist, wherein progress comes out of the dialectical opposition of forces; instead it reflects the Eastern Taoist tradition, where the emphasis is on the wholeness stemming from balance and the mutuality of *yin* and *yang*. Jungian archetypes and the tenets of Taoism illuminate her work, but it is important to refrain from applying such theories in a reductionist fashion: there are more things in her 'heavens and earths' than can be captured in the abstractions of philosophy. Rather, her narratives may fruitfully be approached in the manner of poetry, with an openness to the discovery of previously unearthed riches.

CHAPTER 3

Terry Pratchett

Peter Hunt

Of all fatiguing, futile, empty trades, the worst, I suppose, is writing about writing.
Hilaire Belloc (Winoker, 1987: 103)

Critics say good things, and sometimes dumb things, and occasionally nasty things. The books sell, so I don't mind.
Terry Pratchett (Pratchett and Briggs, 1997: 467)

'All right,' said Susan. 'I'm not stupid. You're saying humans need ... *fantasies* to make life bearable.'
REALLY? [said Death] AS IF IT WERE SOME KIND OF PINK PILL? NO. HUMANS NEED FANTASY TO BE HUMAN. TO BE THE PLACE WHERE THE FALLING ANGEL MEETS THE RISING APE.
'Tooth fairies? Hogfathers? Little-'
YES. AS PRACTICE. YOU HAVE TO START OUT LEARNING TO BELIEVE THE *LITTLE* LIES.
'So we can believe the big ones?'
YES. JUSTICE. MERCY. DUTY. THAT SORT OF THING.
Terry Pratchett (Hogfather: 422)

Approaching Terry Pratchett

There is a scholarly edition of *Gulliver's Travels* in which the editor devotes erudite footnotes to proving that the Lilliputians and Brobdignagians could not have existed – because of the number of cortical cells, bone structure, and so on (Turner, 1986: 310, 325). This has always struck me as being a rather foolhardy annexe to a book by a master satirist, which contains the rather nasty account of the Professors at the Academy at Lagado ('in my Judgement wholly out of their Senses'), and one of whose most famous *obiter dicta* was that 'satire is a sort of glass, wherein beholders do generally discover everybody's face but their own'.

And so any academic venturing to write anything about Terry Pratchett's books, might, if not actually on something not altogether legal, pause to reflect that here we have a satirist every bit as incisive and erudite and wide-ranging as Swift. If Pratchett's contemplation of human foibles is on the whole as much a matter of amusement as of anger, it nevertheless resides in a mocking intelligence and a cordial (and not always genial) contempt for useless activities. Such as literary criticism.

Academics have suffered a long-running lambasting in the Discworld novels, which feature, very frequently and uncharitably, the activities of the Wizards at Unseen University:

> Often they lived to a timescale to suit themselves. Many of the senior ones, of course, lived entirely in the past, but several were like the Professor of Anthropics, who had invented an entire temporal system based on the belief that all the other ones were a mere illusion.
>
> Many people are aware of the Weak and Strong Anthropic principles. The Weak One says, basically, that it was jolly amazing of the universe to be constructed in such a way that humans could evolve to a point where they make a living in, for example, universities, while the Strong One says that, on the contrary, the whole point of the universe was that humans should not only work in universities but also write for huge sums books with words like 'Cosmic' and 'Chaos' in the titles. (*Hogfather*: 144, n)

And just don't think you can sneak under the wire masquerading as an honest scholar:

> I save about twenty drafts ... Once [the final one] has been printed out ... there's a cry of 'Tough Shit, literary researchers of the future, try getting a proper job!' and the rest are wiped. (Pratchett Quote File v5.1 @ alt.fan.pratchett)

But having a live author to deal with is probably the least of a critic's worries, because the approach to Pratchett is stalked by legions of experts and scholars, otherwise known as devotees and fans. The friends of the Discworld seem, even on a brief acquaintance, to be every bit as erudite, expert, committed (not to say obsessive), meticulous, scholarly, defensive – and subtly disdainful of outsiders as, for example, the members of the Arthur Ransome Society, or the Beatrix Potter Society: the only difference is that there are many more of them.

My own technologically inept research on the Web produced several hundred Discworld/Pratchett-linked sites worldwide. Quite characteristic seems to be the *Discworld Monthly*, with a circulation of over 20,000, in which (Issue 39, July 2000) William Barnett sardonically reviewed the first book of criticism on Pratchett, *Terry Pratchett: Guilty of Literature* (Butler *et al.*, 2000). This book falls over itself (rather as I have done) to justify its curious activity, especially in the light of the experience of the Librarian of Unseen University, negotiating the infinite L-space:

> Creatures evolve to fill every niche in the environment ... He waited patiently as a herd of Critters crawled past, grazing on the contents of the choicer books and leaving behind them piles of small slim volumes of literary criticism ... And you had to avoid clichés at all costs. (*Guards! Guards!*: 190–1)

But for all that *Guilty of Literature* is solidly pro-Pratchett, and written by fans, it does not escape, because, as I suspect with all such followings, the Pratchett books belong directly to the fans – each and every one individually. They do not need critics and are rather affronted by them (as I was advised when walking to the podium at the first Literary Weekend of the Arthur Ransome Society: 'Tread softly for you tread on my dreams' (Hunt, 1992)). Thus Barnett is not going to let any self-appointed expert get away with anything. The 'various luminaries from the sci-fi and academic worlds' (he says wryly) who wrote this are (naturally enough) 'guilty of telling you things you already know', and, anyway 'most of them only do criticism, not actual fiction.' And, just to make sure they're nailed into their place, Barnett ends: 'Fancy that.' Of course, one riposte might be that most Pratchett fans only do reading (fancy that) – or, apparently, construct web-sites – but, in fact, they do more than that: they act exactly like the academic literary scholars who have excluded Pratchett from their reckoning.

The idea of an annotated edition of a Pratchett novel, with 25 per cent of the pages devoted to 'notes' might, as things stand in the literary world – especially given the status of comic fantasy (*Gulliver's Travels*, *Gargantua and Pantagruel*, and their ilk, aside) – seem to be a particularly improbable flight of fantasy, and almost certainly a risibly undesirable one. And yet, on the Web can be found a site that lists, at immense length (some of) Pratchett's allusions in his novels, and the intricacy of the detective work is no less impressive (or pointless) than any annotation of *Gulliver's Travels*, for all that the cross-references are to *Twin Peaks* or 'Star Trek' or 'Peanuts', or *Alien*, and that they exist as web-links rather than footnotes.

As these annotations prove, it would be idle for the intellectual snob to dismiss Pratchett as 'merely' a web-meister of popular culture. For example, in *Men at Arms*, the Patrician reflects on the stupidity of people:

> They do things like open the Three Jolly Luck Take-Away Fish Bar on the site of the old temple in Dagon Street on the night of the Winter solstice when it also happens to be a full moon. (197)

As Leo Breebart points out (www.us.lspace.dorg/books/apt/men-at-arms.html), Dagon 'is the Hebrew name for the Philistines' God Atergata, whose temple Samson destroyed (Judges 16: 23); Dagon was half woman, half fish.

Here, then, is modern fantasy at its most successful, most integrated into modern culture. Its range of reference, its allusions, its very concept of what is fantastic and what is real (most strikingly seen in *Only You Can Save Mankind* and *Johnny and the Bomb*) are all fused into the way it is received, interpreted, and talked about. The text and the single reader's imagination are no longer what the reading experience is about. Pratchett's Discworld 'exists' as much in the *Discworld Map*, the *Companion*, the *Quiz Book*, and the dialogues and discussions and speculations on the Web by thousands of reader-authors, as much as it does in what Pratchett actually wrote in the novels. Imaginations, as never before, are *combining* to form a fluid, corporate fantasy.

Pratchett caters for this, in a way, by his use of the ideas of alternative futures and alternative pasts. The history of the Discworld (like the history of the real world – although this is seldom acknowledged) is continually changing; the books continually emphasize possibilities:

> There was another of those long pauses, wherein may be seen the possibilities of several different futures. (*Men at Arms*, 1994: 370)

In *The Carpet People*, Culaina, the mystic wight, is in touch with these possibilities:

> She passed through future after future, and there they were, nearly all alike ... They streamed past her. These were all the futures that never got written down – the futures where people lost, worlds crumbled, where the last wild chances were not quite enough. All of them had to happen, somewhere.
> But not here, she said.
> And then there was one, and only one. She was amazed. Normally futures come in bundles of thousands, differing in tiny

little ways. But this one was all by itself. It barely existed. It had no right to exist. It was the million-to-one chance that the defenders would win. (181)

And the idea is developed formally into the alternative, parallel worlds of *Johnny and the Bomb*:

Everything you do changes everything. And every time you move in time you arrive in a time a little bit different to the one you left. What you do doesn't change the future, just a future.

There's millions of places when the bombs killed everyone in Paradise Street.

But it didn't happen here. (219)

If Pratchett's fantasies are not bounded by the books, are never static, what, then, does the peripatetic critic have usefully to say about them? Criticism will be (more obviously than usual) a reductive intervention. But if it was ever thus, we might fall back on the idea that to write about books at all is an act of faith: to say, in effect, that this kind of intellectual exercise is worthwhile of itself. It is part of the natural discourse that revolves around books, not an extraneous, parasitic activity; it may well become absorbed into the fantasy. Equally, for all his best-seller status, I come across more people who have not read Pratchett than who have – and, as a gesture of gratitude to a writer who has restored my waning faith in the written word, I have an evangelical urge to share the pleasure.

But that ambition has nothing to do with literature as commonly understood. *Guilty of Literature* sees itself as 'the opening salvo in the campaign to admit Pratchett to the canon of literature' (viii). This essay has no such questionable ambition; as we have seen, literature is not a useful concept in that it excludes and confuses, and this is particularly the case with children's books. Canonical literature generally excludes fantasy, marginalizes comedy, and regards children's books as beneath notice. To try to accommodate that way of thinking into the encouragement of the excitement of reading by young readers (or anybody) leads, demonstrably, to unhelpful comparisons. Fantasy, and especially children's fantasy, does not need an elitist relativism imposed upon it.

The distinction between children's books and adults' books is also important in this context, and it is not merely a piece of academic hair-splitting. What people think children's books should be is generally what they turn out to be. Not merely the content, but the attitude to the audience – the construction of the audience – the tone, and even the quality of thought, is governed and distorted by this. Pratchett's children's books, however, are *not* entirely what children's books are expected to be. To look at them critically is to see a fascinating demonstration of a writer establishing for himself just what it means to write for children: what should be done, what might be done, what can be done.

And the Discworld novels? Possibly the most intricate and imaginative alternative world ever created? In some editions the list of titles is headed, 'for adults of all ages'. As with most Pratchett jokes, that one requires a certain amount of unpacking, but while the books do not *exclude* the child reader (whatever that may be) it seems clear that children are not the primary audience. Exploring Pratchett's books means exploring questions not so much about what is for children, but more, what exactly constitutes childhood.

Introducing Terry Pratchett

Despite the fact that Pratchett's novels have sold well over 10 million copies – for some time there has been a joke that no British railway train is allowed to depart unless at least one passenger is reading a Pratchett novel – a brief introduction may still be in order.

Pratchett's first novel, *The Carpet People* (1971) was written when he was seventeen (although it was not his first published work), and, as he said, 'in the days when I thought fantasy was all about battles and kings'. It was rewritten in 1992: 'Now I'm inclined to think that the real concerns of fantasy ought to be about not having battles, and doing without kings' (*The Carpet People*: 7). Although *The Carpet People* is now marketed as a children's book, its implied audience remains ambiguous.

The Dark Side of the Sun (1976) and *Strata* (1981) established him with a promising reputation for humorous 'science fiction'. The first Discworld book, *The Colour of Magic* (1983) has been followed by more than twenty others, appearing recently at the rate of two a year (*The Truth* was published in 2000); there have been a relatively limited number of high-quality 'spin-offs', and some dramatizations and television adaptations – and despite their huge popularity, the Discworld books have managed to retain a cult status, a kind of intimate relationship between writer, readers and imagined world.

Part of this may well be to do with the richness of Pratchett's imagination. Colin Manlove said of *The Colour of Magic*,

> In a sense, the real narrative of the book is Pratchett continually outdoing himself ... Pratchett's fantasy, in this book at least, is a

magnificent entertainment, a display of inventive pyrotechnics. (1999: 136)

While Pratchett's imagination seems to be inexhaustible, it is difficult to agree with Manlove's conclusion that the book 'asks only that we enjoy, it does not seek to change us' (137). None of Pratchett's books are innocent in this way: even the extract that Manlove quotes, on the problems disposing of active spell-books ('burial in deep caves was ... ruled out after some districts complained of walking trees and five-headed cats') has obvious real-world applications. Pratchett's books are a sustained crusade for intelligent living, and models of intellectual awareness – always pursuing the complex, oblique answer. Their moral structure can be seen to rest on

> a conviction that only personal integrity is a useful foundation for free will and true choice; all else is self deception. Ideologies which deny individuality and the value of the individual life are masks for immorality ... Pratchett is *not* trying to assert that morality leads to success, nor that moral actions provide moral outcomes, rather to make it clear that it is morality which makes us who we are. (Butler *et al.*, 2000: 161)

Pratchett's basic target may be (or may have been initially – for his fantasy has taken on a life of its own) the world of fantasy fiction and science-fiction (which, for this reader at least, is hard to take seriously after reading Discworld), but any social absurdity or human folly is fair game. For example, as the Lord Vetinari observes in *Jingo* (1998):

> 'Putting up a statue to someone who tried to *stop* a war is not very, um, statuesque. Of course, if you had butchered five hundred of your own men out of arrogant carelessness, we'd be melting the bronze already.' (405)

What singles Pratchett out is that he carries this constant attitude of attack into his children's books; just as in the Discworld novels he seems always to be testing the limits of fantasy to carry polemic, so in his children's books he seems to be pushing at the limits of what limited conceptions of childhood assume that children can understand (*Johnny and the Dead* is perhaps the classic example of Pratchett's social indignation).

The complexity of these shifting borderlines can be illustrated by the example of *Tom Brown's Schooldays* (1857). In the Discworld novel *Pyramids*, Teppic is sent to the Assassins' school, (where a boy called Fliemoe is mentioned in passing (58), much as Speedicut is in Thomas

Hughes's book (1.5)). Pratchett gently parodies the older book, but who is the joke actually *for* – the reader who has read *Tom Brown* (and who has?) – and is the joke the same for a (generalized) child reader as for a (generalized) adult reader (or for someone who does not know that 'Flymo' is a brand of lawn mower).

In *Tom Brown's Schooldays* Arthur, the new boy, is a member of Tom's dormitory:

> Arthur finished his washing and undressing, and put on his night-gown. He then looked round more nervously than ever. Two or three of the little boys were already in bed ... It was a trying moment for the poor lonely little boy; however, this time he didn't ask Tom what he might or might not do, but dropped on his knees by his bedside, as he had done every day from his childhood, to open his heart to Him who heareth the cry and beareth the sorrows of the tender child, and the strong man in agony.
>
> Tom was sitting at the bottom of his bed unlacing his boots, so that his back was towards Arthur, and he didn't see what had happened, and looked up in the sudden silence. Two or three boys laughed and sneered, and a big brutal fellow, who was standing in the middle of the room, picked up a slipper and shied it at the kneeling boy, calling him a snivelling young shaver. (2.1)

In *Pyramids*, the new boy is also called Arthur, but religion is a little different on the Discworld:

> The door at the end of the room swung open slowly and Arthur entered, backwards, tugging a large and very reluctant billy-goat ... Adopting the shiny, pink-faced expression of someone who is going to do what they know to be right no matter what, Arthur drew a double circle around his bed and ... filled the space between them with as unpleasant a collection of occult symbols as Teppic had ever seen ... He drew a short, red-handled knife from the jumble on the bed and advanced towards the goat –
>
> A pillow hit him on the back of the head.
> 'Garn! Pious little bastard!' (37)

Enthusiasts for literature often make great play with resonance and intertextuality: with Pratchett, not only is such allusion self-conscious – his characters (especially in some of the children's books) are aware of the allusions too.

The 'children's' books

Apart from *The Carpet People*, Pratchett has (thus far) published six books marketed for children. *The Bromeliad*, consisting of *Truckers* (1989), *Diggers* (1990) and *Wings* (1990), and the three Johnny Maxwell books, *Only You Can Save Mankind* (1992), *Johnny and the Dead* (1993), and *Johnny and the Bomb* (1996). Enthusiastic classifiers might argue that the first three at least are essentially 'science fiction' rather than 'alternative world' fantasies. The four-inch-high Nomes may occupy an alternative space in our contemporary world, but they are still concerned with that 'real' world; they may be creatures of fantasy, but the central mechanisms for enabling the Nomes to find their way home are a computer and a spaceship, creations of speculative science. The Johnny Maxwell books, on the other hand, evade classification. They are, on one level, contemporary realism, but they all explore alternative worlds, in which science and philosophy and imaginative possibilities and impossibilities have equal weight.

Also, as we have seen, Pratchett's books explore the essential differences between children's and adults' books – and the fact that he writes fantasy complicates matters considerably.

One key point at which children's books and fantasy-adventure frequently overlap is in the use of central characters who are anti-heroes – apparently powerless, marginalized people, who nevertheless triumph. This is the fantasy of many adults – and the fantasy that many adults construct for childhood. Thus characters in Pratchett's books that are marketed as children's books, the unheroic Snibril in *The Carpet People*, the quixotic Masklin in *The Bromeliad*, and the bemused Johnny Maxwell, may seem to serve the same function as, say, the incompetent wizard Rincewind, or the innocent Mort in the Discworld novels (marketed for adults). The people with whom many of us seem to (and are presumably intended to) identify, win through, despite the inscrutable ways of (in the children's books) the adult world, or (in the adult books) the magic world. The difference between the two may well be that the children's book characters are treated with a rather less ironic sympathy (although, as we shall see, this is not always the case with Johnny).

The differences can be subtle. Take the exchange between the tribal king, Brocando, the (ex)general of the Empire, Bane, and Snibril in *The Carpet People*. Brocando says to Bane:

> 'I've brought you to the secret place ... I should have you blindfolded.'
> 'No,' said Bane. 'You want me to fight for you, then I'm

wearing no blindfold.'

'But one day you might come back with an army.'

'I'm sorry you think so,' said Bane stonily.

'As *me*, I don't, said Brocando. 'As a king, I *have* to think so.'

'Ha!'

'This is stupid,' said Snibril. 'Why bother with a blindfold?'

'It's important,' said Brocando, sulkily.

'You've got to trust one another sooner or later. Who are you going to trust instead? You're men of honour, aren't you?' said Snibril.

'It's not as simple as that,' said Brocando.

'Then make it simple!'

He realized he had shouted. (75)

Is there anything in that text that marks it out as 'for children'? The fantasy element which says that the most powerless can bang some sense into the heads of the supposedly powerful is common to books for adults and for children. Perhaps the only tell-tale element is the word 'sulkily', which seems to belong to a certain linguistic set – but, equally, it is an example of 'telling' rather than 'showing': the narrator is not letting us (as 'adults') deduce, he is thinking for us (as 'children' – or as readers who need to be, or wish to be, thought for).

As his children's books develop, Pratchett, to his eternal credit, rarely makes this kind of distinction: to say that his children's books respect their audience by dealing with complex issues is only half of their merit: the other is that he establishes an unpatronizing tone and mode.

Another area in which children's books, adults' books and fantasy overlap is the need for explanation of previously unknown things, the amount you need to explain, and the way you then explain. Pratchett's books have certain built-in advantages. It is a truism that adult writers of children's books cannot avoid educating their audience: in adults' books they can assume a peer knowledge, and can therefore entertain. In the world of fantasy, both adult and child readers are more equally inexperienced – but Pratchett levels the playing field more than many writers. The fact that he is habitually didactic, and a habitual aphorist means that he adopts much the same tone in all his books. For example, would it be possible to tell, out of context, which type of book this comes from?

'After this, no more books. No more history. No more history books.'

'Somehow, that's the worst part' . . .

> 'I'd just like to say that no more history books is not the worst part, young man. Dying's probably the worst part ... History will look after itself.' (*The Carpet People*: 182)

Similarly, as we have seen in considering fantasy in general, certain things – the absence or presence of which might indicate the kind of book being written – are cut out. Thus Pratchett does not describe violence gratuitously, and he does not describe sex, apart from in a highly ironic way. (Of course, this would be a good argument for a sceptic who might then feel that all Pratchett's books could count as children's books.)

But, most importantly, Pratchett assumes an audience whose knowledge of, say, computing, theories of time, and, especially, popular culture are as acute as his. (I'm probably not the first 'critic' to enjoy Pratchett's ingenious allusiveness (even, probably, to feel a little superior at getting the gags) only to have an uneasy feeling about the number of gags I'm missing.) This means that, not only are his books unpatronizing and wide-ranging, but the characters are very *knowing*: *Johnny and the Bomb*, especially, turns this self-awareness into, in effect, a discussion of the boundaries of books.

And so, when Pratchett writes for children, he writes with inherent respect, and the books are as full of ideas and intellectual speculation as any.

This is not to say that he does not relish the small moments of self-indulgent joy that populate almost all fantasy, from David killing Goliath to Sara Crewe demolishing Miss Minchin. There is, for example, the portrait of the consummately cool professional, the Clint Eastwood–John Wayne character of the invincible hero. In *The Carpet People*, this is Bane:

> Snibril ... crept towards the sleeper and made to raise his hat brim with the knifepoint. There was a blur of activity. It ended with Snibril flat on his back, his own knife pressed to his throat, the stranger's tanned face inches from his own.
>
> The eyes opened. *He's just waking up*, Snibril thought through his terror. *He started moving while he was still asleep!* (27)

Bane is also quick on the draw:

> Bane was drawing his sword. He dismounted quietly, and inched forward. With his free hand he motioned Pismire to go on talking ... Bane took one step forward, then whirled round and brought his sword whistling down into the shadows at his side. There was

a grunt, and a body fell silently across the path, a crude black
sword dropping from its hands. (31)

Fantasy is very often subversive because many of us take pleasure in
such incidental displays which are quite unconscionable in any other
literature.

Small concerns: *The Carpet People*

The Carpet People is presented as a children's book – it must be a
children's book, as it is about tribes of small people – actually
minuscule people – who would take an hour to walk across a match,
and live amongst the dust of the carpet. But the settings and characters
are typical of other-world fantasy, and their equivalents can be found
in Tolkien or a thousand other variants. There are dark horrors (such
as the underlay) and dazzling wonders (such as the Woodwall – or
matchstick). The villains are evil, the wise shaman of the tribe
(Pismire) is suitably pragmatic, the anti-hero (Snibril) an intelligent
adolescent, the cool warrior (Bane) almost invincible; there is the dim
but unstoppable warrior (Glurk), and a mystic female (Culaina) – and,
the society is vaguely medieval.

But there is nothing particularly *of childhood* in the book, and, in the
re-written version at least, the preoccupation is, as in the rest of
Pratchett, the defence of both the rational and the imaginative. At the
end of the book, the race that rules the empire appoints the hero Bane:
'since he was considered to be honest and brave and without any
imagination. The Dumii distrusted imagination – they said it made
people unreliable' (169). At what stage in one's acquisition of
knowledge of the world is this comment applicable to grading-
conscious education systems or repressive (or any) governments?

The fact that the characters are small and in 'this' world, rather than
being of normal size in some 'other' world (although, as one character
says, 'We ... are *correctly-built* ... it's no business of ours if everyone
else is ridiculously overgrown' (60)) aligns them with the child-world of
toys; the fact that they are (in cosmic terms) helpless, and are aware
that they do not understand the world 'out there' aligns them with
children. But beyond that, the core of the book could be for any
audience sympathetic to the conventions of fantasy, and sympathetic
to the idea of co-existence rather than confrontation – to the idea of
constructive change. When the evil (religionists) are dispatched,
Pismire reflects on the fact that the real wisdom seems to be coming
from the previously disempowered:

'Snibril's right, though ... Everyone's done things the old way.
Now we'll have to find a new way. Otherwise there won't be *any*

way. We don't want to have to go through all this just to start squabbling over something else, the Empire –'

'I'm not sure there's going to be an Empire again,' said Bane ... 'There might be something better ... I'm thinking about it. Lots of small countries and cities joined together could be better than one big Empire. I don't know.'

'And a voice for women,' said Lady Vortex's voice from somewhere in the crowd.

'Possibly even that,' he said. 'There should be something for everyone.' (186)

In a sense, that change applies to the world of fantasy as well as to the 'real' world that the fantasy reflects. One might suspect that when Pratchett says that 'It's not exactly the book I'd write now' (*The Carpet People*: 7), one aspect that he might have changed would have been the inherent sexism. *The Carpet People* is very largely a male-quest book in the tradition that Ursula K. Le Guin both celebrated and rebelled against in the 'Earthsea' quartet, and which Pullman re-wrote completely in 'His Dark Materials' trilogy. Only towards the end of the book do females begin to assert themselves, but they are either, like Culaina, mysteriously other, or they are surrogate males:

Lady Vortex picked up a sword. She was bristling with anger ... 'And when we get out of this, young man,' she snapped, 'there's going to be some serious talking. If we're going to fight, we're going to have a bit of the future too –' (182–3)

Although Pratchett's other books are male-centred, he considers seriously the idea of the female and the feminine. There are 'strong female characters', Grimma in *The Bromeliad*, and Kirsty in the Johnny Maxwell books. However, Masklin and Johnny, the ostensible heroes, have what are often regarded as feminine characteristics – a talent for sympathy, negotiation, and lateral thinking. The females, on the other hand are (generally) tough, aggressive, and highly efficient. Kirsty has 'the voice of someone who dialled wrong numbers and then complained that the phone was answered by people she didn't want to speak to' (*Johnny and the Bomb*: 37). Grimma is the power behind Masklin:

'What you'll do,' she said sharply, 'is jolly well stop moping and get up and go out there and *get things organised!* ... *Do it now!*' ...
Masklin stood up.
'You shouldn't talk to me like that,' he said plaintively. 'I'm the leader, you know.'

She stood, arms akimbo, glaring at him.

'Of course you're the leader,' she said. 'Did I say you weren't the leader? Everyone knows you're the leader! Now get out there and lead!' (*Truckers*, 155)

Ingenuity and indignation: *The Bromeliad*

The Bromeliad is, equally obviously – and equally not obviously – a children's book. The idea of four-inch high nomes who live ten times faster than humans may provide the opportunity for endless ingenuity, but it is clearly (in literary terms) trivial and unimportant. 'Once you have thought of the big people and the little people,' Dr Johnson, that spokesman for a rational world, is reputed to have said of *Gulliver's Travels*, 'the rest is easy.' These must be childish things because they are small. The underlying premise, which is that the little people live in a world governed by big people to whom they cannot relate and who they can scarcely understand – but whom they can outsmart, is clearly a metaphor for childhood, and this relegates the story to the inferior realm of children's books. But this kind of smallness can be seen in other ways. As Lois Kuznets notes in her totally unapologetic study of animated toys in fiction:

> toy characters in literature, like many other characters in fantasy, often function as subversive forces acting out crises of individual development generally repressed by modern society. This function, shared by toys in life, is familiar to child psychology as well as to psychoanalysis ... [T]oy characters both disguise and express suppressed desires, helping to evade individual and societal censors ... [P]lay and art belong to the same realm. (1994: 7)

A good many fantasies, both for adults and children, are fundamentally regressive, suppressing growth, development, and the imagination by the insistence on conformity to generic patterns and various predetermined codes of behaviour. Children's fantasies (by adults) tend to keep children in their place by imposing closure. *The Bromeliad*, in contrast, has as a basic theme the idea of widening one's conceptions of life: it is a book about growth, exploration, empowerment – the essential stuff (I would hope) of childhood and children's books – and, of course, it is a theme relevant to a good many adults. Thus the central metaphor of the book (put into the mouth of the repressed female, Grimma, as an argument against domestication and marriage) is about continually transcending boundaries that you might not even know are there:

'There's this place, you see. Called Southamerica. And there's these hills where it's hot and rains all the time, and in the rain forests there are these very tall trees and right in the top branches of the trees there are these like great big flowers called bromeliads, and water gets into the flowers and makes little pools and there's a type of frog that lays eggs in the pools and tadpoles hatch and grow into new frogs and these little frogs live their whole lives in the flowers right at the top of the trees and don't even know about the ground.' (*Truckers*: 42)

But Pratchett's intellectual tic, as it were, is always to ask the next question. When even Dorcas, the nome of science, eventually realizes the virtue of imagination, the effect is to put forward the exact opposite of, for example, the world-view of *The Wind in the Willows* or *The Lord of the Rings*:

Of course there were a lot of questions, but right now the answers didn't matter; it was enough just to enjoy the questions, and know that the world was full of astonishing things, and that he wasn't a frog.

Or at least he was the kind of frog who was interested in how flowers grew and whether you could get to other flowers if you jumped hard enough.

And, just when you'd got out of the flower, and were feeling really proud of yourself, you'd look at the new, big, wide endless world around you.

And eventually you'd notice that it had petals around the horizon. (*Truckers*: 153)

That is not to say that, for all *The Bromeliad*'s seriousness of purpose, there is not plenty of wish-fulfilment (or, as Pratchett might just observe, there might be if this didn't happen to be fiction). When Masklin and the 'outside' nomes arrive in the Department Store (already populated (under the floors) by a complicated nome society), and are held up by the Corsetri bandits, there is one of those satisfying scenes (for me, at least) out of innumerable films, from *A Fistful of Dollars* to *Crocodile Dundee*, in which the apparently innocent outsiders demolish the evil insiders. For Masklin, Grimma, and the elderly Granny Morkie and Torrit, the idea of theft is a new one.

'We've decided,' [Masklin said], 'If it's the same to you, we keep what we have. Sorry ... '

Two bandits grabbed Granny Morkie.

This turned out to be a mistake. Her bony right hand flashed out and there were two ringing slaps.

'Cheek!' she snapped, as the nomes staggered sideways, clutching their ears.

A bandit who tried to hold old Torrit got a pointed elbow in his stomach. One waved a knife at Grimma, who caught his wrist; the knife dropped from his hand and he sank to his knees, making pathetic bubbling noises.

Masklin leaned down, grabbed a handful of the chief's shirt in one hand, and lifted him up to eye-level.

'I'm not sure we fully understand this custom,' he said, 'But nomes shouldn't hurt other nomes ... So I think perhaps it would be a good idea if you go away, don't you?' (*Truckers*, 61)

In essence, exactly the same scene has been enacted in those children's books that walk along the edges of fantasy, such as *Little Lord Fauntleroy* or *Pollyanna*, although the violence there is verbal.

If, however, such scenes are taken as a gauge of the lack of seriousness or quality of the book (things are more difficult in real life, in real books) then one might consider the world that Masklin and his rural nomes enter. The nome society of Arnold Bros (est. 1905) may seem at first sight to merely be a source of fun. Not only are they (like Mary Norton's Borrowers) named after where they live – the del Icatessens, the de Haberdasheri, the Stationeri – but (also like the Borrowers) they adapt to their surroundings the Klothians, for example, are a gentle, mystic people, living on tea and biscuits and yoghurt from the Staff Rest Room. And the nomes constantly misunderstand human language around them – Prices Slashed (a monster that stalks the store), Everything Must Go ('"Arnold Bros (est. 1905)'s way of telling us that we must lead good lives because we all die eventually"' (78)), Final Reductions, and, of course, the fire bucket.

But much of this misunderstanding is incorporated into the religion the nomes live by – are controlled by – the religion of Arnold Bros (est. 1905). It is a solipsistic religion; the Stationeri hold the power: they can read. They are a male Priesthood in which the 'outside' does not – cannot – exist. When Masklin and his people arrive, the Abbot and his Monks cannot – will not – see them. The Abbot, however, is a pragmatist, and meets Masklin in private:

'I don't understand!' [Masklin] said. 'You can see me! Ten minutes ago you said I didn't even exist and now you're talking to me!'

'There is nothing strange about it,' said the Abbot. 'Ten minutes ago it was official. Goodness me, I can't go around letting people believe I've been wrong all along, can I? The Abbots have been denying there is anything Outside for generations. I can't suddenly say they were all wrong. People would think I've gone mad ... The important thing about being a leader is not being right or wrong, but being certain ... Of course, it helps to be right as well.' (*Truckers*: 71–2)

Masklin slowly comes to appreciate the practicality (if not the wisdom) of such utterances, in much the same way as many other fantasy heroes, but it is the continual stress on the fact that, as the Abbot also says, '"People are always a lot more complicated than you think ... It's very important to remember that"' (73), that sets Pratchett's books apart. This is fiction, and all fiction simplifies, but the painful progress of the new Abbot, Gurder, and his struggles with his faith are complex and serious. Religion is seen obliquely by Masklin, who had never thought of it. 'There had never been any religion or politics back home. The world was just too *big* to worry about things like that' (79).

According to Gurder, the big pink humans that stood in Fashions, and Kiddies Klothes and Young Living, and never moved at all, were those who had incurred Arnold Bros (est. 1905)'s displeasure. they had been turned into horrible pink stuff, and some said they could even be taken apart. But certain Klothian philosophers said no, they were particularly *good* humans, who had been allowed to stay in the Store for ever and not made to disappear at Closing Time. Religion was very hard to understand. (150)

But Gurder has his doubts, and begins to grasp at straws. When the nomes board a truck to escape the destruction of the store, and the truck first moves, he interprets it as part of his faith.

'We actually moved!' he was whispering. 'Arnold Bros (est. 1905) *was* right. Everything *Must* Go!' (163)

But when he realizes that there is more to the world than the store: that there is an outside:

Gurder was trembling. 'There's no roof!' he moaned. 'And it's so big!'
    Masklin patted him on the shoulder,

'Of course, all this is new to you,' he said. 'You mustn't worry if you don't understand everything.'

'You're secretly laughing at me, aren't you!' said Gurder.

'Not really. I know what it's like to feel frightened.' (171)

Masklin's modest, human and humane response seems to be Pratchett's baseline. Faith, the sub-text seems to say is real, regardless:

'I shall ask Arnold Bros (est. 1905) to guide us and lead us,' said Gurder firmly.

'Yes, good,' said Masklin. 'Good idea. And why not? But now we really must –'

'Has his Sign not said If You Do Not See What You Require Please Ask?' said Gurder.

Masklin took him firmly by the arm. Everyone needs something, he thought. And you never know. (174)

But tolerance is one thing. The next generation evangelical, Nisodemus, who even embarrasses Gurder (*Diggers*: 30), and who eventually 'wasn't able to listen to anything except for little voices deep inside his head' (93) is a chilling portrait of a fanatic, rousing the quiescent majority with his plan to return to the good old days:

It was magnificent in its way, that plan. It was like a machine where every single bit was perfectly made, but had been put together by a one-handed nome in the dark. It was crammed full of good ideas which you couldn't sensibly argue with, but they had been turned upside-down. The trouble was, they were *still* ones you couldn't sensibly argue with, because a good idea was still in there somewhere. (61)

Pratchett's conclusion is rather more gentle than in some of the other books (for example, in *Pyramids*, where Dios, the High Priest, is eternally in charge). In *Wings*, when it is revealed that the original Arnold Bros had actually seen the nomes, Masklin says to Gurder: 'You know you believed in Arnold Bros (est. 1905) . . . Well, he believed in you too' (*Wings* 134).

On the other hand, although Pratchett tends to emphasize that one must make up one's own mind about spiritual matters (as in *Johnny and the Dead*), the innocent eye of the characters is manipulated by a narrator who might not be exactly innocent:

'Do you know, humans think the world was made by a sort of big human?'

'Get away?'

'It took a week.'

'I expect it had some help, then,' said Dorcas. 'You know. With the heavy stuff ... Only humans could believe something like that. There's a good few month's work, if I'm any judge.' (59)

In terms of traditional fantasy, *The Bromeliad* has an explicitly conventional structure. The quest that Masklin has laid upon him by the dying Abbot is quite clear:

'I don't say you're blessed with brains ... In fact I reckon you're the stupid but dutiful kind who gets to be leader when there's no glory in it. You're the kind who sees things through. Take them home. Take them home.' (*Truckers*: 100)

The trilogy, then, may have the trappings of science, but it is a fantasy for humans and for nomes. Pratchett's penchant for allusion links the fantasy and the reality. As Dorcas the technician says: 'Amazing things, levers. Give me a lever long enough, and a firm place to stand, and I could move the Store' (141), and, of course, allusions turn into jokes: Grimma has been reading a lot.

'We're not going to run away again,' she said flatly. 'We shall fight them in the lane. We shall fight them at the gates. We shall fight them in the quarry. And we shall never surrender.'
'What does "surrender" mean?' asked Dorcas.
'We don't know the meaning of surrender', said Grimma.
'Well, *I* don't,' said Dorcas. (73)

Changing ways of thinking: the alternative worlds of Johnny Maxwell

In the Johnny Maxwell books, because they are focalized through children, the distinction between children's and adults' books is much more obvious. This is the world seen through the eyes of street-wise (and street-bewildered) teenagers, Pratchett's indignation at what humans have done to the world is translated into indignation at what adults have done to the world. The nomes may not be able to understand the stupidity of humans, but it is not really any of their business; Johnny and his friends have to come to terms with reality, but at the same time realize the potentialities of a world only half-seen by 'normal people'. Johnny provides the innocent eye:

Normal people just ignored almost everything that was going on around them, so that they could concentrate on important things like, well, getting up, going to the lavatory and getting on with their lives. Whereas Johnny just opened his eyes in the morning and the whole universe hit him in the face. (*Johnny and the Dead*: 7)

It is just such innocence that blurs the distinction between fantasy and reality and between this world and alternative worlds – but in this case it is an innocence mixed with knowingness. Johnny may be a kind of shaman, but there is nothing mystic about him, at least to his friends:

'Huh, you'd have to be mad even to understand time travel,' said Wobbler eventually.

'Job opportunity for you there, Johnny,' said Bigmac.

'*Bigmac*,' said Yo-less, in a warning voice.

'It's all right,' said Johnny. 'the doctor said I just worry about things too much.' (*Johnny and the Bomb*: 21)

These books, then, are addressed to self-aware readers: the teenagers know about psychology and marriage break-ups, and urban living and racism: none of it is a surprise, none of it is for the reader to deduce as a sub-text. The characters are all immersed in the popular culture of science-fiction films, and fantasy computer games, and children's fiction. As Wobbler says, towards the end of *Johnny and the Dead*:

'Well, that's it, then ... Game over. Let's go home. Nasty men foiled. Kids save the day. Everyone gets a bun' (172–3)

But it is exactly this self-awareness that makes the fantasy worlds that the characters enter so striking: these worlds are genuine extensions of a world gone stale, circumscribed by incompetent town-planners and over-competent games-designers.

Absorbing new forms: *Only You Can Save Mankind*

There is a sense, then, in which the Johnny Maxwell books are actually *about* fantasy: the matter is continually discussed – fantasy is not a realm where you find out and follow other people's arcane rules, it is a place where you make your own moral decisions and invent ways of implementing them. In both *Only You Can Save Mankind*, and *Johnny and the Bomb*, the children come to realize that they are in control. When Kirsty and Johnny find familiar controls in their spaceship, Johnny points out that of course they are familiar: '"This is in our *heads*, remember. It has to be things we *know*"' (*Mankind*: 153).

The conventional devices of fantasy writing are kept firmly in place by the fact that the characters know what the generic rules are. *Only You Can Save Mankind* is particularly rich in this, combining as it does personal fantasies set within other people's fantasies – the computer games – and a sardonic realism.

The premise of the book, that the invaders from space in the eponymous game are tired of being shot at and destroyed, and actually surrender, throws up a complex series of moral dilemmas – although reviewers have found the parallels with the Gulf War a little heavy-handed: 'There was a film on the News showing some missiles streaking over some city. It was quite good' (22). Johnny is also going through what he calls Trying Times, and Pratchett, very much in the way that he demolishes whole genres of 'high' fantasy in the Discworld books, takes on the huge and solemn genre of the teenage problem novel. There are toe-curlingly embarrassing talks with his father:

> On top of it all, his father came upstairs to be fatherly. This happened about once a fortnight. There didn't seem to be any way of stopping it. (29)

But the insouciant Johnny develops a stolid cynicism about the whole business, feeding himself, and exploiting the situation with his teachers, apparently without any of the rage or blaming or overt desperation of many of his fictional counterparts.

> Anyway, there had to be a good side to the Trying Times everyone was going through in this house. If you hung around in your room and generally kept your head down, stuff like computers sort of happened. It made everyone feel better. (19)

His friends agree:

> 'You still having trouble at home?' said Yo-less.
> 'It's all gone quiet,' said Johnny.
> 'That can be worse than shouting'
> 'Yes.'
> 'It's not that bad when your mum and dad split up,' said Wobbler, 'although you get to see more museums than is good for you.' (43)

This is the angst of the knowledgeable, postmodernist 1990s: disintegration is the normal state of things. As a result, the device of fantasy being a sublimation of psychological problems is, as it were, exploded. (The most classic British examples of this sub-genre are probably Penelope Farmer's *A Castle of Bone* (1973), Catherine Storr's *Marianne Dreams* (1958: USA – *The Magic Drawing Pencil*), and William Mayne's *A Game of Dark* (1971) – although there are innumerable others. For a discussion of these kinds of texts, see Rustin and Rustin, 1987.) Yo-less, Johnny's friend who is aiming, seriously, to be a doctor, has worked it out.

> 'Well ... your mum and dad are splitting up, right? ... So you project your ... um ... suppressed emotions onto a computer game. Happens all the time ... You can't solve *real* problems, so you turn them into problems you *can* solve. Like ... if this was thirty years ago, you'd probably dream about fighting dragons or something. It's projected fantasy.' (28)

The thematic similarities between A *Game of Dark*, described by Alison Lurie as 'a tale in the tradition of Jorge Luis Borges or Gabriel García Márquez' (184) and usually accepted as a major and serious work of a major and serious children's writer, and *Only You Can Save Mankind* are striking. In both, the protagonists find themselves in moral dilemmas, and in both, in contrast to many other fantasies of this type, there is only a partial resolution. Donald, in A *Game of Dark*, having killed the loathely worm in his fantasy by radical (and thus traditionally dishonourable) means, and having listened to his father die in the real world, 'went to sleep, consolate' (126). Johnny, having freed the ScreeWee fleet, and having killed the gunnery officer, lies in bed:

> He snuggled down, treasuring this time between dreaming and waking ...
> These were still Trying Times. There was still school. Nothing actually was better, probably. No-one was doing anything with a magic wand.
> But the fleet had got away. Compared to that, everything else was ... well, not easy. But less like a wall and more like steps. (172)

Only You Can Save Mankind is, then, a new approach to modern fantasy. It has the same motivations, the same psychology – but these are now mixed with the stuff of the shopping mall, rather than the medieval world, and the rules of computer games rather than the rules of some wizardly culture. The fundamental problems that theorists (at least) have about dreams, are confronted head-on. As Johnny ponders, 'You get so much better graphics in your dreams' (22). And we do, after all know what's really going on in dreams:

> He wondered why people made such a fuss about dreams ... when you got down to it dreams were often horrible, and they felt *real*. Dreams always started out well and then they went wrong, no matter what you did. You couldn't trust dreams. (58)

The philosophical problem that Carroll touches on in *Through the Looking Glass*, of who is actually doing the dreaming, is mirrored – and taken one step further, when Johnny dreams himself into the spacecraft.

> Right. So he was back in real life again. When he got back to ... when he got back to ... He'd have to have a word with the medics about this odd recurring dream that he was a boy in –
>
> No! he thought. I'm me! Not a pilot in a computer game! If I start thinking like that then I'll *really* die! (74)

But, unlike most of its predecessors, *Only You Can Save Mankind* has characters who are fairly down to earth:

> 'Look, have you ever wondered what's real and what isn't?'
> 'Bloody stupid thing to wonder,' said Bigmac. (96)

It takes a very confident writer to, as it were, expose the nuts and bolts of his craft – to mock the very conventions that he's using. But to do anything less, Pratchett seems to imply, would be to underestimate the readers – and to do less than the other media do.

> The trouble with all the aliens he'd seen was that they either wanted to eat you or play music at you until you became better people. You never got the sort who wanted to do something ordinary like borrow the lawn mower. (41)

And, besides these complex areas, Pratchett's satirical finger is always itching on the 'fire' button of the literary joystick: Australian Soap Operas (*Cobbers*), plastic models in cereal packets, the Neil Armstrong Shopping Mall, education, mindless language (' "Way to go, eh?". "Way to go where?" ... "We're really kicking some butt!" "Some but what?" ' (43)) – and TV journalists who trivialize death. And often several targets get hit at once.

> There was an extended News, which meant that *Cobbers* was postponed. There were the same pictures of missiles streaking across a city that he'd seen the night before, except that now there were more journalists in sand-coloured shirts with lots of pockets talking excitedly about them.
>
> He heard his mother downstairs complain about *Cobbers*, and by the sound of the raised voices that started Trying Times again.
>
> There was some History homework about Christopher Columbus. He looked him up in the encyclopaedia and copied out four hundred words, which usually worked. He drew a picture

of Columbus as well, and coloured it in. (29)

All of this keeps readers on their toes, but it should not be overlooked that Pratchett's characters are (and increasingly are) three-dimensional. From Bigmac the aspiring skinhead, whose mates are killed (we assume) in a stolen car, to Kirsty the superconfident, highly intelligent girl with a shelf of awards and no friends, his characters challenge clichés – and are all, by implication, vulnerable. His technique even allows – or requires – his readers occasionally to judge even the most sympathetic of them. When the (female) commander of the invading fleet asks Johnny what the word sexist means, Johnny does his best:

> 'Oh, *that*. It just means you should treat people as people and, you know ... not just assume girls can't do stuff. We got a talk about it at school. There's lots of stuff most girls can't do, but you've got to pretend they can, so that more of them will. That's all of it, really.'
> '*Presumably there's, uh, stuff boys can't do?*'
> 'Oh, *yeah*. But that's just girls' stuff,' said Johnny. 'Anyway, some girls go and become engineers and things, so they can do proper stuff if they want.' (83)

It is possible to argue that *Only You Can Save Mankind* is a children's book because its morals are too obviously stated for 'adult' taste: 'I'm not even sure there *are* aliens. Only different kinds of us' (171). But, as ever, Pratchett stays awake:

> Kirsty looked thoughtful.
> 'Do you know,' she said, 'there was an African tribe once whose nearest word for "enemy" was "a friend we haven't met yet"?'
> Johnny smiled. 'Right,' he said. 'That's how –'
> 'But they were all killed and eaten in eighteen hundred and two,' said Kirsty. 'Except for those who were sold as slaves. The last one died in Mississippi in eighteen sixty-four, and he was *very* upset.'
> 'You just made that up,' said Johnny. (124)

Intermission: *Johnny and the Dead*

Johnny and the Dead is perhaps the least fantastic of all Pratchett's novels, but as before, the fantasy (of the cheerful dead protesting about the sale of their graveyard) works because of the realism that it overlays. Perhaps most importantly, the characters of Wobbler, Bigmac, Yo-less and Johnny have been deepened and detailed; their endless, oblique conversations – similar to those in Jan Mark's *Enough is Too Much Already* (1988) – both add subtlety to their portraits and allow Pratchett to pepper his usual targets for derision.

The book's fantasy actually operates most forcefully on quite another plane – that of the small forces of good overcoming the impersonal multinational company. In the set-piece public inquiry scene, the platform party is routed by Johnny and old Mr Atterbury:

'The boy is right. Too much has been taken away, I do know that. You dug up the High Street. It had a lot of small shops. People lived there. Now it's all walkways and plastic signs and people are afraid of it at night. Afraid of the town where they live! I'd be ashamed of that, if I was you. (125)

But, characteristically, in the end, the victory is only symbolic: the dead, liberated, no longer need the graveyard.

Pratchett's guns are trained on the past horrors of the Pals' Regiments, but he also spares some shot for other targets. There is the 'traditional English pub, with a "Nuke the Gook" video machine that Shakespeare himself might have played' (117), the Joshua N'Clement Block (' "People have got to live somewhere," said Yo-less. "Reckon the man who designed it lives here?" ' (31)), television (Grandad watches *Video Whoopsy* incessantly), and, of course *Cobbers* ('tonight Janine is going to tell Mick that Doraleen took Ron's surfboard –' (29)). And racism:

'I've got a question, too,' said Yo-less, standing up.

The chairman, who had her mouth open, hesitated. Yo-less was beaming at her, defying her to tell *him* to sit down.

'We'll take the question from the other young man, the one in the shirt – not, not you, the –' she began.

'The black one,' said Yo-less helpfully. (120)

As before, Johnny is passing through Trying Times ('There was a vague feeling that it might all work out, now that people had stopped trying to be sensible. On the whole he tried not to think about it' (8)) and his ability to see the dead produces a rational explanation from his friends: Yo-less says,

'Now, *personally*, I think you're very nearly totally disturbed and suffering from psychosomatic a and hearing voices and seeing delusions . . . and probably ought to be locked up in one of those white jackets with the stylish long sleeves. But that doesn't matter, 'cos we're friends.'

'I'm touched,' said Johnny.

'Probably,' said Wobbler, 'but we don't care, do we guys?' (49)

The fantasy, the social concern, and the satire all converge and overlap. When Johnny is thinking of telling Mr Attebury that he has seen the ghostly Pals' Regiment march by, Mr Vicenti, one of the dead, stops him:

'If you did something like that a few hundred years ago you'd probably be hung for witchcraft. Last century they'd lock you up. I don't know what they'd do now.'

Johnny relaxed a little ...

'Put me on television, I expect,' he said, walking along the road.

'Well, we don't want that,' said Mr Vicenti. (103)

Johnny and the Dead is, as ever, multi-referential (even one of the Discworld characters, Death, makes a guest appearance), and by the end of the book, Pratchett has laid the foundations for another remarkable, intellectual, multilayered, and multi-accessible book, *Johnny and the Bomb*.

The trouser legs: *Johnny and the Bomb*

In the *Discworld Companion*, Pratchett and Briggs observe that

There is probably a law, or at least a pretty strict guideline, that says that every book with the word 'Chaos', 'Time' or 'Fractal' in the title must, on some page, include an illustration of the Trousers of Time ... The trousers are used to demonstrate for very slow people the bifurcating nature of Time – how, for example, one simple choice can cause the universe to branch off into two separate realities. (1997: 393–4)

Or, an infinite number of parallel universes: 'Everything that happens ... stays happened. Somewhere. There's lots of times side by side' (*Johnny and the Bomb*: 156). The conventional wisdom of time travel, that you cannot change anything, is replaced by the idea that you must inevitably change things, and when you do, you produce different, parallel worlds. Although, naturally enough in a book that proceeds largely by discussion, not everyone agrees:

'Let's face it,' said Yo-less, '*anything* we do changes the future ... Any little thing changes the whole of history.'

'That's daft,' said Bigmac. 'I mean, rivers still flow the same way no matter how the little fish swim.' (166)

The next question then, is how you travel between these parallel times, and the mode of travel is provided by the old bag-lady who pushes the supermarket trolley loaded with black plastic sacks, Mrs Tachyon, whom we have already briefly encountered in *Johnny and the Bomb*. (Also naturally enough, Johnny, who has read the books and seen the films, has trouble with a time machine that doesn't have flashing lights (65).) At this point, in Pratchett-land we might well expect to encounter a footnote on the lines of:

The *Oxford Concise Colour Science Dictionary* (Oxford University Press, 1997, 713) defines (in part), Tachyon as 'a hypothetical particle that has a speed in excess of the speed of light ... No such particle has yet been detected'.

This isn't as Johnny says, magic, '"It's probably just very, very very strange science"' (161) although, as the others observe, what is the difference? Mrs Tachyon, who speaks a continual flow of catchphrases from random years of the twentieth century, is thought to be mad – but in her 'lucid' moments (and everything is relative), she gives Johnny the key idea. Whereas Kirsty assumes that it is Mrs Tachyon's fault that there is no communication, Johnny is totally open-minded, in his innocently shaman-like way:

She nodded at Johnny.
  'What's the word on the street, mister man?'
  Johnny tried to think like Mrs Tachyon.
  'Er ... "No Parking?"' he suggested.
  'That's what *you* think. Them's bags of time, mister man. Mind my bike! Where your mind goes, the rest of you's bound to follow. Here today and gone yesterday. Doing it's the trick! Eh?' (49)

And so Johnny is liberated into sampling the various versions of time by opening his mind. When we get a glimpse into Mrs Tachyon's mind we find, as it were, the ultimate advanced Zen: 'Mrs Tachyon remembered everything, and had long ago given up wondering whether the things she remembered had already happened or not' (237). Johnny can tap into this world because his imagination 'is so big that it's outside his head' (156), and all of this contrasts strongly with the real, 'rational' world of Trying Times and adult behaviour:

She probably is mad, he thought. Or eccentric, anyway ... Yes. Eccentric. But she wouldn't do things like dropping bombs on

Paradise Street. You have to be *sane* to think of things like that. She's totally round the bend. But perhaps she gets a better view from there. (227–8)

The implication of the theory, that whatever changes the characters make to events are only changes to one version, and do not stop anything unpleasant happening in another version, is left hanging. Which is perhaps just as well, as we are close to the determinism which so undercuts the drama of C. S. Lewis's books – and much other high fantasy.

But, needless to say, there is so much else going on in *Johnny and the Bomb* that it is easy to overlook this (or at least to store it away for later consideration) and one of the things that is going on is the thorough demolition of the clichés of children's fantasy. One of these is that children are not believed by adults, or by other children. This doesn't happen with the redoubtable Kirsty – although she does believe for the wrong, media-induced, reasons:

'I've read books and books about that sort of thing, and they're full of unintelligent children who go around saying "gosh". They just drift along having an *adventure*, for goodness' sake. They never seem to think of it as any kind of opportunity.' (64)

As we have seen, this leads us to the knowingness of the characters. When the group first travels (in time, or into a different version of time) there is a virtuoso display of self-referentiality:

Johnny opened his eyes. the ground sloped up all around him. There were low bushes at the top.
'If I asked what happened,' said Yo-less, from somewhere under Bigmac, 'what'd you say?'
'I think we may have travelled in time,' said Johnny ...
'Which way did we go?' said Yo-less, still talking in his deliberate voice. 'Are we talking dinosaurs, or mutant robots? I want to know this before I open my eyes.'
Kirsty groaned.
'Oh dear, it's going to be that kind of adventure after all,' she hissed, sitting up. 'It's just the sort of thing I didn't want to happen. Me, and four token boys. Oh, dear. Oh, dear. It's only a mercy we haven't got a dog.' She sat up and brushed some grass off her coat. 'Anyone got the least idea where we are?' (86)

The Johnny Maxwell books are remarkably economical, in that even the smallest detail helps to round out the characters: Pratchett disproves the theory that the novel of character and the story of fantasy cannot coexist. The characters may exist primarily for the service of the story or the ideas, but that does not make Yo-less's negotiation of the swamps of racism any less affecting, or Kirsty's gradual humanization any less subtle. Nor is there ever any intellectual compromise, as when it is revealed that Kirsty has a collection of 'Star Trek' videos:

> 'Just shut up! Just because the programme happens to be an accurate reflection of late 20th century social concerns, *actually*, it doesn't mean you can go around winding people up just because they've been taking an academic interest! ... So I watch some science fiction films ... At least I do it in a spirit of intelligent deconstruction. I don't just sit there saying "Cor, lasers, brill!"'
>
> 'No-one said you did,' said Yo-less, managing to sound infuriatingly reasonable.
>
> 'You're not going to let me forget this, are you?' said Kirsty. (165)

The alternative worlds of Terry Pratchett's books may be as much in his characters' heads, and as much in the overlap between other writers' and readers' imaginations as 'elsewhere'. But he epitomizes the way in which fantasy is deeply and inevitably embedded in some kind of 'realism' – bearing in mind that what exactly constitutes realism is infinitely difficult. When this is wedded to a combination of innocent character and sardonic narrator, the complexity is considerable.

> [Johnny] hadn't expected time travel to be this hard. He thought of all those wasted lessons when they could have been telling him what to do if some mad woman left him a trolley full of time. School never taught you anything that was useful in real life. There probably wasn't a single text book that told you what to do if it turned out you were living next door to Elvis Presley. (125)

Or, as Sergeant Comely reflects in *Johnny and the Bomb*, 'Just because they made silly films about aliens and things didn't actually mean, did it, that it couldn't ever happen' (134).

For anyone who can understand/for adults of all ages. A note on the Discworld

The two somewhat gnomic pronouncements that appear in some editions of Pratchett's books might best be seen as inclusive invitations to readers, or an attempt to pick a fight with those who equate fantasy with childishness and children's literature with an even more intense form of childishness.

As we have seen, children's books and adults' books, if they can be separated at all, can be separated by point of view, and the point of view taken in the Discworld novels generally assumes an adult audience. For example, take Pratchett's ideas about stories and childhood. In *Hogfather*, one of his ironically competent female heroes, Susan Sto Helit (Death's grand-daughter) has become a governess, somewhat in the ruthless mode of Mary Poppins:

> It was a quiet day for Susan, although on the way to the park Gawain trod on a crack in the pavement. On purpose.
>
> One of the many terrors conjured up by the previous governess's happy way with children had been the bears that waited around in the street to eat you if you stood on the cracks.
>
> Susan had taken to carrying the poker under her respectable coat. One wallop generally did the trick. They were amazed that anyone else saw them.
>
> 'Gawain?' she said, eyeing a nervous bear who had suddenly spotted her and was now trying to edge away nonchalantly.
>
> 'Yes?'
>
> 'You meant to tread on that crack so I'd have to thump some poor creature whose only fault is wanting to tear you limb from limb.'
>
> 'I was just skipping –'
>
> 'Quite. Real children don't go hoppity-skip unless they are on drugs.'
>
> He grinned at her.
>
> 'If I catch you being twee again I will knot your arms behind your head,' said Susan levelly ...
>
> The previous governess had used various monsters and bogeymen as a form of discipline. There was always something waiting to eat or carry off bad boys and girls for crimes like stuttering or defiantly and aggravatingly persisting in writing with their left hand. There was always a Scissor Man waiting for a little girl who sucked her thumb, always a bogeyman in the cellar. Of such bricks is the innocence of childhood constructed. (*Hogfather*: 36–7)

The whole attitude here is of adult addressing adult – and constructing a certain kind of adult, sympathetic to the ideas. It does not exclude children (only, perhaps those who do not know about *When We Were Very Young* and *Struwwelpeter* – or whose oral cultures interweave with those books), but it invites readers to regard children from an adult point of view.

It is, after all, not whether one recognizes the denotations that makes one a mature (or adult) reader, but the recognition of connotations, and the sharing of an attitude of mind – or the acceptance of the attitude of mind implied by the narrator. When, therefore, the narrator describes the intelligence of the troll Detritus in *Jingo* as 'falling somewhere between a cuttlefish and a line dancer' (21) readers have to be quite quick on their mental feet.

Consequently, without implying a single actual boundary, we will visit the Discworld only briefly, and only to point out some of its more obvious delights. Here is a complete (or at least potentially complete) other world, carried (famously) through space on the shoulders of four giant elephants who are standing on the back of the Great A'Tuin, a ten-thousand-mile-long star turtle. It has a strong magic field which slows down light, and distorts virtually everything: it has villages and cities, countries and continents, with their own climates and laws and legends and science; it is populated by a vast array of characters and species borrowed from a vast range of mythologies and legends and imaginations ...

Or, to put it another way, here is a setting where literary genres and social movements can be satirized, gently or savagely, according to need, and where Pratchett's constant linguistic and philosophical awareness, not to say cynicism, can be matched against the 'real' world.

For newcomers, the city of Ankh-Morpork would be a good place to start. As Pratchett describes it, it is a great deal more subtle and intricate than many places of fantasy, just as his characters are more subtle and intricate than the genre seems to require.

> I needed a working background. I wanted to get the feel of a real society operating ... of a city actually *working*. Ankh-Morpork is almost, now, what a city like London would be if no one had built anything new since about 1600, no one had discovered steam or electricity, and all the classic fantasy creatures had turned out to be real and wanted a job. The dwarfs have an Equal Heights pressure group and trolls have started the Silicon Anti-Defamation League to beat up people who suggest that, well, trolls beat up people.
>
> [In creating a fantasy city] you had to start out by wondering how the fresh water got in and the sewage got out ... World building from the bottom up, to use a happy phrase, is more fruitful than doing it from the top down. (Pratchett and Briggs,

1997: 474–5)

If we feel that certain things are *more likely to be the concern of* adults than of children, such as the principles of civil government, the behaviour of academics, or the ethics of the movie business, then the Discworld is more likely to be seen as adult reading matter. But it is difficult to tell: there may well be children fascinated by the habits of pieces of luggage – like the homicidal magical Luggage which attaches itself to the wizard Rincewind:

> The Luggage might be magical. It might be terrible. But in its enigmatic soul it was kin to every other piece of luggage throughout the multiverse, and preferred to spend its winters hibernating on top of a wardrobe. (*Sorcery*: 22)

Equally, the battle between witches' and wizards' magic in *Equal Rites*, which echoes, anarchically, but no less seriously, the theme of Le Guin's *Tehanu*:

> 'I don't think there's ever been a lady wizard before,' said Cutangle. 'I rather think it might be against the lore. Wouldn't you rather be a witch? I understand it's a fine career for girls.'
> (181)

And at what point does an ironic aside on titillating graphics become funny to an adolescent? The second of the Discworld novels, *The Light Fantastic* (which introduces, for example, Cohen the Barbarian) features the freelance woman with a sword, the red-headed Herrena the Harridan:

> Now, there is a tendency at a point like this to look over one's shoulder at the cover artist and start going on at length about leather, thighboots and naked blades.
> Words like 'full', 'round' and even 'pert' creep into the narrative, until the writer has to go and have a cold shower and lie down.
> Which is all rather silly, because any woman setting out to make a living by the sword isn't about to go around looking like something off the cover of the more advanced kind of lingerie catalogue for the specialized buyer.
> ... She was currently quite sensibly dressed in light chain mail, soft boots, and a short sword.
> All right, maybe the boots were leather. But not black.
> Riding with her were a number of swarthy men that will certainly be killed before too long anyway, so a description is

probably not essential. There was absolutely nothing pert about any of them.

Look, they can wear leather if you like. (117)

The narrative stance, which implies a complicity between narrator and readers, allows an allusive playfulness: in *Guards! Guards!* for example, chunks of dialogue are lifted (with slight modifications) from *Dirty Harry* and *Casablanca* – as well as the conversation between various heroes, assembled to fight the dragon, and lamenting the state of the modern world:

> 'Monsters are getting more uppity, too,' said another. 'I heard where this guy, he killed this monster in this lake, no problem, stuck its arm up over the door –'
>
> 'Pour encourjay lays ortras,' said one of the listeners.
>
> 'Right, and you know what? Its mum come and complained. Its actual mum come right down to the hall next day and complained. Actually complained. That's the respect you get.' (114)

Of such trivial tales, of course, are winners of the British Whitbread Award made. Nothing is, as they say, sacred, perhaps especially the ancestors of Pratchett's own genre. Here is a cheerful aside on ancient poetry:

> Five generations ago one of her ancestors had halted his band of nomadic cutthroats a few miles from the mound of Sto Lat and had regarded the sleeping city with a peculiarly determined expression that said: this'll do. Just because you're born in the saddle doesn't mean you have to die in the bloody thing.

A footnote adds:

> The speech [that he made] has been passed on to later generations in an epic poem commissioned by his son, who wasn't born in the saddle and could eat with a knife and fork. It began:
>
> > 'See yonder the stolid foemen slumber
> > Fat with stolen gold, corrupt of mind.
> > Let the spears of your wrath be as the steppe fire on a windy day in the dry season ... '

And went on for three hours. Reality, which can't usually afford to pay poets, records that in fact the entire speech ran:

'Lads, most of them are still in bed, we should go through them like kzak fruit through a short grandmother, and I for one have had it right up to here with yurts, okay?' (*Mort*: 114–15)

But if academia and high culture have not really come to grips with the playful, for all its theoretical validity, they might appreciate Pratchett for the complete course in narratology that the Discworld novels provide. Academics who have laboriously catalogued and pondered on narrative devices, ways of telling, and authorial stance, along with its encyclopaedia-load of terminology, might reflect on what is going on in a passage such as this from *Mort* (the first of a sequence featuring Death (who always speaks in CAPITALS) as a central character). At one point, the Princess Keli is talking to Cutwell the wizard in the city of Sto Lat; elsewhere, Death is about to talk to his apprentice, Mort.

'You're a wizard. I think there's something you ought to know,' said the princess.
THERE IS? said Death.
(That was a cinematic trick adapted for print. Death wasn't talking to the princess. He was actually in his study, talking to Mort. But it was quite effective, wasn't it? It's probably called a fast dissolve, or a crosscut/zoom. Or something. An industry where a senior technician is called a Best Boy might call it anything.) (116)

Reading Terry Pratchett, then can be an unnerving as well as an invigorating experience, as if he is cheerfully cutting off the literary branch on which he is sitting, but managing to efficiently levitate at the same time. He can be read for his ingenuity or his insights (The Geneva Convention is 'like finding a tiny bit of the Middle Ages in the middle of all the missiles and things' (*Only You can Save Mankind*: 60)); for his satire or his philosophy ('All the witches who'd lived in her cottage were bookish types. They thought you could see life through books but you couldn't, the reason being that the words got in the way' (*Carpe Jugulum*: 31–2)); or even his bad jokes: 'It would seem that you have no useful skill or talent whatsoever ... Have you thought of going into teaching?' (*Mort*: 185)).

But, whatever the reason, we are reading a writer committed to expanding the mind:

So let's not be frightened when children read fantasy. It is compost for a healthy mind. It stimulates the inquisitive nodes ...

[T]here is some evidence that a rich internal fantasy life is as good and necessary for a child as healthy soil is for a plant, and for much the same reasons ... Like the fairy tales that were its forebears, fantasy needs no excuses. ('Let there Be Dragons': 7)

References

Butler, A. M., James, E. and Mendleson, F. (nd [2000]) *Terry Pratchett: Guilty of Literature*, Reading: The Science Fiction Foundation.

Hunt, P. (1992) '"Tread softly for you tread on my dreams": Academicising Arthur Ransome', *International Review of Children's Literature and Librarianship* 7(1): 1–10.

Kuznets, L. R. (1994) *When Toys Come Alive. Narratives of Animation, Metamorphosis and Development*, New Haven: Yale University Press.

Lurie, A. (1990) *Don't Tell the Grown-Ups*, London: Bloomsbury.

Mayne, W. (1974) *A Game of Dark*, (Hamish Hamilton, 1971), Harmondsworth: Penguin.

Manlove, C. (1999) *The Fantasy Literature of England*, London: Macmillan.

Pratchett, T. (1987) *Equal Rites*, London: (Gollancz, 1987), Corgi.

Pratchett, T. (1988) *Mort*, London: (Gollancz, 1987), Corgi.

Pratchett, T. (1989) *Sorcery*, London: (Gollancz, 1988), Corgi.

Pratchett, T. (1990) *Guards! Guards!*, London: (Gollancz, 1989), Corgi.

Pratchett, T. (1993) *The Carpet People*, (Colin Smythe, 1971), London: (Doubleday, 1992), Corgi.

Pratchett, T. (1993) *Only You Can Save Mankind*, London: (Doubleday, 1992), Corgi.

Pratchett, T. (1994) *Johnny and the Dead*, London: (Doubleday, 1993), Corgi.

Pratchett, T. (1994) *Men at Arms*, London: (Gollancz, 1993), Corgi.

Pratchett, T. (1994) *The Light Fantastic*, (Colin Smythe, 1986), London: Corgi.

Pratchett, T. (1995) 'Let there be dragons', *Books for Keeps*, 83, 6–7.

Pratchett, T. (1997) *Hogfather*, London: (Gollancz, 1996), Corgi.

Pratchett, T. (1997) *Johnny and the Bomb*, London: (Doubleday, 1996), Corgi.

Pratchett, T. (1998) *Jingo*, London: (Gollancz, 1997), Corgi.

Pratchett, T. (1998) *The Bromeliad*, London: Doubleday [*Truckers*, London: Doubleday, 1989; *Diggers*, London: Doubleday, 1990; *Wings*, London: Doubleday, 1990].

Pratchett, T. (1999) *Carpe Jugulum*, London: (Doubleday, 1998), Corgi.

Pratchett, T. and Briggs, S. (1997) *The Discworld Companion*, London: Vista.

Rustin, M. and Rustin, M. (1987) *Narratives of Love and Loss*, London: Verso.

Turner, P. (ed.) (1986) *Gulliver's Travels*, Oxford: Oxford University Press.

Winoker, J. (1987) *Writers on Writing*, London: Headline.

CHAPTER 4

Philip Pullman

Millicent Lenz

I'm trying to write a book about what it means to be human, to grow up, to suffer and learn.
(Philip Pullman, 'Achuka Interview')

His Dark Materials: alternative worlds for the twenty-first century

Pullman's *His Dark Materials* trilogy consists of *Northern Lights* (NL) (1995), *The Subtle Knife* (SK) (1997), and *The Amber Spyglass* (AS) (2000). *Northern Lights* was published in the USA as *The Golden Compass* (1996). Page references to all books in the trilogy cite the US editions.

The 'Big' Questions In *His Dark Materials*

'Where is God ... If he's alive? And why doesn't he speak any more?' (Mrs Coulter in *The Amber Spyglass*: 328)

In the contemporary world, stories on themes 'too large for adult fiction [can] only be dealt with adequately in a children's book'. So said Philip Pullman in his Carnegie Medal acceptance speech. Authors of books for children do not disdain to satisfy the universal human hunger for 'story, plot, and character', and their works provide a spin-off benefit, a social one, for stories are much more potent than moral precepts in teaching 'the world we create ... the morality we live by ... We don't need lists of rights and wrongs, tables of do's and don'ts: we need books, time, and silence. Thou shalt not is soon forgotten, but once upon a time lasts forever'.

His Dark Materials interweaves an engrossing, breath-taking adventure story with a deeply felt examination of existential questions, such as Mrs Coulter's anguished plea to know whether God is, as Nietzsche asserted, 'dead', or why, if he still lives, he has grown mute. In his bold willingness to take on this and other 'big' questions (such as the nature of sin, the fall, the war between the Kingdom of Heaven and the rebel angels), Pullman differs from more timid contemporary writers. His intellectual audacity has been praised by Nick Gevers, who remarks that his occasional didacticism (inevitable in children's books and never in Pullman's case patronizing) is offset by the deep metaphysical implications of his 'playing with John Milton's dark materials, with all their grounding in Biblical and Calvinist ontology and moral philosophy ... so dogmatic conceptions of God are interrogated, as is the magnetism of Satanic evil' (Gevers, *Northern Lights*). The subject of *His Dark Materials* is nothing less than the story of how human beings, at this critical time in history, might evolve towards a higher level of consciousness.

The trilogy speaks to the existential state of humanity at the beginning of the new millennium, a condition where 'the maps no longer fit the territories' (Houston, 2000: 1). Pullman's many-layered story works on one level as a suspenseful fantasy adventure for children, yet read reflectively, it also yields for an older audience a new map to define our place in the universe. It is a wake-up call to respond to the threat of disasters on the individual and collective levels: widespread despair and soul-loss, social chaos, political upheaval, ecological ruin, massive wars, a catastrophe of apocalyptic dimensions. All this is expressed in the overarching metaphor – the toppling of the 'Kingdom' of Heaven – so the 'Republic' of Heaven may be built in its stead.

His Dark Materials: Intertextuality, Influences

Pullman at the close of *The Amber Spyglass* describes his process as 'Read like a butterfly, write like a bee.' Three nectar-rich sources have fed his imagination: *On the Marionette* [Puppet] *Theatre* by Heinrich von Kleist; John Milton's *Paradise Lost*, and the works of William Blake. All of these are (to shift the metaphor) woven into the tissue of the three novels and give depth to his treatment of 'big' metaphysical questions. *His Dark Materials*, a phrase drawn from Milton's *Paradise Lost* (II, 910–20) describes the chaotic mix of the four elements – water, earth, air and fire – left over from the creation of Earth, now swirling around in the 'wild abyss'. This massive chaos is the cauldron of unbridled Energy, where the forces of life struggle against the forces of death, seen through the eyes of the watchful, 'wary fiend', who thinks that the 'almighty maker' may use this cosmic junk 'to create more worlds'. By this rich borrowing from *Paradise Lost*, Pullman sets the scene for a drama of cosmic scope: the destinies of entire worlds hang in the balance.

Pullman realigns the 'hero' and 'villain' roles: his 'Satan' (Lord Asriel) and the 'fallen' angels are engaged in a morally justified battle to unseat a corrupt 'Authority'. In aligning the rebellious angels with good and freedom, 'rather than authority, repression, and cruelty', Pullman says, 'I'm in a long tradition. William Blake consciously and Milton unconsciously wrote about this, so I'm in a line with the English dissenters' (Cooper, 2000: 355). He also draws upon Kleist's essay 'On the Marionette Theater', deriving metaphors for the Fall – 'the business of losing innocence and finding experience' (quoted in Parsons and Nicholson, 1999: 117–18). He recalls with pleasure the moment when his writerly imagination connected the paradox 'that the loss of innocence is the beginning of wisdom' (Pullman, 1999: 31) to distinguishing between the daemons of children (making them 'shape-shifting'), and those of adults (who settle into one fixed form (Parsons and Nicholson, 1999: 128)).

Kleist uses three *exempla* to explain the Fall from natural grace: a story of a puppet; a parable of a boy's 'fall' into self-consciousness on discovering his resemblance to a certain Roman statue; and a story about a man who fenced, unsuccessfully, with a chained bear. Kleist's narrator meets a Mr C., a dancer, who elaborates upon his theory that a dancer should learn from a puppet, for in its lack of self-consciousness, the puppet is wholly attuned to 'its centre of gravity' – the line that traces '*the path of the dancer's soul*'. Therefore the puppet is 'incapable of affectation': affectation occurs only 'when the soul (*vis matrix* – '*moving force*') is located at any other point than the center of gravity of a movement'. Unhappily, humans lose their graceful balance when they eat from the tree of knowledge and become self-conscious and 'affected'. Henceforth, as for Adam and Eve, 'Paradise is locked and bolted and the cherub is behind us. We must make a journey around the world, to see if a back door has perhaps been left open.' Only through an unguarded back door might a human have another chance at regaining paradise and a new innocence (Kleist, 1982: 211–13). Puppets have a second advantage over humans: *countergravity*, or 'the force that lifts them into the air [which is] greater than that which pulls them to the ground'. Thus they can achieve an inhuman lightness, only *touching* the solid platform below them and thereby 'reanimating the spring of their limbs'. No mere human being can do this (214).

The second tale is from the narrator's own experience: he once saw a youth lose his innocence of movement when by a glance in a mirror he happened to perceive his resemblance to a Roman statue, 'Spinario', depicting a youth removing a thorn from his foot. From that time forward, his self-consciousness put him out of line with his centre of gravity, resulting in gracelessness.

The third story of a fencing match between Mr C. and a bear is the source of the fencing scene between Lyra and the armoured bear Iorek Byrnison, in *Northern Lights* (225 ff.). Mr C. is easily outdone by the animal, who seems able to read his soul and can not be fooled (Kleist, 1982: 216). This anecdote also supplies the germ of the idea that bears in their natural state are immune to trickery: as Iorek says, ' "We see tricks and deceit as plain as arms and legs. We can see in a way humans have forgotten" ' (*NL*: 226). (The pretentious Iofur Raknison, who tries to become 'human', thus sacrificing his integrity, can however be deceived, and Lyra tricks him by pretending to be a daemon and falsely offering to serve him (334 ff.).)

From Kleist, Pullman derives his 'theory of grace': Grace 'appears most strongly in those parts of nature that are inanimate (the puppets), or animal (like the bear), or innocent and unformed (like the child)'. Humans lose this grace as they mature, but it can be regained through 'discipline, pain, suffering', and the regained grace is more valuable, for it is accompanied by *wisdom*. In contrast to C. S. Lewis, whose view of the Fall is 'pessimistic and defeatist', Pullman much prefers Kleist's optimistic view – sometimes called 'the fortunate fall' by theologians. This perspective underlies his portrayal of Lyra as an Eve figure. The narrator of von Kleist's story expresses the paradox: 'That means ... that we would have to eat of the tree of knowledge a second time to fall back into the state of innocence' (Kleist, 1982: 216). The idea that regained grace is more valuable than the grace lost in the Fall is reflected in Lyra's loss of the ability to read the alethiometer and the angel Xaphania's comforting words: ' "You read it by grace ... and you can regain it by work ... Grace attained like that is deeper and fuller than grace that comes freely" ' (*AS*: 491).

Pullman also draws heavily upon William Blake's dialectic of contraries: innocence/experience, heaven/hell, as well as what this dialectic implies – that the soul must pass through the fallen world to achieve its salvation in a new, higher innocence, thereby fitting it to enter the New Jerusalem of the redeemed imagination (see Blake's *The Marriage of Heaven and Hell*).

There are other, less lofty influences on Pullman's writing: his boyhood love for the comics – 'Superman' and 'Batman', for example, gangster and cowboy serials, movies and stories of adventurers. He took Lee Scoresby's first name from Lee Van Cleef, the actor who appears with Clint Eastwood in the 'spaghetti' westerns, and his last from 'an Arctic explorer called William Scoresby' ('Darkness Visible,' part 1). From his earliest days he has been fond of 'a good yarn,' and he speaks affectionately of the power of his grandfather's eclectic mix of everything from Bible stories to tales told by the murderers to whom, as chaplain to the inmates of Norwich Jail, his grandfather had ministered. Remembering how he was 'gripped' as an eight-year-old by a teacher's reading of Coleridge's 'The Ancient Mariner', he honed his skills of storytelling by retelling such classics as the *Iliad* and the *Odyssey* to his own middle-grade students. Thus he developed his bardic technique (interview with Fox, 1997: 12).

This accumulated wealth of story gives *His Dark Materials* an astonishing degree of intertextuality, which reaches its zenith in *The Amber Spyglass*. Lyra and Will are co-protagonists in a quest that takes them through several alternative worlds, including the barren landscape of the world of the dead. Throughout, Pullman weaves in allusions to various masterpieces, notably Dante's *Inferno* and the story of the 'Harrowing of Hell' (popular in Old English poetry and Middle English drama, wherein Christ descends into Hell and frees the souls held captive since the beginning of the world). The stark personification of Death is reminiscent of the medieval mystery play, *Everyman* ('Lyra and Her Death'); the children's quest then connects with the Miltonic struggle between the forces of oppression (the cohorts of the 'Authority') and those of liberation (led by Lord Asriel and Xaphania – a Sophia or 'Wisdom' figure). In the book's closing chapters, the myth of the Garden of Eden is re-interpreted through the dawning sexuality of Lyra and Will, posing the Energy of Eternal Delight against its contrary, the Endless Night that will ensue if Dust (consciousness) seeps out of the world.

His Dark Materials thus portrays what is means 'to be human, to grow up, to suffer, and to learn', in the face of daunting odds: two near-adolescents face world-shattering adversaries, narrowly escape falling into the abyss of despair, and return to their respective worlds transformed by their experiences. The kiss that marks their 'fall' into sexual awareness is more properly an *ascent* into a revelation, as the author says, 'of the myriad possibilities of life' (Cooper, 2000: 355).

Settings in *His Dark Materials*: parallel worlds in an indeterminate time

His Dark Materials inhabits a number of alternative worlds, settings that mix the familiar and the startling, blending features from the historical late nineteenth and twentieth centuries with others from an imagined 'elsewhere' or a hypothetical near future. Opposite the 'Contents' page of *Northern Lights* a note places the action in 'a universe like ours, but different in many ways'; the setting of *The Subtle Knife* is projected to be in 'the universe we know'; and that of the third novel – *The Amber Spyglass* – will move 'between the universes'. Pullman modified this plan when he realized the need to go 'back and forth' between worlds in Book Two (<http://www.achuka.co.uk/ppint.htm> – question five).

The most crucial difference between Lyra's world and our own is a 'doubling' of the human form and psyche through the visible 'souls' – daemons. Bolvanger, site of the cruel scientific experiments in severing the daemons of prepubescent children (shades of the Mengelian horrors of the Nazi era) is situated in the Far North, which the lascivious and misogynist priest, Father Semyon Borisovitch, calls a habitat of 'devilish' things – accursed bears and seductive witches (AS: 100), of which more will be said later.

The Subtle Knife, opening in Will Parry's world (recognizably 'ours,' where humans have no external daemons) moves quickly into an otherworld setting – a strange, deserted tropical city, 'Cittagazze' (Italian *citta* = city, gazza = magpies, 'the city of magpies'), where again humans lack visible daemons, but are haunted by 'Spectres', who feed upon the internal souls of adults. *The Amber Spyglass* follows Dr Mary Malone on her quest to fulfil her 'Serpent' role into the alternative world of the marvellous creatures called the *mulefa*, wheeled creatures with the power to see Dust: with their help and their shared creation of the amber spyglass, she discovers the true nature of Dust. Its most searing dramatic action takes place in the world of the dead, to which Will and Lyra gain entrance at a terrible cost.

The events of these alternative worlds 'sideshadow' actual happenings in our own time: 'intercision', for instance, mirrors the actual abuse of children, including genital mutilation (SK: 49–50) in some contemporary cultures, bearing out Peter Hunt's point that 'the one thing that can rarely be said of fantasy is that it has nothing to do with reality' (Introduction).

The historical 'time' of the narratives is indeterminate; as Jane Langton remarks in a review of *Northern Lights/The Golden Compass*, 'Time here is edgy' (1996: 34). Thus certain details – 'naphtha lights', zeppelins, and the powerful centralization of authority in the Calvinistic 'Consistorial Court of Discipline' are indicative of earlier technologies and eras, whereas some aspects of scientific knowledge (the Barnard–Stokes hypothesis, for instance) are recognizably derived from today's quantum physics.

'The Idea of the North'

'The Idea of the North' has special significance in the trilogy. The Northern Lights, with all their associations of danger, mystery, and otherworldliness, contribute much to the power of place. It is also the place where the 'veil' between the worlds is 'thin', and in *The Amber Spyglass* it is revealed to be where Lyra and Will unwittingly experience a rite of transformation, gaining the power to separate from their daemons without soul-death (AS: 472–3). Early in the first book, the North radiates magnetic power: Lord Asriel's photograms, which Lyra hears about as she hides in the cupboard in Jordan College, include

> a magnificent one of the Aurora Borealis, and even of a glowing city visible beyond the Aurora. By means of a special emulsion, he also has captured the all-important Dust streaming from an adult and absent from an adjacent child. (NL: 2)

From this point onward, Lyra's internal compass points North: she *will* go there, and it is her ability to read the alethiometer that convinces the 'Gyptian' John Faa to take her along on the perilous arctic expedition. Frieda Bostian notes how 'Geographically, the region has few recognizable boundaries' (ice sheets complicate making distinctions, and moreover, the magnetic North Pole actually moves, and watersheds – another usual means of geographical demarcation – are absent): 'the usual boundaries and rules simply don't apply' (4).

The intensely luminous language in which Pullman portrays the heavenly city illustrates his word-painting technique at its finest. Seen through Lyra's eyes,

> The sight filled the northern sky; the immensity of it was scarcely conceivable. As from Heaven itself, great curtains of delicate light hung and trembled. Pale green and rose-pink, and as transparent as the most fragile fabric, and at the bottom edge a profound and fiery crimson like the fires of Hell, they swung and shimmered loosely with more grace than the most skilled dancer. (NL: 184)

The beauty is almost 'holy,' and Lyra's response to the sublime sight is to enter 'the same kind of trance as when she consulted the alethiometer' (NL: 184).

The power and glory of the Aurora have so bewitched Lord Asriel that he is willing to sacrifice Roger to his bridge-building (an instance of the horror that results when the cerebrum is severed from the heart). In a stunningly Mephistophelean scene, replete with musical and poetic allusions, he proclaims that his piercing of the vault of heaven means '"The end of all those centuries of darkness! Look at that light up there: that's the sun of another world! Feel the warmth of it on your skin, now!"' (394). The poetic apogee comes a moment later, when he sees the palm trees waving on a shore in the new world and asks, '"Can you feel that wind? A wind from another world! Feel it on your hair, your face"' (394). As Pullman wrote in a posting to <child_lit listserv> (27 July 2000), this passage echoes the German poet Stefan George, in his poem 'Entrueckung' [Transcendence]: 'Ich fühle luft von anderem planeten' [I feel an air from other planets blowing]. Pullman gives a musical analogy: 'Schoenberg's String Quartet No. 2 in F Sharp Minor ... incorporates a setting of the poem for soprano. It's the point at which the composer finally leaves tonality altogether and launches into the new world of no fixed keys: a profoundly dramatic moment.' The literary parallel is equally dramatic, as Asriel has opened new worlds of unimaginable wonders and – though yet undefined – equally unimaginable terrors.

Alternative worlds in *His Dark Materials*: conceptual bases

The Barnard–Stokes 'business' and the Church

Paul Witcover notes Pullman's use of the 'many worlds' theory from today's quantum physics, which holds that 'every possible outcome of an action or event – no matter how large or small – spawns a universe of its own' (para. 2). The eavesdropping Lyra, hiding in the wardrobe of the Retiring Room in the opening scene (the image that Pullman has called the germ of *Northern Lights* (Nilsen: 217)) overhears an allusion to the 'heretical' 'Barnard–Stokes' business, in response to Lord Asriel's slide showing a city in the sky (contemptuously dismissed by the Dean as '"A city in another world, no doubt?"'). The 'other-world theory' comes up again in 'The Idea of the North' when the Master of Jordan College explains the 'Barnard–Stokes business' to the Librarian, telling how the two renegade theologians after whom the theory is named postulated '"the existence of numerous other worlds like this one, neither heaven nor hell, but material and sinful. They are there, close by, but invisible and unreachable"' – heresy in the eyes of the Church, which holds instead that '"there are two worlds: the world of everything we can see and hear and touch, and another world, the spiritual world of heaven and hell."' Thus, Barnard and Stokes were 'silenced' (*NL*: 34) for daring to venture a scientific hypothesis inconsistent with Church doctrine.

Lord Asriel's discourse on science and theology in *Northern Lights*
Prior to the climax of *Northern Lights* (Chapter 26, 'Lord Asriel's Welcome'), Pullman offers, through Asriel, the most complete and coherent explanation of the key scientific and theological notions woven into the fabric of *His Dark Materials*. Asriel, in exile and under house arrest in rather lavish accommodations in Svalbard, has been shocked by the appearance of Lyra, who has dared many dangers to deliver the alethiometer, mistakenly supposing this to be her 'mission'. Asriel's reception of her and Roger is exceedingly strange – first eager and 'triumphant', then, as he realizes who she is, displays the utmost horror. Too late Lyra realizes the truth: he requires a child to sacrifice for the sake of his bizarre scientific experiment, and he momentarily believed an accursed fate had sent him his own daughter to be the victim. Roger becomes the surrogate (366). Asriel coldly dismisses Lyra's 'sentimentality' (369) but listens to her story and finally allows her to question him. His answers provide a scientific and theological framework for alternative worlds, Dust, and 'sin'.

First, Rusakov particles, or Dust, the Dust that makes the alethiometer work. A Russian researcher, Rusakov by name, discovered a new kind of elementary particle – peculiar for its propensity to cling to adolescents and adults, though it ignored children. Distressed by Rusakov's strange discovery, the Consistorial Court of Discipline first persecuted him, but faced with the irrefutable scientific evidence, had to admit Dust existed. They then turned it to their own purposes, declaring it evidence of original sin (371).

Not surprisingly, the bible of Lyra's world has its own slant on Original Sin based on a Genesis 3 consistent with her universe. The familiar plot of the Adam and Eve story remains, but details differ: the humans are promised by the Serpent that their daemons *'shall assume their true forms, and ye shall be as gods, knowing good and evil'* (372). Predictably, when the couple eats the forbidden fruit, all transpires as the Serpent had promised, and as Lord Asriel says, '"Sin and shame and death [came into the world]"'. The connection to Dust comes from the Biblical admonition, *'Dust thou art, and to dust shalt thou return'* (373). Thus, the loss of innocence and its consequence, death, became inseparably linked with Rusakov's 'Dust', and the Particles became known by the metaphorical name.

Lyra has heard of Dust before, in Mrs Coulter's declaration that it is '"an emanation from the dark principle itself"' (96). With the medieval precedent of 'oblates' (offerings), children given to the church to be monks or nuns, Mrs Coulter formed the 'Gobblers' (the hideous General Oblation Board) to kidnap pre-pubescent children and subject them to 'intercision' in the obscurity of the Far North. Citing precedent, the Church did not object, for in earlier times, it was common practice to mutilate boys for the purpose of providing *castrati*, '"great singers, wonderful artists"' (374). (Compare the making of eunuchs in Le Guin's *The Tombs of Atuan*, where sexual mutilation is similarly a sign of the evil and sterility of the culture.) The brutality of intercision is not limited to children in Mrs Coulter's alternative world: the making of *zombies* is practised in Africa; there are intercised staff workers at 'The Station' (euphemism for Bolvangar), adults who make perfect cogs in a war machine. The verbal associations with 'The Killing Fields' and the surgical operation known as 'lobotomy' in our own world underscore Pullman's social/political criticism of 'real' world atrocities.

The 'other universe' behind the Northern Lights is, as Asriel tells Lyra,

> 'One of uncountable billions of parallel worlds. The witches have known about them for centuries, but the first theologians to prove their existence mathematically were excommunicated fifty or more years ago.' (*NL*: 376)

Using the mundane example of tossing a coin, he illustrates how when one possibility collapses in this world, another world splits off from this one, where the other 'possibility' – the one that did not happen here – springs into being (*NL*: 377).

There is an analogy here with a writer's creation of alternative fantasy worlds: by posing 'what if?' questions, the writer brings these 'possible' other worlds into being imaginatively, through the astonishing 'energy' of words, happily an enterprise requiring no blood sacrifice.

Alternative worlds in *The Subtle Knife*
In *The Subtle Knife* the speculation on alternative worlds continues when Will and Lyra think about

> how many tiny chances had conspired to bring them to this place. Each of those chances might have gone a different way. Perhaps in another world another Will had not seen the window in Sunderland Avenue, and had wandered on tired and lost toward the Midlands until he was caught. And in another world another Pantalaimon had persuaded another Lyra not to stay in the retiring room, and another Lord Asriel had been poisoned, and another Roger had survived to play with that Lyra forever on the roofs and in the alleys of another unchanging Oxford. (*SK*: 265)

Thus Pullman engages with the 'what if?' questions over the Roads Not Taken. His thoughts on this concept, termed the 'phase space' in dynamics, and how it applies to his choices as a writer, are further elaborated in his Patrick Hardy Lecture, 'Let's write it in red' (1998: 47 ff.).

In the close of *Northern Lights*, Asriel makes a Promethean pledge to destroy ' "all the Dust, all the death, the sin, the misery, the destructiveness in the world ... Death is going to die" ' (377) – a statement he disavows in *The Amber Spyglass*, telling Marisa Coulter that he knew she would prefer a lie to hearing his true intention (AS: 381). (His stated intention to destroy death compares with Cob's attempt to escape mortality in Le Guin's *The Farthest Shore*, where similarly the hubristic denial of natural processes bodes colossal disaster, including irreversible damage to the world's ecology.)

Alternative worlds in *The Amber Spyglass*

Besides expanding on the alternative worlds of the preceding two books, *The Amber Spyglass* reveals the existence of a time limit on the individual's survival in an alien world. Will's father's ghost warns in their parting scene:

> 'Your daemon can only live its full life in the world it was born in. Elsewhere it will eventually sicken and die. We can travel, if there are openings into other worlds, but we can only live in our own.' (AS: 363)

Lord Asriel's 'great enterprise' will fail, for this reason: ' "We have to build the Republic of Heaven where we are, because for us there is no elsewhere" ' (AS: 363). Thus he states a key theme of *His Dark Materials*: there are limits, and the survival of human beings and their daemons is linked to a 'local' universe. The speech foreshadows the destinies of Lyra and Will as star-crossed lovers, whose separation is sealed by their births into different worlds.

Dr Mary Malone's adventures continue in a new universe of the Mulefa, the lovable deer-sized, wheeled mammals with horned heads and short trunks like elephants (AS: 90). Pullman remarks that the Mulefa 'embody harmony with the environment' and laughingly likens their approach to life to that of Californians – 'a state of happy fulfillment in the physical processes of life' ('Darkness Visible', Pt. 2). In their respect for the integrity of nature, their sustainable energy source (the 'renewable' seed pod 'oil'), and their creatively synergistic relationship with other sentient beings, they are living exemplars of ideal ecologists. In their world, Malone becomes a cultural anthropologist (*à la* Margaret Mead), learning their language, compiling a dictionary, and through their mutual 'invention' of the amber spyglass, finally coming to an understanding of how 'sraf' (their equivalent of 'Dust' or shadow particles) connects with her own research into the nature of consciousness (AS: 131, 235–6).

Yet another alternative world enters the narrative at the close of the first chapter, through the italicized passage narrating Lyra's dream. She lies, Sleeping-Beauty-like, in the cave where she is protected – and drugged and imprisoned – by Mrs Coulter (one of a number of fairy-tale elements that add texture to the story). The ghost of Roger cries to her out of a company of shadowy, voiceless figures, situated on '*a great plain where no light shone from the iron-dark sky*', a place out of time where millions of feet had flattened the ground, 'the end of all places and the last of all the worlds' (AS: 8). A dismal place, evocative of the classical limbo, complete with a Charon-like boatman, 'crippled and bent ... aged beyond age' (AS: 280). The hapless inhabitants are tormented by harpies, as Lyra discovers later. The cinematic technique of 'cutting' from Lyra's world to Roger's continues, effectively creating the dramatic expectation that the worlds will converge. The 'ghosts' dramatically contrast with the live, warm presences of Will, Lyra, the Gallivespians, and their dragonfly steeds (supposed to be daemons by the bereft ghost-children); the living feel the 'light and lifeless' shades pass through their bodies, 'to warm themselves at the flowing blood and the strong-beating hearts' and hear their whispers 'no louder than dry leaves falling' (AS: 296–7). (Compare the poignancy of the scene from Homer's *Odyssey* wherein Odysseus tries to embrace the shade of his dead mother in Hades (II, 204 ff.).)

V.S.

Human nature in *His Dark Materials*

> Human is that moment when the universe becomes aware of itself. (Teilhard de Chardin)

Pullman's depiction of human nature contradicts the view of mainstream Christian theology, which views the child as intrinsically 'sinful' by nature. Rather, if Lyra may serve as a guide, the child is 'mischievous', rebellious against adult authority, but in a state of unconscious 'grace'. There is no sentimentality in Pullman's view, however, as may be seen in the abandoned children of Cittàgazze, who behave in a lawless, bloodthirsty manner towards Will and Lyra (compare William Golding's teacher-less children in *Lord of the Flies*). These abandoned urchins are a special case, but the children of Will's world also exhibit cruelty in their treatment of his emotionally disturbed mother: as he tells Lyra, 'She was just different and they hated her' (*SK*: 262). On the other hand, Will and Lyra, though still children themselves, show compassion; Lyra, for example, overcomes her instinctive revulsion and holds the 'hideously mutilated creature' safe as she clings to Iorek Byrnison on their return to the campsite of Farder Coram (*NL*: 216). Will similarly shows compassion for his mother. The simplistic categories of 'good' and 'evil' do not fit. Rather, the children display the *capacity* for both good and evil acts. Dr Malone's observation applies: 'good' and 'evil' are ' "names for what people do, not what they are ... People are too complicated to have simple labels" ' (*AS*: 447).

From Pullman's perspective, 'Sin, or what churches have called sin, is in fact a very important stage in human development' (Parsons and Nicholson, 1999: 124). He says in his interview with Julia Eccleshare:

> What I really wanted to do was *Paradise Lost* in 1200 pages. From the beginning I knew the shape of the story. It's the story of the Fall, which is the story of how what some would call sin, but I would call consciousness, comes to us. (1996: 15)

The 'fall' into consciousness is 'good,' and thus it follows that Eve *must* be tempted. Satan in this scenario 'is understood to be good rather than evil'. In the Biblical story (Genesis 3), Satan was instrumental in bringing about what Pullman calls 'the best thing, the most important thing that ever happened to us, and if we had our heads on straight on this issue, we would have churches dedicated to Eve instead of the Virgin Mary' (Parsons and Nicholson, 1999: 119).

Much has been written about John Milton's and others' treatments of this idea of 'the fortunate fall' ('*felix culpa*'), but it can be summed up in the words of the medieval hymn, 'O *Felix Culpa*,' paraphrased by Salandra: 'O happy Sin|O blessed crime|O precious theft|Dear disobedience! Adam, blest thief not of the Apple|But of Mercy, Clemency, and Glory' (quoted in Milton: 465 as note to Adam's cry in *Paradise Lost*, XII, 469–78). Pullman's view does not posit the necessity of a divine redemption, nor of the 'Mercy' and 'Clemency' of medieval theology; rather, a young girl – Lyra – unwittingly plays the role of 'saviour' of humanity (with Will's participation), in ignorance of her importance in the grand scheme of things, and with the blessing of Dr Malone, the rebel angels, the witches, Lee Scoresby, and indeed all those who love her.

The Amber Spyglass elaborates on human nature as tripartite. After the alethiometer tells Lyra the knife will enable her and Will to visit the Land of the Dead, Will declares there has to be 'a third part': a part different from the body and its daemon (*AS*: 166). Later, in another context, Dr Malone draws a parallel with Catholic teaching: St Paul said the human is composed of ' "spirit ['ghost'] *and* soul ['daemon'] *and* body" ' (AS: 439).

Mary Malone as 'Serpent' and visionary

Mary plays the Serpent by telling Lyra and Will the story of her own awakening to sexual awareness, in which a taste of marzipan plays a pivotal part (AS: 441 ff.). The marzipan calls for comparison with Marcel Proust's taste of *madeleine* in Marcel Proust's *A la recherche du temps perdu* – where it functions to represent the simultaneity of past and present in memory. Here, Mary's story of its role in stirring her sexual desires serves as a catalyst for the arousal of sensual awareness in Lyra and Will. This is rendered in a striking metaphor in Lyra's case:

> [She] felt as if she had been handed the key to a great house she hadn't known was there, a house that was somehow inside her, and as she turned the key, deep in the darkness of the building she felt other doors opening too, and lights coming on ... [It] stood waiting, quiet, expectant. (AS: 444)

Mary Malone's spiritual autobiography prepares the groundwork for the resolution of *The Amber Spyglass*. From the time she is first introduced in *The Subtle Knife*, it is evident that she seeks answers to questions of what Paul Tillich calls 'ultimate concern'. Finding institutional religion empty, she has left the Roman Catholic Church, sought enlightenment in Eastern spiritual practice, experienced mystical communication with 'Angels' through her computer (with Lyra's help), and had an out-of-body experience among the *mulefa*. During the latter, she gains insight into the nature of Dust, realizing the shadow particles *are* conscious, and moreover, every conscious creature is composed partly of 'shadow-matter' or Dust (AS: 367–8). If consciousness continues to seep from the world, all will dissolve into oblivion.

With these insights, Mary is 'ripe' for a mystical vision. In a unitary moment under a night sky blazing with stars, she sees the entire world as 'alive and conscious,' a sight that restores her lost conviction that 'the whole universe was alive, and that everything was connected to everything else by threads of meaning' (AS: 449). Yet she wonders what her own purpose in relationship to the universe may be. Her experience with the *mulefa* and observation of their 'feedback system' – their means for keeping 'thought, imagination, feeling' from withering away – yields an answer. Suddenly she intuits her life's purpose: to help nature itself, 'wind, moon, clouds, leaves, grass, all those lovely things', in their struggle to keep the Shadow-particles in this universe' and maintain the loving bond between Matter and Dust. In exultation, she shouts, 'There is [a purpose] now!' (AS: 452): she vows to become the 'Catcher' of Consciousness. Her soul-growth is joyfully fulfilled when Serafina Pekkala helps her to see her daemon through a kind of 'double-seeing' (AS: 505 ff.).

Pullman's view of human nature compared with 'creation theology'

Taken in its entirety, *His Dark Materials* validates a view of human nature congruent with what theologian Matthew Fox calls 'creation theology,' in contrast to fall/redemption theology. Creation theology draws upon a mystical tradition that emphasizes 'original blessing' over 'original sin', 'biophilia' (love of life) over 'necrophilia' (love of death). Fox speaks in favour of 'the ongoing power of the flowing energy of the Creator', rejecting the 'redemption theology' emphasis on sin, and observes:

> Let there be no question about it: what has been most lacking in society and religion in the West for the past six centuries has been a Via Positiva, a way or path of affirmation, thanksgiving, ecstasy. (1983: 33)

Alhough Pullman leaves the 'creator' mysterious, he nonetheless aligns with the path of 'affirmation, thanksgiving, ecstasy'. In a pastoral 'Garden of Eden' scene, Will and Lyra share a picnic – first bread and cheese, then some little red fruits – evoking the apple of the Tree of the Knowledge of Good and Evil. The description is laden with blissful sensuality: their lips touch, they kiss, and they passionately declare their love (AS: 465–6). Their small act of loving awareness attracts Dust and – like a 'single pebble' placed in exactly the right spot to start diverting 'a mighty river' into a different course (AS: 478), they cause the Dust to reverse its direction and flow back into the world of conscious beings. Dust begins to fall 'like snowflakes', a 'golden rain', and Mary Malone, in a moment of Blakean vision helped by her amber spyglass, sees their true natures:

> They would seem to be made of living gold. They would seem the true image of what human beings always could be, once they had come into their inheritance.
> The Dust pouring down from the stars had found a living home again, and these children-no-longer children, saturated with love, were the cause of it all. (AS: 470)

Unwittingly, Lyra and Will are fulfilling their heroic missions, not through conscious striving, but through being the microcosmic means of saturating the macrocosm with loving awareness. Later in the book, Pullman portrays their mutual attraction more fully through a scene in which their daemons 'settle': Will, fully aware of the meaning of what he is doing, strokes the 'fur of [Lyra's] red-gold daemon' (Pantalaimon, now a lithe, sinuous, graceful ferret), causing her to gasp with pleasure, and she reciprocates by caressing Will's now visible silky, warm, cat daemon, and the two daemons settle into their 'shapes for life':

> So, wondering whether any lovers before them had made this blissful discovery, they lay together as the earth turned slowly and the moon and stars blazed above them. (AS: 498–9)

With a delicacy and subtlety rare in contemporary literature, Pullman preserves an aesthetic distance and ambiguity in his treatment of the rapture of first love.

Returning to *Original Blessing*: Fox notes how the medieval mystic Julian of Norwich (credited with inventing the world *enjoy* in English) 'calls those who dwell on sinfulness 'foolish', and he adds:

> Joy beyond measure is part of everyone's potential experience. It is part of recovering an erotic God who plays, takes pleasure, births, celebrates, and feels passion. Eros and hope are part of the blessings of existence. (Fox, 1983: 19)

The 'Authority' in Pullman's cosmology

King Ogunwe shocks Marisa Coulter when he says the 'Authority' came into being by usurping power over the angels (AS: 209–10), thus establishing the Kingdom of Heaven. This revelation begins Mrs Coulter's movement towards allying with Lord Asriel and the rebels against the Authority. When questioned in an interview about his depiction of 'YHWH' (one of many names for the Authority – see AS: 31 ff.) as 'an ancient, useless, befuddled god' Pullman made several points. The Bible portrays God as ageing (companionable to Adam and Eve in Genesis, but becoming the 'Ancient of Days' by the book of Daniel); also, 'befuddlement' is an inaccurate characterization of the 'final glimpse', which shows the Authority departing in his chariot 'with profound and exhausted relief'. Lyra expresses compassion for him (AS: 410–11). Pullman observes: 'The depiction doesn't end on a note of antipathy, but sympathy' (Cooper, 2000: 355). The Authority won his place by deceit (AS: 32) and is thus hardly worthy of honour. Will and Lyra, avenging the cliff-ghast's attack on the valiant Chevalier Tialys, witness the Authority's end: 'demented and powerless', he dissolves in the wind after blinking his eyes at Lyra in 'innocent wonder' (AS: 410–11).

The contemporary proliferation of phantasmical creatures: Why?

At the beginning of the twenty-first century, many popular books for children and young adults feature protagonists caught in dramatic interplay with mythical, folkloric, phantom-like beings: vampires, witches, daemons, wizards. Consider the Harry Potter books by J. K. Rowling, the Earthsea books, the Chrestomanci novels by Diana Wynne Jones, and – hardly to be mentioned in the same breath – the Goosebumps and Fear Street series of R. L. Stine. For over a decade, Stephen King's horror novels, replete with phenomena such as extra-sensory perception and telekinesis, have topped the informal reading interest polls of young adults, and Buffy the Vampire Slayer reigns supreme in the television spin-off category. Why this proliferation of marvellous characters at this particular point in time? Is it a phenomenon in tune with the dark side of our *fin de siècle* collective unconscious, still fraught with apocalyptic fears despite the nearly glitch-free passing of Y2K into history? Are stories of encounters with fearsome phantoms a way of engaging our deep-seated anxieties, putting our spectral enemies to rest by battling them in our imaginations – calling at the same time on friendly spirits (such as Pullman's good witches or Le Guin's wise dragons) to help us survive, and perhaps even to evolve to a higher level of consciousness?

This blossoming of the shadow side of consciousness in books for the young has a brighter side as well. Pullman has noted in his Patrick Hardy lecture how contemporary children's literature has a 'spacious-ness' not found in adult literary fiction:

> Children's books, for various reasons, at this time in our literary history, open out on a wideness and amplitude – a moral and mental spaciousness – that adult literary fiction seems to have turned its back on. (1998: 44)

This may serve as an apt characterization of his own spacious imaginative landscape in *His Dark Materials*.

Varieties of wondrous and spectral beings

Daemons

In Pullman's universe of uncountable billions of parallel worlds, the marvellous beings are broadly speaking of two types: the first are friendly allies, helpers in the struggle for survival, such as the witch Serafina Pekkala, the armoured bear Iorek Byrnison, the *mulefa*, and the Gallivespians; the second are embodiments of dangerous and destructive alien forces, most notably the Spectres and Mrs Coulter's army of intercized soldiers. Daemons may belong to either category, allies or enemies, for they are extensions of their human counterparts and in keeping with the human's spiritual intention, as for instance Mrs Coulter's golden monkey, whose every appearance heralds an evil purpose (until late in *The Amber Spyglass*). Daemons are souls in animal form, each twinned for life with a human being, 'a thinking, talking, feeling, animal-shaped being [usually] of the opposite sex' (Bethune: 58). Until a person attains the age of puberty, his or her daemon can shift shape freely; with puberty, daemons become 'fixed' in shapes that represent their respective human's established soul states. Thus Pullman artfully conveys the fluidity of the child's nature versus the rigidity of the adult's, and at the same time communicates to the reader an immediate impression of a character's essence or, in the case of the child, the current state of the soul: eleven-year-old Lyra's daemon, Pantalaimon, is constantly shape-shifting. Daemons are visible in Lyra's world, hidden within in Will's world ('a silent voice in the mind', as John Parry says, *The Subtle Knife* (213)), though it is possible to learn to see them (*AS*: 505) much as some people can learn to see 'auras'. They may be, like John Parry's osprey daemon, Sayan Kötör, 'female, bird-formed, and beautiful,' (*SK*: 214), or slitheringly horrid, like Sir Charles'/Lord Boreal's snake, concealed in his sleeve (*SK*: 164).

Daemons are speaking, palpable, dialogic presences, perfect allies against loneliness; it is as though (drawing for a moment on Jungian theory), each person's *anima* or *animus* were an embodied presence, the perfect *alter ego* or soul-mate. They may be viewed in the light of the Jungian 'anima' and 'animus', the opposite sexual energy in the male and female psyches, respectively. The bond between the person and his or her daemon is a sacred one, as shown by the unspoken 'law' that no one should *ever* touch another's daemon (*NL*: 142). If the emotional bond to one's daemon is broken, as Gerard J. Senick has observed, the break will cause extreme damage, even death (1999: 151). However, in *The Amber Spyglass* Serafina Pekkala instructs Pantalaimon in witch lore, revealing how certain humans can, like the witches, separate from their daemons without soul-loss (*AS*: 472–3). The delight Mary Malone shows on perceiving her daemon (revealed to be an Alpine chough (*AS*: 506), similar to Will's sweet wonderment on finally seeing his daemon (*AS*: 482), dramatizes the rightness of cherishing these 'soul' guides. Serafina Pekkala sums up the purpose of daemons when she tells Pantalaimon, ' "You must help your humans, not hinder them. You must help them and guide them and encourage them towards wisdom. That's what daemons are for" ' (AS: 473).

Pullman said of his use of daemons, in the context of the stark 'psychological' realism of his fantasy, ' "I use them to embody and picture some truths about human personality which I couldn't picture so easily without them" ' ('Achuka Interview,' section 4); these words connect well with Serafina Pekkala's answer to Lyra's question about *why* people have daemons, first, that no one knows, but ' "It's what makes us different from animals" ' (NL: 316). Where the life of the soul is concerned, fantasy is more 'real' than the literature of so-called 'realism', and daemons are part and parcel of Pullman's psychological realism, no mere fantasy devices. The genesis of his daemons was 'sudden' and 'unexpected', but they do have 'a sort of provenance'. One clear origin is Socrates' daemon. Another is the old idea of 'guardian angel' (<http://www.achuka.co.uk/ppint.htm>section 9). *His Dark Materials* is 'not fantasy but stark realism' in the sense that 'it is realistic, in psychological terms' ('Achuka Interview'). (It is interesting to compare the 'truth' of the soul expressed through the daemon with the concept of the person's 'true' name as the individual's true essence in Ursula K. Le Guin's Earthsea books.)

There is actually a long tradition of using animals to symbolize moral qualities of humans – think for example of Aesop's fables, or of myths in many traditions which use animals as totemic representations of human personality types, as for example the wolf for a 'predator'-type person, the snake for the duplicitous, and so on. The daemon is reminiscent of the animal guide in folklore, and like the animal guide, the daemon 'knows the way', instinctively, the right path for the character to travel.

In *Northern Lights*, Jerry, the able seaman, explains the difference between child and adult daemons to Lyra at the point where she needs reassurance that growing up and having your daemon become 'settled' is not to be feared. At any rate you then know what kind of person you are. When Lyra objects that a person's daemon might settle in a shape repulsive to the individual, Jerry responds that there are plenty of folk who wish they had a lion daemon yet end up with a poodle (NL: 167). Being an adult entails accepting the narrowing of one's potential possible 'shapes', learning to live with a diminishment of the protean possibilities inherent in the child. As the wise seaman implies, there may be some comfort to an adult in having a firmer basis for self-trust and a clearer awareness of limits. Pullman emphasizes, however, that the fixing of the daemon is not morally deterministic: one whose adult daemon is a snake still for example has the choice of being a 'good snake person' or a 'bad snake person' (Parsons and Nicholson, 1999: 128). Individual moral responsibility remains, regardless of the form in which the daemon may 'settle'.

Spectres

In contrast to the soul-twin daemons, Pullman's Spectres, first introduced in the world of Cittagazze, are soul-eaters, phantoms who snatch and devour the daemons of any hapless adults who fall into their clutches. Stanislaus Grumman, explaining Spectres to Lee Scoresby, the aeronaut, compares them to vampires, but their diet is not carnivorous; instead of blood, ' "the Spectres' food is attention. A conscious and informed interest in the world" ' (SK: 280). Thus children, less focused and intense in their attention, are not so attractive to these predators. Since it is 'attention', consciousness, which creates the world and makes it possible to delight in the energy and worth of the phenomena presented to the mind, Spectres rob humans of all that makes life valuable, leaving their victims dead-in-life.

Spectres came into the world of Cittagazze through the misuse of the technology of the Knife: Giocomo Paradisi explains how they appeared when the intelligentsia of the Guild of the Torre degli Angeli – 'alchemists, philosophers, men of learning', were probing into the deepest secrets of 'the bonds that held the smallest particles of matter together'. (The parallel with nuclear research that resulted in splitting the atom is unmistakable. There may also be an allusion here to the medieval idea that certain knowledge is 'God's *privetee*', in Chaucer's expression – not to be revealed to mere humans.) Pullman plays upon the dual meanings of the word 'bonds' as 'something that binds' and 'something that could be bought and sold and exchanged and converted' – bonds in the mercantile sense (SK: 187). The implication is clear: another aspect of the misuse of knowledge is its corruption by commercial interests. By undoing the 'bonds,' these scholars with more knowledge than wisdom and more desire for gain than for protecting the sanctity of relationships, let the Spectres into the world of Cittagazze – though the actual origin of the Spectres remains a mystery.

Later, in *The Amber Spyglass*, Lyra and Will learn from their daemons the truth revealed by the witches – the connection between the Subtle Knife's wounds to nature and the genesis of Spectres (AS: 483). In *The Subtle Knife*, they are thought to come from another world, or from the darkness of space (*SK*: 187). Joachim Lorenz explains in his history of his world that the Spectres had caused the people of Cittagazze to become thieves, like the magpies for which their city is named, for they have lost their capacity to create (*SK*: 135). Once Cittagazze had been a rich and thriving city, replete with arts and crafts, a cornucopia of harmony and plenty for its happy citizens, an earthly paradise. The Spectres changed all that (134).

The Spectres are brought into close association with 'our' world (Will Parry's world in *The Subtle Knife*) shortly after Will's battle with Tullio to obtain the knife, which cost him two fingers of his left hand – the sign of the bearer. Will sees that Tullio's obsessive behaviour resembles that of his mother, and remarks that the Spectres in his world may be called 'something else' (*SK*: 224). This seems to allude to the hallucinations of paranoid schizophrenia. Just as daemons are interiorized in Will's world, Spectres also are hidden within. *The Liber Angelorum* (which Pullman cleverly attributes to an unreliable narrator, leaving its authenticity in doubt) states the 'Spectres are corrupted angels' (<http://www.randomhouse.com/features/golden-compass/subtleknife/angelorum.html>).

Witches

Pullman's witches are tantalizing creations, and most of them belong to the 'allies' category, with Serafina Pekkala the most prominent and pivotal witch character (her name deriving from *Seraph*, a celestial being who hovers above the deity's throne in ancient Hebrew belief). Serafina responds to Lyra's curiosity about Serafina's seeming immunity to the cold: witches *feel* the cold, but it doesn't harm them, and they refrain from wearing heavy clothing because they love the sensations of '"the bright tingle of the stars, or the music of the Aurora, or best of all the silky feeling of moonlight on our skin"' (*NL*: 313).

Besides having such potential for ecstasy, the witches have life spans of as much as a thousand years: Serafina herself, at three hundred, is a paragon of beauty. The deaths of witches are administered by the goddess of the dead, Yambe-Akka, 'older than the tundra', whose approach to the one whose time has come, all smiles and tenderness, offers a gentle passage out of life (*NL*: 314), far preferable to a rendezvous with Dr Kevorkian. This longevity has its downside, for it renders the love between a witch and a human (for example, Serafina Pekkala and Farder Coram) inherently tragic (*NL*: 315). Unlike human beings, witches have never been 'worried about Dust', and indeed, they have none of the troublesome propensity of humans to pry into the secrets and strangenesses of the universe, such as the Tartars' practice of making holes in their skulls (*NL*: 318).

Witches are at the centre of some of the novels' most transcendent moments, as well as some of their most appallingly hideous. Pullman's emotional range, from the height of *joie de vivre* to the depths of hellish despair, can be illustrated in the contrast between the painful scene in which Mrs Coulter tortures Lena Feldt in an effort to wring from her the true name of Lyra, with the scene depicting the ecstatic experience of Ruta Skadi, flying through the brilliance of the night sky with the angels, possessed by a 'fierce joy' that is both spiritual and sensual (*SK*:142). Pullman conveys her highly charged sexual energies when he describes her as living 'so brilliantly in her nerves that she set up a responding thrill in the nerves of anyone close by' (*SK*: 270).

In contrast to Skadi's buoyant joy in life is the agony of Lena Feldt under torture. Trying to save herself, she screams out the true name of Lyra: 'Eve! Mother of all! Eve, again! Mother Eve!' (*SK*: 314), but it is all in vain, for the Spectre devours her daemon anyway, and then feeds on Lena Feldt herself. This is Pullman's consummate description of death-in-life:

> She felt a nausea of the soul, a hideous and sickening despair, a melancholy weariness so profound that she was going to die of it. Her last conscious thought was disgust at life; her senses had lied to her. The world was not made of energy and delight but of foulness, betrayal, and lassitude. Living was hateful, and death was no better, and from end to end of the universe this was the first and last and only truth. (*SK*: 314–15)

Witches are mortal, but because they live for hundreds of years, they stand in contrast to 'short-lives', ordinary humans. They are however like humans in their fallibility and pride, as Juta Kamainen illustrates when she kills Stanislaus Grumman because he spurned her love. Ironically, this occurs just moments after Grumman/Parry and Will experience their epiphany of recognition, and the passionate witch kills herself in remorse for mindlessly depriving Will of his father.

Cliff-ghasts

Cliff-ghasts are the ghastly beings that live on cliffs in the northern regions of Lyra's world (*NL*: 224). They have 'leathery wings and hooked claws ... A flat head, with bulging eyes and a wide frog mouth' plus an 'abominable stink' (*NL*: 320). They enter into the action of *The Subtle Knife* when 'a beast of leathery skin and matted fur' falls from the sky and lands at the feet of Will and Lyra, shot down in a battle with the witches (*SK*: 269). Rudi Skadi tells of overhearing the cliff-ghasts talk gleefully of *Aesahaettr* (*SK*: 272). *Aesahaettr* is mistakenly thought by Ruta Skadi and the other witches to be a person but is actually the subtle knife. A spiteful pseudo-oracle, the 'Grandfather' of the cliff-ghasts, nastily prophesies victory for 'The Authority' over Lord Asriel because the latter 'hasn't got Aesahaettr. Without Aesahaettr, he and all his forces will go down to defeat. And then we shall feast for years, my children!' (*SK*: 273).

Pullman's evocation of disgust at this point is in the tradition of Jonathan Swift's depiction of the Yahoos, or better, his portrait of the *Struldbrugs* of Laputa, cursed with perpetual life at the cost of degeneracy. There is however a great difference: Pullman's spacious, lyrical habit of mind has nothing in common with Swift's obsessive, ingrained mood of savage indignation.

Armoured bears

Pullman's carefully crafted balancing of the portraits of the two armoured bears, Iorek Byrnison and Iofur Raknison, exemplifies his signature technique of 'doubling' (even the names have a certain suggestion of 'twinning') – balancing the true princeliness of the former with the pretensions of the latter, a usurper of the throne: the dignified 'father figure' is posed against the buffoon. The *'panser-bjorne,'* great white sentient armoured bears, are introduced in *Northern Lights* as the guards of the fortress of Svalbard, where Lord Asriel has been imprisoned for his heretical stance *vis-à-vis* the Church (*NL*: 95). Lyra comes to love Iorek passionately, and he gives her the love and protection Lord Asriel, her biological father, denies her. The doubling of Iorek and Iofur in a structural sense demands their duel, and that is brought about by Lyra's clever ruse – to pose as Iofur's 'daemon' in an attempt to see Iorek restored to his rightful place as king of the bears. In his portrayal of the physical rottenness of Iofur Raknison's dung-covered fortress, which reeks with perfume that fails to cover up the stench, Pullman shows both the foolish bear's moral corruption and his own command of the art of satire, including a Swiftian finesse in the use of scatological imagery.

Iorek Byrnison, being a bear, has no daemon, but he has so wonderfully crafted his own armour that it might as well be one. He says to Lyra, ' "A bear's armour is his soul, just as your daemon is your soul" ' (*NL*: 196–7). Thus, when it is stolen, he suffers as deeply as a human severed from his or her daemon. He demands the restoration of his armour as a condition of joining the campaign against Bolvangar (*NL*: 182). Lyra actually restores the armour to him, with the help of Scoresby (*NL*: 197ff.). Later, in a conversation with Lyra, Iorek tells how he made his own armour from 'sky metal', essentially, as Lyra observes, making his own soul, something no human can do.

The starkest contrast between Iorek and Iofur comes through the description of their clothing: Iofur Raknison and his courtiers vie for merit with their outward trappings of 'plumes and badges and tokens', and some carry little dolls that seem to be pretend-daemons; in contrast, Iorek Byrnison is 'pure and certain and absolute' in his demeanour even though his armour is 'rusty and dented' (SK: 345, 349), for 'he had made it and it fitted him. They were one. Iofur was not content with his armour; he wanted another soul as well. He was restless while Iorek was still.' As Lyra realizes, she is not seeing just two bears, but 'two kinds of beardom ... two futures, two destinies' (SK: 349). Iofur can be tricked because he lacks the 'grace' of a true internal compass; hence Lyra's success in fooling him, and Iorek's victory over him in their unequal contest.

When Iorek Byrnison gives Lyra a new name – 'Lyra Silvertongue' – which she wins through her rhetorical skill in tricking Iofur Raknison – he is acting in the tradition of mentor figures in fantasy, who bestow new names at a pivotal point in the protagonist's life. Thus the moment marks a new self-awareness on Lyra's part, a strengthening of the bond between her and the princely bear, and by foregrounding Lyra's rhetorical skill, it foreshadows the storytelling theme so central to The Amber Spyglass.

In The Amber Spyglass Iorek first reappears in 'Scavengers,' introducing the theme of ecological disaster: 'The whole of nature was overturned' (AS: 37) and King Iorek is preparing to move his bears south to escape starvation. Serafina Pekkala's news of Lee Scoresby's death persuades the armoured bear to go first in pursuit of Lyra to the scene where Scoresby's uncorrupted remains lie preserved by the witch's spell; once there, he shows his reverence by accepting the last 'gift' that Scorseby can give – his flesh and blood, in a kind of sacramental meal (AS: 42). In a fortuitous meeting, Will's and Iorek's paths cross as they are both seeking Lyra. Initially enemies, Will and Iorek join their quests when Will's demonstration of the power of the subtle knife enables him to play the role of peacemaker (AS: 106 ff.).

'The Forge' shows Iorek at his finest, a mythic, Hephaestus- or Vulcan-like figure, reforging the broken subtle knife (broken when Will loses his concentration, seeing his mother's face in Mrs Coulter's (AS: 153)). Iorek's pure, clear perceptions lead him to mistrust the knife, and prophetically, he speaks, in Aristotelian fashion, of its unknown 'intentions': ' "The intentions of a tool are what it does. A hammer intends to strike, a vice intends to hold fast, a lever intends to lift. They are what it is made for. But sometimes a tool may have uses that you don't know"' (AS: 181). The oracular 'reading' Lyra receives in response to a question posed to the alethiometer (should Iorek repair it or not?) helps little: '"The knife would be the death of Dust, but ... it was the only way to keep Dust alive"' (AS: 183). It is Lyra's pleading on behalf of Roger that moves the faithful bear to carry out the task. Ironically, he feels he may be '"as foolish as Iofur Rakinson"' in doing so – and he is so troubled by doubt (not a 'bear thing') that he fears he is becoming human, denying his true, bear nature (AS: 191). His integrity is reflected in the Zen-like advice he gives Will: he must keep his attention on his task, for '"If your mind is divided, the knife will break"' (AS: 194). Indeed, Iorek's bear 'conscience' seems purer than any human's: yet his reluctant act, dubious in the light of his scrupulosity, makes Lyra's and Will's epic journey to the World of the Dead possible.

Iorek's reappearance in 'Authority's End' seems anti-climactic, though the reunion with Lee Scoresby's ghost gives the scene a human warmth in contrast with the violence of the struggle. The aëronaut is given a kind of 'apotheosis':

> The last little scrap of the consciousness that had been the aëronaut Lee Scoresby floated upwards, just as his great balloon had done so many times ... [and] passed through the heavy clouds and came out under the brilliant stars, where the atoms of his beloved daemon Hester were waiting for him. (AS: 418)

Angels

Angels are introduced in *The Subtle Knife*, where they respond to questions posed through the computer of Dr Mary Malone; they also guard Stanislaus Grumman (up to a point), and later Lyra and Will. Pullman's angels have a Blakean 'feel' about them, reminiscent of the illuminated, architectonic figures of the great poet's artwork. They are known to themselves as *bene elim* [Hebrew, sons – or progeny – of the gods], as Joachim Lorenz, leader of a group of ill-starred exiles from Cittagazze, explains to Serafina. Others call them 'Watchers.' They are beings of spirit, and if they have flesh, it is of an ethereal sort different from that of humans. Their calling is to carry messages from heaven to earth (SK: 137). It is tempting to compare them, in their role as liminal beings (intermediaries between the divine and the human realms) with Le Guin's dragons; there is a further parallel in that both Pullman's angels and Le Guin's dragons have intermingled with men and women and had offspring by the latter, so that as it is written in *The Liber*

Angelorum, 'we can all claim to be descendants of angels' (though in the case of Le Guin's Earthsea inhabitants, only some have dragon lineage).

The Liber Angelorum purports to set down in a systematic fashion a digest of angel lore, but its contents are spurious and its provenance suspect. The dedicated bibliophile who patched it together had no way of telling 'what was truth, what was speculation, or even what was stark heresy, set down only in order to be refuted' (a description to arouse torment in the mind of any archivist). Pullman has created an admirable example of a postmodern text, a text with no fixed meaning. Moreover, he shows how an author in a digital world can 'play' in his own 'phase space'. 'Phase space' is 'the untrackable complexity of changing systems ... to serve as a metaphor for ... the notional space which contains not just the actual consequences of the present moment, but all the possible consequences' (Pullman, 1998: 47). In 'Playing in the phase space: contemporary forms of fictional pleasure,' Margaret Mackey has pointed out that the concept of 'phase space' can help us conceptualize how in the contemporary world stories have 'nebulous' boundaries, and are subject to forms of textual 'play' that often cross media boundaries. New technologies make possible 'hybrid' story forms: as for example, adaptations for film, television, audio, video games, CD-ROMS, collaborative online fiction, web sites, and so on. (In addition to the hypertext on the *Liber Angelorum,* there is a hypertext giving the history of the alethiometer, instructions for how to read it, and a glossary of its symbols <http://www.randomhouse.com/features/goldencompass/goldencompass/aleth.html>). Mackey points out how Pullman offers 'An example of textual play that challenges our thinking about literary practice' in our era, as well as providing 'useful critical vocabulary for discussing these matters' (1999: 17). Peter Hunt's comments (89 above) on the extensions to Pratchett's *Discworld* in cyberspace – where thousands of readers are combining their imaginations to create 'a fluid, corporate fantasy' – deal with the 'phase space' phenomenon: the cyberplayground where co-created hypernarratives are spawned.

The Liber Angelorum points out the 'envy' of angels for 'the power and brilliance of our senses,' which should fill us humans with 'bliss' (a central theme of the trilogy) as well as the angels' lack of all passions or affections, except one – 'curiosity, or intellectual passion' (contradicted incidentally by the passionate attachment between Balthamos and Baruch in *The Amber Spyglass,* though as Baruch was 'once a man' (*AS:* 16), this may explain the apparent discrepancy).

Aesthetically, the most important quality of the angels is that they are 'lighted beings' (*SK*: 139); they inspire some of Pullman's most shimmering language, as when he calls their true form 'more like architecture than organism, like huge structures composed of intelligence and feeling' (*SK*: 140–1).

More word-painting occurs when Serafina, observing the angels guarding the sleeping Will and Lyra, intuitively understands 'the idea of pilgrimage' (though there is no word for it in her world): she suddenly knows 'why these beings would wait for thousands of years and travel vast distances in order to be close to something important, and how they would feel differently for the rest of time, having been briefly in its presence.' The vivid and cadenced language gives substance to these 'beautiful pilgrims of rarefied light' (*SK*: 276) in a scene heavy with overtones like those of a painting of a sacred scene from the high Renaissance.

The two closely bonded angels who guard over Will (seen initially without being named at the close of *The Subtle Knife*), are Balthamos and Baruch. Pullman sensitively portrays their passionately homoerotic relationship (*AS*: 26). Lacking physical bodies, they seem psychically almost one, as when Balthamos knows telepathically of Baruch's death.

Baruch's fraternal relationship to the terrible Regent Metatron (once Enoch) was broken for reasons not explicitly stated (*AS*: 63). Pullman draws upon the apocryphal tradition, which 'suggests that Enoch the Patriarch was taken into heaven and transformed into the angel Metatron' (Cooper, 2000: 355); Metatron has become the 'Regent', who acts for the now enfeebled 'Authority'. He first appears in *Spyglass* when he makes a vicious attack on Will (*AS*: 28 ff.). Balthamos' final act – holding the stunned Father Gomez's head under water until he is dead – is both a grotesque inversion of a baptismal rite and a kind of heroic memorial to the memory of Baruch (*AS*: 469).

The Amber Spyglass introduces another angel of great importance, Xaphania. She is initially referred to only as 'One of those who came later ... Wiser than he' (the Authority); she was banished for perceiving that the emperor had no clothes. The rebel angels have served her from the time of the first War in Heaven (*AS*: 32). Pullman's portrait of Xaphania may owe something to the gnostic belief in the 'divine Mother', or 'Wisdom' (Greek 'Sophia'), in turn a translation of the Hebrew *hokhmah* (Pagels, 1981: 64). 'Sophia' is identical to the Latin 'Sapientia', derived from the verb *sapère* ('to taste'), a significant etymology, for it suggests 'wisdom' means knowing how to *savour* life, how to respond to it with a sensuous appreciation and gusto – a view of life in harmony with the values that emerge from *His Dark Materials* in its entirety. Xaphania is unclothed, signifying perhaps her total naturalness and lack of pretence; her countenance is ageless, 'austere and compassionate', and she knows 'hearts' intuitively, as Will and Lyra sense (AS: 490). She shares her ancient and arcane knowledge about Dust with Lyra and Will: Dust can be created by the 'thinking and feeling and reflecting' of conscious beings, by their 'gaining wisdom and passing it on', a lesson in what psychologist Eric Erickson calls 'generativity', a gift to coming generations. With Will and Lyra, she is sorrowful over the necessity of closing the windows between worlds (all but one, to be kept open so the 'ghosts' may emerge from the World of the Dead) (AS: 492).

Xaphania expresses an important theme when she distinguishes between true 'imagination' – it is not *pretending*, as Lyra first thinks – but rather 'a form of seeing' (AS: 523). One might compare the Romantic idea of the imagination as, in the words of Percy Bysshe Shelley, 'the great instrument of moral good', which possesses the power to create what the Romantic poets called 'a heterocosm – a world other than this one – which, once alive imaginally, can inspire action' (Watkins, 1987: 72, 74–5). Pullman's characterization of Xaphania may take some inspiration from the gnostic idea of the deity as a 'dyad whose nature includes both masculine and feminine elements'. It thus can serve as a corrective to what Elaine Pagels, in her historical study of metaphors for the divine, calls the virtual disappearance of the feminine from the orthodox Christian tradition (Pagels, 1981: 68).

The shaman, and the place of Lyra and Will in 'witch lore'

Will's long-lost father, Stanislaus Grumman/John Parry, becomes a shaman through the process of trepanning (making small holes in the skull), an initiation rite practised by the Tartars (SK: 214). His shamanic powers have enabled him to travel to many worlds, to gain knowledge of the subtle knife and its powers, and to practise herbal healing (particularly by means of bloodmoss, which heals Will's knife wound). Trepanning induces mystic consciousness, opening the mind to messages from beyond; it seems to be an ancient technology for communicating with 'Dust', a theory supported by a concentration of Dust (or shadow particles) on the trepanned skulls in the Royal Geological Museum (SK: 77).

Whereas Will's father achieved shaman-status by means of a deliberate act, Lyra and Will unwittingly earn their 'witch-power' by passing through a desolate region of the north, where no daemons can enter – the very point on the shores of the world of the dead, where they were obliged to leave their daemons before entering the netherworld. Henceforth, they are like the witches, whose daemons can remain part of 'one whole being; but now they can roam free' (AS: 472–3).

The act of leaving Pan is Lyra's prophesied 'betrayal,' yet despite the great suffering they both had to endure, this is paradoxically also the means whereby she and Will were initiated into their 'witch-power', which they must keep secret from other mortals (AS: 516).

Gallivespians, *mulefa*, harpies and ghosts

The Amber Spyglass introduces the Gallivespians – Lord Roke, Lady Salmakia, and Chevalier Tialys – with their lodestone resonators, devices enabling them to communicate through a remarkable technology that seems related to physicist Rupert Sheldrake's theory of 'morphic resonance'. Sheldrake builds upon a 'vibrational' theory of nature wherein forms and behaviours are transmitted across both space and time by means of repetition, thus forming 'habits': the more similar the forms, the greater the degree of resonance (Sheldrake, 1989: 371). 'Quantum entanglement' – so-called in the novel – reflects Pullman's penchant for science as well as his fascination with sound (witness his analogies between his work and 'a piece of music' with contrasting 'loud' and 'quiet' passages ('Darkness Visible,' Pt. 1). Gallivespians are no more than a hand-span in height (about the size of Jonathan Swift's Lilliputians, their possible literary ancestors), and are 'short-lived,' with a nine- to ten-year lifespan. They never age, but instead die in the 'full strength and vigor of their prime' (AS: 75). Their small size makes them ideal spies; their short lifespans make them inherently tragic figures. Allies of Lord Asriel and his rebel angels, they help Will and Lyra liberate the ghosts of the World of the Dead as well. Their Dragonfly steeds are ironically thought to be daemons by the ghost-children of the netherworld who long to connect again with their own daemons (AS: 296); they also bring out Lyra's dawning maternal instincts. The noble Madame Oxenteil rescues Lyra and Will from Metatron's forces and restores them to their daemons (AS: 411 ff.).

The charming *mulefa* are introduced in *The Amber Spyglass*, when Mary Malone enters their world in flight from the Spectres. The *mulefa*'s evolutionary path has diverged from that of humans in Mary's world: they are strongly communal beings who live in synergy with the seed pod trees. They look back on an idyllic, a Golden Age (AS: 132; compare the world of *Cittàgazze*) but their natural world is now in decline. Mary becomes a kind of cultural anthropologist in her efforts to help solve the mystery of why their trees, so essential to their pastoral life, are dying. Their lives are based on sound ecological values, which recognize their interdependency with nature. Mary comes to understand them intuitively and love them for their wisdom, eventually seeing how they connect with the question that has preoccupied her for several years – the nature and significance of Dust (*sraf* in their language, meaning '*us*'). Their creation story, which includes a 'snake' (*make-like*) (*AS*: 223–4), suggests how their evolution of consciousness parallels that of humans in Mary's world, though with a stronger sense of community (*AS*: 223 ff.). Pullman has said they 'stand for a state of happy fulfillment in the physical processes of life – they manage their world completely – because they have what we call consciousness' ('Darkness Visible', Pt. 2). Their respect for the integrity of their environment, their gentleness for all sentient beings underscores Pullman's strong ecological theme. Mary's experiences in the *mulefa* world help to characterize her as a physicist of the Fritjof Capra variety – a scientist-mystic. Appropriately, the *mulefa* are given the honour of planting and maintaining the grove around the 'holy' place where the ghosts emerge from the world of the dead (*AS*: 502), a joyful assignment befitting their natures.

Harpies have a long literary tradition, going back to classical mythology; they also occur in Dante's *Inferno* (XIII, 101), where they feed on the living sprouts that grow from the torn souls of suicides. In Pullman's underworld, they are at first hostile to Lyra and Will but are gradually won over by Lyra's 'silver' tongue. 'No-Name' (the chief harpy) embodies the universal desire for stories, has no time for fanciful tall tales and the echoes from her scream – ' "*Liar! Liar! Liar!*" ' give the impression she is screaming Lyra's name, 'so that *Lyra* and *liar* were one and the same thing' (*AS*: 293). Through the harpies Lyra comes to comprehend the vast difference between spinning idle tales and speaking stories of heartfelt passion and truth. Whereas the latter are life-changing and life-giving, the former are worthless. When No-Name saves Lyra from the abyss, Lyra christens her 'Gracious Wings' in gratitude (*AS*: 386). These events are vital to the storytelling theme of *Spyglass*. In Pullman's words,

> Lyra's fantasy doesn't satisfy the harpies. They're only satisfied when she tells them the truth. And I *mean* that ... Books which satisfy us and feed us and nourish us have to have this substratum of genuine truth in them. And I don't see much of that in most fantasy. ('Darkness Visible', Pt. 1)

The proud harpies also hunger for meaningful work, and through the negotiations of the gallant Chevalier Tialys and Madame Salmakia, they are given the 'honorable place' of serving as guides through the land of the dead, delivering the ghosts to the new opening into the world – in exchange for *true* stories (AS: 318).

Roger plays the central role among the ghosts of the world of the dead, and his haunting voice, first heard in Lyra's dreams, is the impetus for her underworld journey. Pullman artfully captures the pathos of the ghostly state, contrasting the live Lyra, Will and the Gallivespians with the bodiless shades of those who long for a return to a palpable world of sensuous experiences. The ghosts drive home one of the central themes of the trilogy: the great blessing humans enjoy (and so largely take for granted), in contrast to the ethereal angels.

LYRA: 'The first believable little girl since Alice'

The opening sentence of the *Northern Lights* engages the reader's interest by the striking conjunction of Lyra and her *daemon*. Curiosity is aroused: what is a daemon, and what sort of world have we entered?

At first glance, the eleven-year-old protagonist is a trespasser, yet a sympathetic one, as she endeavours – like a young Nancy Drew – to outwit the stuffy Jordan College officials and their servile, petty servants. Her name suggests her nature, being a near-homonym of 'liar', though it has more direct associations of a celestial sort, 'Lyra' being the name of a constellation containing a star of the first magnitude (Vega). Lyra also suggests 'lyre,' an ancient musical instrument of Greece, used as an accompaniment to the recitation of heroic poetry. Her shapeshifting daemon, Pantalaimon, further characterizes her as a mercurial pre-adolescent; she cherishes him, and in retrospect he seems to compensate somewhat for the absence of family in Lyra's life.

By giving Lyra a temporary orphan status (she has falsely been told her parents had died in an airship accident (NL: 121)), Pullman draws upon an honoured tradition in children's literature and folklore. Orphans are appealing as lead characters partly because they express a paradox: 'They are a manifestation of loneliness, but they also represent the possibility for humans to reinvent themselves' (Kimball, 1999: 558). Certain folkloric motifs persist in children's stories featuring orphan protagonists – such as a birth under unusual circumstances; a prophecy of an unusual destiny; an assigned task or quest; a 'helper' – sometimes in the form of an 'animal guide'; punishment of the villainous characters who mistreat the orphan; and (usually) a happy resolution including a 'reward' that may take the form of marriage, wealth, and position. Lyra's story at the outset incorporates several of these motifs, most obviously her oracular 'destiny' and the 'animal guide' or companion in the form of her daemon. The shrouded circumstances surrounding her birth are unveiled later by John Faa, King of the 'Gyptians' (121–4), one of her several surrogate father-figures, along with the armoured bear Iofur Raknison and the aëronaut Lee Scoresby.

Despite her privileged social status (clear from her relationship to Lord Asriel), the predominant image is one of a brilliant, spirited, but emotionally deprived girl on the verge of adolescence, who is seeking her identity and purpose. Thus she is open to the romance of adventure in the mysterious North (offered, or so she initially believes, by the glamorous Mrs Coulter) and to the 'mission' of delivering the alethiometer to the romantically daring Lord Asriel, as well as her epic quest into the world of the dead to speak with Roger. Loyalty is one of her primary virtues – to Roger, to Will, and to Pantalaimon – and the pain she experiences when she separates from 'Pan' is one of the most vividly realized emotions in the trilogy. Having been nursed by a 'gyptian' woman and neglected by her biological mother, the lonely Lyra experiences a revelatory moment in the underworld when the soothing voice and maternal qualities of the Lady Salmakia cause her to 'wish in her heart to have a child of her own, to lull and soothe and sing to, one day, in a voice like that' (AS: 277–8) – one of many signals of her emotional growth.

Lyra as chosen 'Eve' and Pullman's variations on the heroic quest pattern in fantasy

Heroic quests featuring male protagonists traditionally adhere to a pattern, containing some or all of the following features: a humble birth; orphan status; being the subject of a mysterious prophecy; exceptionality – a special gift; being apprenticed to a teacher or mentor with magical powers (who may bestow upon the neophyte a new name); being endowed with a weapon of supernatural prowess; committing an act of disobedience or hubris which brings on a disaster, for which the hero must seek cure or remedy; suffering a dramatic temptation, which he may either resist or succumb to (like Odysseus to Circe's charms), but which he ultimately overcomes; waging a battle with a dragon, or some similar supernatural opponent (for example, *Beowulf*); winning a victory over the evil adversary; and finally returning to his community, with a boon (as Joseph Campbell termed it) or gift, ultimately restoring the society to wholeness. On all these points except the humble birth and the hubris, Lyra comes close to qualifying (stretching 'teacher' a bit to include Iorek), with two important differences: she *must* succumb to the temptation in order to fulfil her destiny, and she has a partner in her heroic exploits, Will Parry.

In a sort of androgynous blend of the male and female patterns, Lyra's quest shares most features of the traditionally male pattern, but draws also upon critic Bruce Lincoln's three-stage female pattern of initiation: enclosure, metamorphoses, and emergence (quoted in Attebery, 1992: 91). Secreted in the wardrobe of the Retiring Room, she is literally enclosed in the opening scene, but as a ward of Jordan College, Lyra has a fair amount of superficial freedom to roam about and explore. She is 'enclosed' in a deeper sense by the strictures on female roles in her world (contrast Mrs Coulter and a female scholar of Will's world, Dr Mary Malone, in their range of options). Prepubescent, she enjoys the latitude allotted to the tomboy at this age. *The Amber Spyglass* carries her to the threshold of womanhood, in her realization of her life purpose and her deepening feelings for Will.

The explicit prophecy of her special destiny adds tension to the narrative: the Master of Jordan College speaks of the important part she will play (though he seems oblivious of the details), known presumably from the alethiometer (*NL*: 30 ff.). Dr Lanselius, counsel to the witches, tells of their centuries-old knowledge of a prophecy about ' "this child of . . . rare destiny . . . Without this child, we shall all die" ' (*NL*: 176).

Pullman uses the technique of gradual revelation to build suspense. Serafina Pekkala embroiders on the details of the 'curious prophecy':

> 'She is destined to bring about the end of destiny. But she must do so without knowing what she is doing . . . If she's told what she must do, it will all fail; death will sweep through all the worlds; it will be the triumph of despair, forever. The universes will all become nothing more than interlocking machines, blind and empty of thought, feeling, life.' (*NL*: 310)

Her metamorphosis begins when Iorek names her 'Lyra Silvertongue,' though others contribute to her 'apprenticeship' as well – Fader Coram, for example, and Ma Costa, who declares (meaning it as a compliment) that she has 'witch oil in her soul' (*NL*: 112). The witches know, of course, that Lyra is an avatar of the mythical Eve (*SK*: 314) and that this knowledge must be kept from Mrs Coulter. The alethiometer is Lyra's metaphorical sword, arming her with magical power. Complications arise in *The Subtle Knife* when the alethiometer commands her to give priority to helping with Will's quest for his father. Pullman is depicting what Riane Eisler might call a 'partnership' quest, the male and female sharing equally and (in some details at least) assuming non-traditional gender roles (for example, Will cooks, Lyra operates the 'technological' tool, the alethiometer). Both seek to free themselves from the perverted cultures of their respective worlds. A mythic archetype is preserved in Mrs Coulter, who though she is Lyra's biological mother, plays the fearsome stepmother role. She is better understood as a kind of fairy-tale figure than as a realistic mother; her near-total perversity makes her a tantalizing but flat character, until she switches loyalties in *The Amber Spyglass* and sacrifices herself to preserve Lyra's life.

Pullman presents in Lyra a highly individualized variation on the female hero: charmingly mercurial, at one moment a 'coarse and greedy little savage' (*NL*: 36), at another an inventor of tall tales (her defensive mechanism to deal with her insecurities after she discovers Asriel is not her uncle but her father (*NL*: 130)). At yet another time she is as sensitive as a Romantic poet to the splendours of nature, as when the sight of 'a majestic line of great hills in the distance' gives her 'the same deep thrill she'd felt all her life on hearing the word *North*' (*NL*: 133).

The Amber Spyglass furthers Lyra's character development, as she and Will learn of the sorrows of mortality, the wonder of first love, and ultimately, of the heart-rending sacrifice they must make for their daemons' survival. Lyra's heroic 'tasks' are many: the harrowing descent into the underworld, during which she must 'betray' Pan; acknowledging her omnipresent Death, about which she learns from 'Peter' – the man waiting in limbo with other ghosts to enter the underworld, who says to her, in words that might have come straight out of *Everyman* itself, that

> 'We had 'em [our deaths] all the time, and we never knew. See, everyone has a death. It goes everywhere with 'em, all their life long, right close by ... The moment you're born, your death comes into the world with you, and it's your death that takes you out'. (*AS*: 260)

Or in the words of *The Book of Common Prayer*: 'In the midst of life we are in death'. Lyra must confront the personification of her own Death, overcoming her instinct to recoil; eventually she heeds the wisdom of the old grandmother's death, who tells them all not to hide, but ' "Say welcome, make friends, be kind, invite your deaths to come close to you, and see what you can get them to agree to" ' (*AS*: 264). Without her Death at her side, in fact, she cannot enter the underworld, nor can Will. In addition, she must grow, with 'No-Name's help, into a teller-of-truth; she must recognize her own feelings for Will, including her emerging identity as a young woman transformed by love; finally she must commit herself to an 'ultimate concern' ('building the

Republic of Heaven where you are').

Lyra's growth towards adulthood and wisdom is evident in her home-coming scene, when she is amazed to find the Master's manservant, Cousins, warm and affectionate (*she*, not he, has changed), and second, when the Master sees through her loss of 'unconscious grace' to 'the beautiful adult she would be, so soon' (AS: 512, 514).

Will and his father's 'mantle': 'don't argue with your own nature'

Will has certain traditional characteristics of the hero of fantasy: his lineage is remarkable, in that his explorer father has disappeared in mysterious circumstances and become a shaman in another world; lacking a visible daemon, he has a surrogate animal guide, the cat that leads him through the 'window' into the world of Cittàgazze and helps in the 'theft' of the alethiometer from Sir Charles; he acquires a knife with magical powers, through his and Lyra's daring; he is recognized as the mythical 'Bearer,' his destined role; his mother foretells his heroic path, referring to taking up his father's mantle (SK: 10). His differences from the pattern are nonetheless significant: he is not hubristic: in fact, he resists heroism and must be convinced of his 'warrior' nature by Stanislaus Grumman (John Parry, 'Jopari'), who asks him the crucial question, has he fought to obtain the knife? When Will answers in the affirmative, the older man adds: ' "Then you're a warrior. That's what you are. Argue with anything else, but don't argue with your own nature" ' (SK: 320). In his heart Will longs for home; still a boy inside, he would like to be comforted, kept safe, praised by his mother, though in fact their roles have been reversed, and he feels responsible for her safety (SK: 307).

Will grows greatly in *The Amber Spyglass*, taking command of his own quest to save Lyra, then joining with Lyra in the underworld journey to seek the ghost of his father. The subsequent key scenes pivotal to Will's coming of age are first, when he plays the role of peacemaker, confronting Iorek and out-manoeuvring him in a David-and-Goliath fashion (AS: 106 ff.); second, when in his farewell to his father's ghost, he affirms his freedom of choice:

> 'You said I was a warrior. You told me that was my nature, and I shouldn't argue with it. Father, you were wrong. I fought because I had to. I can't choose nature, but I can choose what I do. And I *will* choose, because now I'm free.' (AS: 418)

Significantly, John Parry validates his son's self-affirmation. A third key experience comes when Will can see his daemon, the cat-formed Kirjava, signifying that he can see his own soul, and it is beautiful (AS: 482). Finally, he arrives at the truth about the subtle knife, its perilous own 'intentions' (as Iorek had warned), and the necessity of first closing all the windows to stop Dust leaking out of the worlds, and then, of breaking the knife altogether, which he can do only by thinking of something it could not cut – his love for Lyra (AS: 510). His realization of Mary's friendship as they re-enter their own world marks his coming-of-age.

Lyra's and Will's partnership quest

Pullman's innovations on the traditional heroic roles centre on the sharing of quests between Will and Lyra. Just as she subordinates her own quest for Dust to his quest for his father, Will comes to see their paths as inevitably intertwined: each needs the other not only on the level of physical survival, but for wholeness of soul. This is poignantly foreshadowed when Pantalaimon instinctively comforts Will, going against the prohibition of daemon-touching (SK: 182 ff.). Will takes the lead in a number of episodes, such as the rescue of Lyra, and even more dramatically when he uses the knife to prevent the bomb from killing her (by resonating with a hair from her head). These feats are matched by Lyra's own acts of astounding courage, notably finding the self-control to part from Pan for the sake of Roger; reaching out compassionately to the ghosts and committing to the quest to free them; finding a way to connect with the No-Name and transforming their relationship; finally, insisting she and Will must make the painful choice of cultivating their respective gardens in their own worlds, though never forgetting their soul-connection. The 'pure constellations', looking down on the Botanic Gardens in their respective worlds, will connect them always, however far apart.

Pullman's worldview: anti-theological and manichean?

Alan Jacobs ('The Devil's Party') notes that like other great creators of secondary worlds, Pullman offers 'not just a story but a world ... not just a moral, but a worldview.' Secondary worlds help to satisfy the hunger of today's readers for a metaphysics, a cosmology, a mythic pattern to structure human experience, so lacking in many lives. After some opening compliments, Jacobs critiques the trilogy from the standpoint of its 'distinct anti-theology'. Unlike Milton, he says, who was 'of the Devil's party without knowing it', Pullman is acutely conscious of which side he is on.

Although Jacobs praises Pullman's stellar gifts as a storyteller, he cites a lengthy string of transgressions – such as polemic interruptions of the 'momentum' of the narrative; the fact that 'the daemons in Lyra's world always comfort, never burden'; his so-called 'reductive and contemptuous ideology'; and his neglect – in Jacobs' eyes – of 'the tangled consequences of even the most principled revolutions'.

One charge is that Pullman cheats the reader by passing over the 'key theological moment' towards which the narrative has been driving – Authority's 'end', in a few lines, neglecting to explore the dramatic possibilities of the moment, and thus 'diminishing' his story through his attempt to 'diminish God'. This judgement ignores the fact that the 'Authority' has been carefully characterized as a self-appointed and false sovereign, already much diminished. Xaphania clearly sees this, and it is remarkable that Jacobs mentions her only in passing, for she is a pivotal figure in the novel and represents the contemporary need to balance 'masculine' and 'feminine' archetypes (compare Le Guin's *Tehanu* in this respect). As for Jacobs' mention of two supposed 'absurdities', first the enticement of Metatron, the Almighty's Regent, by the seductive 'babe', Mrs Coulter; and second, Asriel's 'Intention Machine', as 'a hovercraft straight out of *Star Wars*', one might retort that absurd things *do* happen to supposedly impregnable heads of state, and that today's film-loving readers will probably relish the allusion to *Star Wars*.

In calling Pullman's theology 'reductive and contemptuous', Jacobs gives little heed to the tradition of exaggeration in satire. Pullman's satire targets the 'Church' of Lyra's world, a gross caricature of institutionalized religion, totally at odds with any values the historical Jesus would recognize. Since this is a dead institution in an alternative world, exaggeration is an effective narrative strategy, in the tradition of Jonathan Swift. As for Pullman's depiction of Christianity in 'our' world, when Mary asserts that ' "The Christian religion is a very powerful and convincing mistake, that's all" ' (AS: 441), a prudent reader must remember who she is: a former nun who has become an atheist.

Pullman has responded plainly to questions about his portrayal of organized religion, admitting he knew it would be troublesome to some:

> 'I knew there'd be a certain amount of critical reaction to my criticism of the churches. But it seems to me, if you look at human history, and if you look at the present day, too, in many parts of the world, that organized religion – especially those religions that have a monotheistic god – have been responsible historically for enormous amounts of persecution, of suffering and cruelty.'

Because young people's fiction especially fails to acknowledge this, Pullman 'wanted to give a sort of historical answer to the, so to speak, propaganda on behalf of religion that you get in, for example, C. S. Lewis' (quoted in Odean, 2000).

Jacobs correctly observes that few people, especially young readers, have the contextual knowledge necessary to critique the novel's perspective from the standpoint of Christian doctrine and the Bible. Sarah Johnson expresses a similar view in her review of *The Amber Spyglass*, stating her contention that young readers will take Pullman's 'Church' for 'the real thing', and many will be so drawn in by the power of the narrative that they will never again be able 'to explore faith without a Pullmanesque bias'. This, she affirms, 'is a greater sadness than this most imaginative of men can imagine'. These remarks cannot be blithely dismissed, yet pleas for a totally balanced and objective perspective make practically impossible demands on a writer who is working in the tradition of dissent.

Others may argue that young readers will simply devour the story and leave the theological and historical world-view to adults. It is also just possible that more discerning teen readers can be provoked to explore these historical and theological questions further. A critically annotated edition of *His Dark Materials*, for these readers, would be highly desirable, for this could enable them to put this remarkable work in its proper context, as Wagner (2000) says, 'with and against Paradise Lost, with and against Blake's depiction of old Nobodaddy.' They could then discover 'the dissenting tradition from which these books spring. This is remarkable writing: courageous and dangerous, as the best art should be. Pullman envisions a world without God, but not one without hope.'

Pullman's own words about his beliefs are enlightening: he affirms his love of 'the language and the atmosphere of the Bible and the prayer book. I don't say I agree with it ... I no longer believe in the God I used to believe in when I was a boy' (Odean, 2000). Nevertheless, his imagination is steeped in Biblical lore (from his childhood with his Church of England clergyman grandfather), an influence he will never escape (and never desires to escape!). 'So although I call myself an atheist, I'm certainly a Christian atheist and even more particularly, a Church of England – what would you say, Episcopalian? – atheist. And very specifically, a 1662 Book of Common Prayer atheist.'

As for the World of the Dead, where all 'ghosts' are condemned to what Jacobs terms 'a horrifically vacuous underworld (very like the one visited in Homer's *Odyssey*)', readers will most likely put this in perspective according to their personal beliefs about immortality. Within the novel, Lyra and Will seek to save these souls – whose agony is powerfully described – by leading them through a new 'window' to the living world, where they will (gladly) disintegrate into atoms (AS: 364). Pullman portrays his characters' obliteration as a kind of joyous merging with the Cosmos, and Jacobs justly points out that some readers may find this a poor sort of 'salvation'. (Abramson has called this the 'fertilizer' theory of immortality: the individual disintegrates, but his or her 'atoms' go on forever, in the death-rebirth cycle of nature.)

Why ?!

Where Jacobs' reading of the narrative definitely misses the point is when he calls Lyra's 'lies' a reflection of 'dishonesty' on the author's part, for this overlooks the significance of the harsh lesson Lyra learns when 'No-Name' the Harpy punishes her for telling lies (AS: 292–3). No-Name explains that true 'news of the world' is nourishing, and all the Harpies hunger for it, and henceforth Lyra must tell the truth, for true stories are liberating. Stories of true life experiences in fact become the basis for the bargain Chevalier Tialys makes with the Harpies: true stories from each 'ghost' in exchange for guidance out of the netherworld into the sunlit world above (AS: 316–18).

The complexity and subtlety of *His Dark Materials* are disregarded in Jacobs' harsh approach, and nowhere is this more evident than when he interprets events near the end of the story as suggesting that 'the positive energy in the world, the Dust, is produced by specifically erotic love'. First, the narrative leaves what takes place between Lyra and Will indefinite (Jacobs may be imagining too much); it is clear that bodily love indeed attracts Dust, but the positive energy in the world is also increased through consciousness and awareness (AS: 491). Xaphania, the angel of wisdom, makes this point, and the implication is that love takes its power from participating in this 'consciousness-generating' process.

In trying to demolish Pullman's concept of the Republic of Heaven on historical–political grounds, particularly through discrediting the rhetoric of Lord Asriel and his ally, the good King Ogunwe, Jacobs writes as if the trilogy were a political–theological manifesto, not a story. He moreover treats the Republic of Heaven as though it were a political entity, rather than what it clearly is – a state of mind, an orientation to life. It hardly seems true that Pullman neglects consequences, as though the (presumed) toppling of Lord Asriel's Adamant Tower (of Babble) and his ignominious fall into the abyss were not punishment enough for his inflated ego and wrong-headed neglect of limits (such as the need for daemons to sustain themselves by dwelling in their own worlds, a suggestion that 'all politics is local', perhaps?). Moreover, the almost mythic Asriel has less in common with the historical 'Liberators' with whom Jacobs identifies him (Robespierre, Stalin) than with Prometheus.

It is helpful to juxtapose Pullman's own remarks on the nature of The Republic of Heaven and the related theme of 'celebrating the senses and ... the human body in the here and now – building ... The "Republic of Heaven" where we are'. He points out how religions traditionally have attempted to control human behaviour by 'apportioning ... punishment and reward in an afterlife', leading some people to neglect to live in the here and now, which is 'the only world we can be certain of'. His concern is with celebrating life in the moment, leaving the political theory to those who 'murder to dissect'. As John Parry says in his farewell to Will: 'For us there is no elsewhere' (AS: 363). Pullman defines 'Republic' as a state of consciousness, not a polis: 'This is all there is; and it is extremely beautiful and full of the most exquisite delight. That's what I mean about the republic of heaven. It's already around us. I just wanted to make that a bit more explicit, to give it a name' (quoted in Wagner, 2000).

[handwritten margin note: Buddhist]

[handwritten margin note: ? Convincing]

The shrivelling conclusion to Jacobs' article rejects what he terms 'the Manicheanism of Pullman's moral vision: closed versus open minds, tyrants versus liberators, the vicious Church versus its righteous opponents'. To accuse Pullman of Manicheanism (a dualistic religious system blending elements of Gnostic Christianity, Buddhism, and Zoroastrianism) seems ludicrous: its belief in Matter as 'evil' and 'dark' (in contrast to Spirit, seen as 'good' and 'light') could scarcely be more at odds with Pullman's celebration of body–soul–ghost – the tripartite human nature he depicts so vividly. Pullman has said in an interview with Ilene Cooper that his 'myth' owes something to Gnosticism, through Harold Bloom's *Book of J* and *Omens of the Millennium* as well as Gnostic writings, but his world-view differs in

> one essential characteristic. The Gnostic worldview is Platonic in that it rejects the physical created universe and expresses a longing for an unknowable God who is far off. My myth is almost the reverse. It takes this physical universe as our true home. We must welcome and love and live our lives in this world to the full. (Cooper, 2000: 355)

To charge Pullman with 'crudity', with encouraging simplistic, 'binary' thinking in young adults, as Jacobs does, is to miss his qualities of mind and art altogether. Far from being falsely accused for telling adolescents 'that good folks are distinguished from evil ones on the single criterion of religious belief' (Jacobs, 2000), Pullman should be thanked for increasing the degree of 'consciousness' on our planet, leading us to examine our beliefs and lives, and to practise vigilance in the perilous process of testing our 'stories' against the realities of our experiences.

Though *His Dark Materials* shows the demise of an antiquated 'Authority,' it is by no means nihilistic in its world-view. Implicitly it affirms certain humanistic values or 'principles', such as the few that follow, together with their 'pragmatopian' implications (*pragmatopia* = Gr. for 'a realizable future' (Eisler, 1987: 198, 239, n. 65)): (1) the principle that soul-survival is world-specific: daemons need to live in the world into which they have been born. The implication: live and love and work in the present place and moment; (2) the principle of heartfelt devotion to expanding human consciousness, resisting the forces that lessen mindfulness. The implication: practice your own 'ecology of mind,' in Gregory Bateson's wonderful phrase; (3) the principle of balance, both in the macrocosm (the total environment) and in the microcosm – between individuals, especially male and female. The implication: move from the exploiter model to the 'co-creator' model; (4) the principle of 'generativity'. The implication: the wiser or more knowledgeable person passes on the gift of wisdom or knowledge to another (for example, Dame Hannah mentoring Lyra, or Mary Malone befriending Will); (5) the principle of conservation of mental and emotional energy. The implication: rather than expending your consciousness on exploring illimitable windows to different worlds, develop the wisdom to know when to close them and experience the world around you, so your stock of true stories may increase; (6) the principle of *truth* in storytelling. The implication: like Lyra, learn to shape your own experiences into meaningful and emotive narratives, and tell your 'truth' to others – or as has been said, 'Don't die with your music in you'.

Pullman's contributions to the fantasies of alternative worlds

Nick Gevers calls *Northern Lights* 'an immediate, certain classic, head and shoulders above virtually any competitor': what features give *His Dark Materials* its outstanding quality? I think that it is a seamless blending of the following:

1. A *distinguished style and sensuous use of language*, capable of conveying a sense of the sublime, as at the climax of *Northern Lights*, when Lord Asriel harnesses the energy of Roger's separated daemon:

At the moment he [Roger] fell still, the vault of heaven, star-studded, profound, was pierced as if by a spear.

A jet of light, a jet of pure energy released like an arrow from a great bow, shot upward from the spot where Lord Asriel had joined the wire to Roger's daemon. The sheets of light and color that were the Aurora tore apart; a great rending, grinding, crunching sound reached from one end of the universe to the other; there was dry land in the sky – sunlight. (*NL*: 393)

Additionally, an abundant intertextuality, enabling a reader to make 'hypertextual' jumps to a metaverse of other narratives.

2. *Intellectual daring and inventiveness.* Pullman is like a Lord Asriel among writers, boldly taking on the 'authorities' of conventional children's literature, tackling the most challenging and unconventional themes.

3. A *metaphysical imagination,* endowing the superficially common objects of the world with a high charge of mystery and emotional energy – as for example a seemingly 'ordinary looking dagger' (*SK*: 180), though on closer inspection 'swirling with colors' and sporting delicate angel-formed designs. This ability to render the supposedly commonplace rich and strange and cognitively vibrant puts him in the company of the metaphysical poets (compare John Donne's use of the compass in 'A Valediction: Forbidding Mourning').

4. *Breath-taking action scenes interlaced with the philosophical,* as for example the episode of the Silver Guillotine, where the white-hot suspense over Lyra's fate is balanced against the moral and political implications of what the Guillotine represents: the attempt to render humans less than human – soulless – in order to have power over them.

5. *Presenting a dialogue between highly speculative scientific and spiritual ideas, often omitted from literature for children or adults in the contemporary world.* For instance, concepts from physics, such as 'shadow particles' and alternative worlds, are sometimes fused, sometimes in dialogue with concepts from religious thought, such as 'original sin' and angels. It seems that 'the very setting of *His Dark Materials* is a metaphor for the free will the rebels seek: all options realized, in parallel, rather than the stable monolithic reality Authority desires' (Gevers). On the other hand, there is evidence in favour of 'balance' (compare Le Guin's concept of Balance in *Earthsea*), for as Gevers continues, Pullman's interest is

primarily in the down-to-earth Lyra and Will, not in their ambitious parents; and 'the Spectre-afflicted world seems very much like an Eden destroyed by the alchemic meddling that created the subtle knife. Perhaps there are proper limits to knowledge and aspiration; perhaps Authority has a place'.

6. *Achieving an intergenerational appeal through a technique of double-coding* – writing to appeal on several levels, as for instance the plot-driven level of mystery and romance, alongside the other level of 'metaphysics and philosophy' (Parsons and Nicholson, 1999: 121). 'Double coding' also describes the way Pullman conveys adult sexuality in a manner that makes it unmistakable to adult readers but (probably) invisible to the pre-pubescent child, as when Ruta Skadi tells how she made her way, invisible, into Asriel's 'inmost chamber' as he was preparing to sleep, and how all the witches knew what followed, but neither Will nor Lyra dreamed of it (SK: 271). Pullman has remarked that he doesn't want his books to be pigeonholed by age, but to have the 'largest audience possible ... I'd like to think that I'm telling the sort of story that holdeth children from play and old men from the chimney corner, in the old phrase of Sir Philip Sidney' (Quoted in 'The Man Behind the Magic').

7. *Portraying young protagonists endowed with the psychic energy sufficient to sustain them through the fears and sorrows of life.* At least three basic fears are portrayed in the trilogy: the fear of soul loss; the fear of abandonment, and the fear of the loss of one's 'world'. It may be argued that the second of these fears is a stock-in-trade in children's literature, and many stories are designed to assuage it, bringing the protagonist 'home' after the 'wild things' adventure (Sendak, 1963). The other two fears are however not common fare for children, and it is part of Pullman's achievement to deal with them, in a multilayered story whose child protagonists, despite their gifts, are believable characters with foibles enough that readers can identify with their anxieties and participate in their triumphs.

8. *Depiction of alternative modes of consciousness, language-, rather than drug-induced, fashioned from mind-stretching metaphors: a linguistically-altered consciousness.* Many in today's world are seeking new modes of consciousness or expanded awareness, not necessarily for 'escape', but as a means of psychological survival in a world devoid of certainties. The open, receptive mode of consciousness ('negative capability') Lyra needs to use the alethiometer has its perils (who knows what dreams may come?), but it may also hold

the best hope for learning to live in a world of extremes, where the feelings of isolation and depersonalization exist in tension with the 'collective' consciousness made possible (and hardly avoidable) by 'connections' to strangers in cyberspace. It may suggest a mental and emotional capability to hold the individual, private realm in balance with the 'pooled' imagination.

9. *Modelling of a 'partnership' quest, giving balanced roles to Lyra and Will.* In an era of increasingly fluid gender roles, Pullman shows masculine and feminine qualities in a balanced yin–yang relationship, neatly expressed through the cooperative use of tools – the subtle knife and the alethiometer. The story moves away from the lethal 'blade' (which ends up demolished), and Lyra's alethiometer-reading 'competence' is lost (to be relearned). That leaves the amber spyglass, Mary's 'tool', suggesting perhaps that her scientific quest may yield a sustainable vision on which to build the world's future.

10. *Celebrating, through story, the role of stories in 'redeeming' or re-enchanting the imagination of human beings in a world where many have lost the traditional comforts of religion and the safe haven of a loving family.* Through his young co-protagonists, Pullman shows how human beings can, with courage and loving cooperation, survive the nightmares of history. Along the way, they develop their resilience and talents for improvisation, to become at last enlightened and whole individuals, able to move with compassion and joy through the sorrows of their complex worlds. Their 'negative capability' guides them through this 'vale of soul-making' (to borrow from Keats) and they emerge in a golden halo of Dust, conscious of the possibility of a heaven such as even atheists can believe in. We need heaven, Pullman affirms, though there may be no supreme being, for we need

> Joy ... Delight ... A belief that our lives mean something and have significance in the context of the universe and that they are connected to the universe and connected to each other ... All of this is part of what used to be called heaven. [Thus the necessity] ... to create a republic of heaven because that's the only way we can live at all. (Cooper, 2000: 355)

11. *Giving the world an unforgettable love story,* stretching from the infinite spaces of the macrocosm to the individual microcosms of two forever-bonded hearts. For countless readers, two stars of equal magnitude have an enduring place in the constellation Lyra.

References

Abramson, J. (1974) 'Facing the other fact of life: death in recent children's fiction,' *School Library Journal* 21(4): 31–3.

Attebery, B. (1992) *Strategies of Fantasy*, Bloomington, IN: Indiana University Press.

Bethune, B. (1996) 'Daemons and dust: a fantasy writer creates a haunting world'. Review of *The Golden Compass*. *Macleans*, **109** (30), 58.

Bostian, F. (2000) 'Philip Pullman's Northern exposure: the role of the Arctic in *His Dark Materials*,' presented at the Children's Literature Association, 27th Annual Conference, Roanoke, VA., 22 June. Unpublished.

Cooper, I. (2000) 'Pullman on the theology of "His Dark Materials,"' an interview, *Booklist* 97(3) (1 October): 355.

Eccleshare, J. (1996) 'Northern Lights and Christmas miracles,' *Books for Keeps*, 100: 15.

Eisler, R. (1987) *The Chalice and the Blade: Our History, Our Future*, San Francisco: Harper and Row.

Fox, G. (1997) Authorgraph 102: Philip Pullman, *Books for Keeps* 102: 12–13.

Fox, M. (1983) *Original Blessing: A Primer in Creation Spirituality*, Santa Fe, NM: Bear and Company.

Gevers, N. (Accessed 4 July, 2000) 'Philip Pullman: *Northern Lights*: an infinity plus review' <http://www.iplus.zetnet.co.uk/nonfiction/northern.htm>.

Gevers, N. (Accessed 4 July, 2000) 'Philip Pullman: *The Subtle Knife*. an infinity plus review' <http://www.iplus.zetnet.co.uk/nonfiction/subtle.htm>.

Gordon, E. V. (1957) *An Introduction to Old Norse* (2nd edn, revised by A. R. Taylor), Oxford: Clarendon Press.

Houston, J. (2000) *Jump Time: Shaping Your Future in a World of Radical Change*, New York: Jeremy Tarcher/Putnam.

Jacobs, A. (2000) 'The Devil's party: Philip Pullman's bestselling fantasy series retells the story of Creation – with Satan as the hero,' *The Weekly Standard*, 6(6): 23 October, Books and Art section. <http://www.weeklystandard.com/magazine/mag_6_6_00/jacobs_b-kart_6_6_00.asp> (Accessed 20 September, 2000).

Johnson, S. (2000) ' "On the dark edge of imagination," Review of *The Amber Spyglass* by Philip Pullman', *The Times of London*, 18 October. <http://www.thetimes.co.uk/article/0,,20824,00.html> (Accessed 19 October, 2000).

Kimball, M. A. (1999) 'From folktales to fiction: orphan characters in children's literature,' *Library Trends* 47(3): 558–78.

von Kleist, H. (1982) 'On the puppet theater,' in *An Abyss Deep Enough: Letters of Heinrich von Kleist, with a Selection of Essays and Anecdotes*, (ed and trans, P. B. Miller), New York: Dutton: 211–16.

Langton, J. (1996) 'What is dust?' *NYTBR*, 19 May: 34.

Lincoln, B. (1981) *Emerging from the Chrysalis: Studies in Rituals of Women's Initiation*, Cambridge, MA: Harvard University Press.

Mackey, M. (1999) 'Playing in the phase space: contemporary forms of fictional pleasure,' *Signal* 88: 16–33.

Milton, J. (1957) *John Milton: Complete Poems and Major Prose* (ed. Merritt Y. Hughes), New York: Odyssey Press.

Odean, K. (2000) 'The story master,' *SLJ Online: Articles*, 6 October, <http://www.slj.com/articles/articles/20001001_9064.asp> (Accessed 21 October, 2000).

Pagels, E. (1981) *The Gnostic Gospels*, New York: Random House/ Vintage.

Parsons, W. and Nicholson, C. (1999) 'Talking to Philip Pullman: an interview,' *The Lion and the Unicorn* 23: 116–34.

Pullman, P. (1989) 'Invisible pictures,' *Signal* 60 (September): 160–86.

Pullman, P. (1995) *Northern Lights: His Dark Materials, Book One*, London: Scholastic; *The Golden Compass*, New York: Knopf, 1996.

Pullman, P. (1997) *The Subtle Knife: His Dark Materials, Book Two*, London: Scholastic; New York: Knopf.

Pullman, P. (1998) 'Let's write it in red: the Patrick Hardy Lecture,' *Signal* 85 (January): 44–62.

Pullman, P. (1999) '*Götterdämmerung* or bust,' *Horn Book Magazine* 75(1) (January/February): 31.

Pullman, P. (2000) *The Amber Spyglass: His Dark Materials, Book Three*, London: Scholastic; New York: Knopf/Random House.

Pullman, P. (n.d.) excerpt from Carnegie Medal Acceptance Speech, <http://www.randomhouse.com/features/goldencompass/subtle-knife/speech.html>

Pullman, P. (n.d.) 'A letter from Philip Pullman,' <http://www.doubleday.com/features/goldencompass/subtleknife>

Pullman, P. (n.d.) *Liber Angelorum*, <http://www.randomhouse.com/features/goldencompass/subtleknife/angelorum.html>

Pullman, P. (Accessed 14 February, 2000) 'Achuka interview,' <http://www.achuka.co.uk/ppint.htm>

Pullman, P. (Accessed 6 October, 2000) '*The Amber Spyglass: His Dark Materials, Book Three*, author interview,' <http://barnesandnoble.com>

Pullman, P. (Accessed 6 October, 2000) 'Darkness Visible: an interview with Philip Pullman,' in two parts <http://www.amazon.-com/exec/obidos/tg/feature/-/94589/104-4404176-4842313>

Pullman, P. (Accessed 6 October, 2000) 'The man behind the magic,' author interview, <http://shop.barnesandnoble.com/booksearch/isb-ninquiry.asp?>

Random House web site for *Northern Lights*, with supplementary materials: <http://www.randomhouse.com/features/goldencompass/ goldencompass /aleth.html> (accessed 17 February, 2000).

Sendak, M. (1963) *Where the Wild Things Are*, New York: Harper and Row.

Senick, G. J. (1999) 'Pullman, Philip,' in *Something about the Author Vol. 103*, (ed. Alan Hedblad), Detroit: Gale: 146–54.

Sheldrake, R. (1989) *The Presence of the Past: Morphic Resonance and the Habits of Nature*, New York: Random/Vintage.

Wagner, E. (2000) 'Divinely inspired,' *The Times*, 18 October, <http://www.thetimes.co.uk/article/0,,20758,00.html>

Watkins, M. (1987) '"In dreams begin responsibilities": moral imagination and peace action,' in *Facing Apocalypse*, (ed. V. Andrews, R. Bosnak, and K. Walter Goodwin), Dallas, TX: Spring Publications.

Witcover, P. (Accessed 11 February, 2000) Ballantine Teacher's Guide for *Northern Lights*, <http://www.randomhouse.com/BB/teachers/ tgs/goldencompass.html>

Philip Pullman

Philip (Nicholas) Pullman was born in Norwich, Norfolk, England, 19 October 1946, the son of Alfred Outram Pullman and Audrey (Merrifield) Pullman. He was brought up in Rhodesia, Australia, London and Wales. His father was an airman. Philip was educated at Oxford University; he married Judith Speller (a hypnotherapist), 15 August 1970, and they have two children, James and Thomas. Before becoming a full-time writer, he worked for the Oxfordshire Education Authority, Oxford, England, as a teacher, 1972–88; he continued to do part-time lecturing at Westminster College, Oxford, 1988–96 and is active as a public speaker and lecturer. He describes himself as 'left' in his politics. His avocational interests include music and drawing. He is the author of many highly acclaimed books for young readers, from contemporary fiction to Victorian thrillers, in addition to plays and picture books for readers of all ages.

Books

Ancient Civilizations, Exeter, England: Wheaton, 1978.

Galatea. New York: Dutton, 1979.

Count Karlstein, or the Ride of the Demon Huntsman, London: Chatto and Windus, 1982; New York: Knopf, 1998.

The Ruby in the Smoke, Oxford: Oxford University Press, 1985; New York: Knopf, 1987.

How to Be Cool, London: Heinemann, 1987.

The Shadow in the North, Oxford: Oxford University Press, 1987; New York: Knopf, 1988.

Spring-Heeled Jack: A Story of Bravery and Evil, London: Transworld Publishers, 1989; New York: Knopf, 1991.

The Broken Bridge, London: Macmillan, 1990; New York: Knopf, 1992.

The Tiger in the Well, Harmondsworth: Penguin, 1992; New York: Knopf, 1990.

The White Mercedes, London: Macmillan, 1992; New York: Knopf, 1993.

The Tin Princess, London: Penguin, 1994; New York: Knopf, 1994.

The Firework Maker's Daughter, London: Doubleday, 1995; New York: Arthur A. Levine, 1999.

Clockwork: Or All Wound Up, London: Doubleday, 1996; New York: Arthur A. Levine, 1998.

Detective Stories (compiler), London and New York: Kingfisher, 1998.

Plays

'The Three Musketeers' (adaptation of the novel by Alexandre Dumas), produced at Polka Children's Theatre, Wimbledon, 1985.

'Frankenstein' (adaptation of the novel by Mary Shelley), produced at Polka Children's Theatre, Wimbledon, 1987, Oxford University Press, 1990.

'Sherlock Holmes and the Adventure of the Sumatran Devil,' produced at Polka Children's Theatre, Wimbledon, England, 1984, published as *Sherlock Holmes and the Adventure of the Limehouse Horror*, Nelson, 1993.

Index